TechTactics

TechTactics

Instructional Models for Educational Computing

CAROLYN THORSEN
Boise State University

Boston   New York   San Francisco
Mexico City   Montreal   Toronto   London   Madrid   Munich   Paris
Hong Kong   Singapore   Tokyo   Cape Town   Sydney

Series Editor: Arnis E. Burvikovs
Editorial Assistant: Matthew Forster
Marketing Manager: Amy Cronin
Editorial-Production Service: Omegatype Typography, Inc.
Manufacturing Buyer: JoAnne Sweeney
Composition and Prepress Buyer: Linda Cox
Cover Administrator: Kristina Mose-Libon
Electronic Composition: Omegatype Typography, Inc.

For related titles and support materials, visit our online catalog at www.ablongman.com.

Between the time Website information is gathered and published, some sites may have closed. Also, the transcription of URLs can result in typographical errors. The publisher would appreciate notification where these errors occur so that they may be corrected in subsequent editions.

Many of the designations used by manufacturers and sellers to distinguish their products are claimed as trademarks. Where those designations appear in this book, and Allyn and Bacon was aware of a trademark claim, the designations have been printed in initial or all caps.

Library of Congress Cataloging-in-Publication Data

Thorsen, Carolyn.
    TechTactics : instructional models for educational computing / Carolyn Thorsen.
      p. cm.
    Includes bibliographical references and index.
    ISBN 0-205-33594-2
    1. Computer-assisted instruction.   2. Instructional systems—Design.   I. Title.

  LB1028.5 .T52 2003
  371.34'4—dc21

2002023021

Printed in the United States of America

10 9 8 7 6 5 4 3 2   07 06 05 04 03

I would like to dedicate this book to my mother, father, aunts, and uncles, who always believed in the power of knowledge and the joy of learning.

Contents

PART ONE   A STARTING POINT   1

As you read this book, you will learn as much about learning and teaching as you will about computers and other equipment. Educational technology is more than just machines. It is a way of looking at human learning and instruction. The role of technology in teaching is to serve students and teachers transparently rather than be a focus of instruction. The focus of the teaching/learning process is helping students acquire information, problem-solving strategies, and critical thinking skills. To expedite this process for their students, teachers use teaching strategies called models and support them with machines such as computers and their peripherals as well as digital cameras, televisions, calculators, probes, and other devices.

These teaching strategies are especially effective because of the information-processing capabilities of computers. As you learn computer skills, it will be important for you to relate those skills to how they help your students learn.

CHAPTER TWO   An Introduction to Computers for Teaching   **22**

PART TWO   THE INTERNET: INFORMATION RETRIEVAL AND COMMUNICATION   31

Acquiring and judging the value of information and exchanging information are the topics of Part Two of this book. One of the greatest strengths of the Internet is its role as a repository of information. In addition, Internet-based communication, including email and web-based conferencing, helps students acquire information from each other and from experts. It provides opportunities for collaboration during problem-based learning activities. Furthermore, the Internet is becoming a classroom itself. It is a medium in which a broad range of courses and learning activities are available for both children and adults. In addition to its role as a repository for information, the Internet is a powerful tool for communication. You will learn how to design instruction based on communication over the Internet. As your students use the Internet for this purpose, they will improve their writing skills as they acquire information.

CHAPTER THREE   Information Retrieval   **31**

PART THREE   DISPLAYING INFORMATION   79

Before the computer, students had fewer formats in which they could display information. They wrote most reports in text—handwritten or typewritten. Some students would cut pictures out of magazines to include with reports. All charts and graphs were hand made and hand calculated. Students with poor writing skills had limited opportunities to work with many facts and ideas on the higher levels of Bloom's Taxonomy because they had to be more concerned with producing a legible product with passable grammar. This is not to say that legibility and grammar are not important, but a focus on them can keep students from learning other skills that are just as important. Presentation software and word processors allow students to work with large ideas and concepts, much as the calculator shifts students from a focus on computational errors to looking at the large ideas in mathematics.

The process that students use to display information in a computer-based presentation provides opportunities for them to organize and contextualize the information. Organizing information, or, better, finding the organization that is inherent in information, is one way to learn it well (Gagne et al., 1993; Woolfolk, 2000).*

*References for Woolfolk and Gagne et al. appear in Chapters 5 and 6, respectively.

PART FOUR   ANALYZING DATA WITH DATABASES AND SPREADSHEETS   151

Besides giving us increased power to gather and present data, computers also provide us with the tools to analyze data. The two premier tools for data analysis are databases and spreadsheets. A database allows us not only to store and retrieve large amounts of factual information, but also retrieve those facts in such a way that we can see patterns that we would not have seen otherwise. Spreadsheets are to numbers what databases are to words. With spreadsheets, students can summarize numbers from many different perspectives using pivot tables, charts, and graphs, as well as do "what if" simulations. Unlike the word processor and presentation software that yield the product of solitary student work on the computer, databases and spreadsheets are most valuable when groups or whole classes use them to brainstorm solutions to problems that they study. These two tools are unlike any other that students have had access to in the history of education.

Preface

This book is written for pre-service teachers who are being introduced to the uses of educational technology in the K–12 classroom. Unless these students already have had a skills or application course in basic computer tools, this book should be accompanied by a skills book that covers the Internet, presentation software, word processing, databases, and spreadsheets. Although the skills required to understand the information in this book and complete the end-of-chapter exercises are elementary, at least some of your students will need some reference information. One of the difficulties with teaching a course such as "Introduction to Computers in Education" is the variable skill levels of the students. In the courses in which this book has been used, the instructors have required both this book and a supporting skills book. The two, if used together, provide one full semester or two quarters of work.

To provide a link to other coursework that students are taking or will take, the book references some instructional models that students commonly learn and practice in teacher education programs. As a result, students should see the place of technology in the larger context of the teaching and learning environment.

Topics taught in an educational technology course vary from instructor to instructor. Because the focus of the book is on the integration of computers into the teaching/learning process, the main chapters are devoted to the integration of basic tool software. However, there are other important areas that do not necessarily fit into this flow—for example, minor tools and methods, national educational technology standards, file management and how to teach file management, concept mapping, and the complexities of school networks, to name a few. These topics are covered in appendices at the end of the book that can be adapted to short extra readings or extra credit assignments, or a few days' work in class, if necessary. At the Allyn & Bacon website you will find all of the web links noted in each chapter for use by you and your students.

I would like to add a quick note about the order of the chapters. Teachers often begin a class with word processing because that is the tool everyone seems most comfortable with. In this book, word processing is not covered until Chapter 9, but it may stand alone if necessary. Chapter 6 on screen design may also stand alone, and, depending on your teaching strategy, you may want to assign it early in the course.

In addition, other parts of the book include:

- Information retrieval
- Displaying information
- Analyzing information

These parts can be taught in a different order from which they are written. There is one reference in Part Four to information in Part Three, but the students should be able to understand the information nevertheless.

At the ends of many chapters, I have provided annotated resources. These appear in chapters where the flow of the text did not provide for the presentation or discussion of references within the text material itself. For example, there are few annotated resources for the database and spreadsheet chapters because of the many references to information within the chapters themselves. On the other hand, there are many annotated resources for the first and second chapters because I could not cover the breadth of the field within the chapters themselves. The same is true of chapters on the Internet and word processing.

■ ACKNOWLEDGMENTS

I would like to recognize the thoughtful contributions made by the staff of the Educational Technology Outreach Program of Boise State University College of Education. Dr. Robert Barr saw the potential for producing a book in this area. I want to thank Arthur Galus and Donna Vakili as well. They have field-tested and supervised others in the testing of both the text itself and the methods that you will learn from this book. Dr. Connie Pollard adopted the book for her classes early and perhaps before it was entirely ready. Her encouragement and support have been instrumental. Other instructors who have helped test and refine the book include Kerri Whitehead, Todd Van Dehey, Theresa Foster, and Ruth Waller. I want to thank my series editor, Arnis Burvikovs, who worked through the review process with me and provided the title for this book. I would also like to recognize my husband, Dr. Richard Johnson, who supported and encouraged this project, carrying the load while I wrote.

In addition, I would like to thank the following reviewers for their helpful suggestions: Marilyn D. Bowen, Mississippi State University; John V. Connor, Daytona Beach Community College; Kathleen E. Fite, Southwest Texas State University; Sharleen Gonzalez, Baker College; and Sandra W. Sutherland, Carlsbad Unified School District.

TechTactics

Computers in Classrooms

OBJECTIVES

- Identify computer tools that will be discussed in this book.
- Explain the purpose of computing in the K–12 classroom.
- Know and explain six foundational areas relating to computers in which all educators should be proficient.
- Explain three different approaches for using computers in the teaching/learning process.

Education is undergoing dramatic changes. Left behind is the world where a teacher had considerable latitude with the curriculum. Pre-service teachers are entering a profession that is focused on standards and reform. States increasingly set standards and define curricula for districts and competencies for students. Then districts build on state mandates and add their own local standards and requirements. When all of the standards, mandates, and curricula finally reach thirty students and one teacher in a classroom, the success enjoyed by the students, apart from their own diligence, rests largely on the ability of the teacher to present information well and interact skillfully with students. Where does educational technology fit in this demanding setting?

Standards and reform

The premise of this book is that educational technology provides a sophisticated set of both production and cognitive tools that help learners acquire facts as well as providing a fertile and challenging environment for problem solving and critical thinking. Key to this premise is the notion that educational technology is adaptable to the information and problems posed by the standards, curriculum, and competencies required by school districts and states.

■ APPLICATION SOFTWARE: YOUR TOOLS

The information in this book focuses almost completely on the use of **tool software:** Internet, presentation/visualization, word processing, database, and spreadsheet software. Unlike instructional software that is built to teach specific content, tool software is structured to assist a user who wants to create content. Each tool can be used to find, analyze, and present many different kinds of information. Used by a skillful teacher, these tools support content and many teaching methods that districts and states require of their teachers. Educators who read this book should come to it with a fundamental set of computer tool skills or should plan to learn them as they read about the instructional models applicable to each tool. The introduction to each tool will provide you with a list of basic tool skills that you need to know or look up and learn.

The information in this book is not directed toward either Mac or Windows users. The screen shots are taken from a Windows operating system, but all concepts apply to the Mac as well. Tool software transcends these environments. You may use Word Perfect or Word as your word processor, Excel or Lotus as your spreadsheet, and PowerPoint or Hyperstudio as your presentation software. The same flexibility is true of your web browser (Netscape or Explorer) and database (Access and Filemaker Pro). You may be using another tool not named above, such as Works. You can apply the principles you will learn in the following chapters to any brand of application software. This ability to design lessons based on tools rather than a specific brand name of software should help you when you go to a classroom that may not use the same kind of software that you are using in your training.

■ PURPOSE OF COMPUTING
IN K–12 CLASSROOMS

This book is full of narrative examples of classroom life. You will be an invisible observer that can get into both students' and teachers' heads as we go on virtual field trips to see how teachers integrate technology into the teaching/learning process. The primary goal is to demonstrate good strategies for using technology to support teaching, but another goal is to expose the misconceptions that lead to the failure of computer-supported teaching and learning. Some common attitudes and misunderstandings account for how both children and teachers react to computers.

When you are working on activities suggested in this book (called "Checking Your Understanding"), be sure to note where you have problems with either your computer skills or your conceptualization of the instructional problem on which you are working. If you have difficulty, you can be sure that some of your future students will have a similar experience. One of the very best qualities of a computer-using teacher is to have experienced repeated attempts and even failure to solve problems with a computer. This preparation will help you anticipate your own students' experiences.

Using a computer in your teaching should promote improved analytical thinking and information management skills among your students. The point is not to teach

Observing your
own learning

tool software
Software that has no content
of its own. Also called *application* software.

them computer skills, though sometimes this is necessary. Rather, the point is to teach them to acquire, process, and present information better using the computer as a tool. It is important to recognize that although computers are wonderful machines capable of motivating and challenging students with the **cognitive tools** they provide, they are only one tool among many. Other cognitive tools include outlines and Venn diagrams. Used systematically, databases, spreadsheets, and presentation software also are cognitive tools. Although computers can help students learn facts as well as improve their problem-solving strategies and critical-thinking skills (Schacter, 1999), so can books, field trips, discussions, and other tools teachers use. Consequently, another goal of this book is to help you know what computers do best and when their use is appropriate.

> The computer as a cognitive tool

■ WHAT MUST I KNOW TO TEACH WITH COMPUTERS EFFECTIVELY?

There are some basic computer skills and tools that you need to have or acquire as you read this book. Although several organizations (The Milkin Exchange and CEO Forum, for example) promote the use of computers in the K–12 classroom, ISTE (International Society for Technology in Education) is one of the largest and perhaps the most influential concerning technology standards for both teachers and students. Six foundational areas of competence are recommended for teachers by ISTE (2000):

> The field of educational technology

- Technology operations and concepts
- Planning and designing learning environments and experiences
- Teaching, learning, and the curriculum
- Assessment and evaluation
- Productivity and professional practice
- Social, ethical, legal, and human issues

As you can see, teachers must have a big picture that includes hardware, software, the instructional process, their own administrative work, and the larger nontechnical or instructional issues that arise from the culture in which we live. As you begin your study of computers in the teaching/learning process, you must always be alert to these issues. In the following sections of this chapter, we explore these themes as a foundation for the technology integration process.

Technology Operations and Concepts

In spite of teachers' best efforts, some students will always know more about how to operate computers and the software that is on them. However, there are some basic standards for students in which teachers themselves should be competent. An excellent definition of these standards is found in ISTE's National Educational Technology Standards for Students (ISTE, 2000). Although teachers may not have explored every

cognitive tool
A structure or process that helps students analyze and retain information.

Skills standards

function on every menu of every computer tool, they should know most of the functions on each menu and be able to work through online or printed Help manuals to solve a problem if necessary. Probably everyone has heard a story about how "the children know more than the teacher about computers and isn't it wonderful that Johnny can show the teacher how." It is wonderful, to a point. Although the role of the teacher is changing from lecturer to guide or even co-learner, it is necessary for teachers to have the same basic skills as students. It is *not* wonderful to watch a second-grade student show the teacher how to cut and paste.

Furthermore, teachers should endeavor to acquire some basic hardware troubleshooting knowledge. Schools do not generally have the technical support they need, and when something goes wrong the teacher should a) know some basic diagnostic strategies, and b) know enough terminology to be able to talk to a technical support person over the telephone and explain a problem. Most of all, the teacher should display a can-do, positive, troubleshooting attitude in front of students when things go wrong. This model will help students develop a positive approach that will be useful throughout their lives.

Learning Environments

Using technology effectively in the classroom requires more than basic computer skills because computers should fit into a larger context: the learning environment. The learning environment is determined by the kinds of tasks students complete, the way teachers and students interact, and how students are exposed to information. The challenge to construct an effective lesson that is well received by students requires much planning and knowledge on the part of the teacher.

Constructivism

One kind of learning environment in which computers fit well is based on the constructivist theory of learning. Although constructivism does not describe just one school of thought, there are some common elements of a constructivist perspective (Woolfolk, 2000). These include:

■ Complex, challenging learning environments and authentic tasks
■ Social negotiation and shared responsibility as a part of learning
■ Multiple representations of content
■ Understanding that knowledge is constructed (Woolfolk, p. 334)

Reiser and Dempsey (2002) further state that in a constructivist learning environment learners "engage in activities authentic to the discipline in which they are learning" (p. 68). In this context, technology is especially appropriate. For example, students can work with real data in spreadsheets and databases as they study the sciences and social sciences. In the arts and in language arts students use the tools that professionals use to display information (audio, video, text, graphics, and animation).

This philosophy of education requires students to be active participants in the learning process while the teacher is an instructional designer. To help you gain further insight into learning environments where computers are effective, we will be even more specific and talk about problem-based learning.

Problem-based learning

Problem-based learning is one concrete expression of how constructivist theory may be implemented at a practical level. In later chapters, much of what you learn about designing instruction that includes computers is based on the understanding that students are solving problems. Problem-based learning "is a teaching and learning model that focuses on the central concepts and principles of a discipline, involves students in problem-solving and other meaningful tasks, allows students to work autonomously to construct their own learning, and culminates in realistic, student-generated products" (Thomas, Mergandoller, & Michaelson, 1999, p. 1). The key words in this definition are:

- Central concepts of a discipline
- Problem solving
- Meaningful tasks
- Construct their own learning
- Student-generated products

Problem-based learning takes place in many formats. Within a single project, students may work alone, in pairs, in small or mid-size groups, and in large groups as well. Each configuration has its advantages for different learning tasks (Thomas et al., 1999). Observe the examples in Table 1.1. Listed there are some typical classroom activities as well as some computer activities. Although you may not yet understand what the computer activities might be or how they would work, it is important to know that you do not always have to have a computer for each student. Some computer activities are more helpful when several students are working at the same computer. In later chapters, you will learn which computer tools are appropriate for group work and which are more appropriate for individual work.

Teaching based on constructivist theory and problem-based learning should not only provide for the acquisition of facts but also stimulate **higher-order thinking skills** among students. Both facts and higher order thinking skills are acquired when students process information. Computers allow students to process a great deal of information in complex ways that were not available to them before the advent of computing. Learning these different approaches to information processing is the focus of this book. This takes us to a discussion of "Teaching, Learning, and the Curriculum." Constructivism and problem-based learning provide a framework for instruction, but what goes into this framework?

higher-order thinking skills
Activities in which students predict outcomes, judge between or among alternatives, or analyze problems or situations.

TABLE 1.1 ■ Examples of Problem-Based Learning

Grouping Strategy	Activities
Individual	Conducting library research; word processing
Pairs	Peer critiques; working with a database or spreadsheet to enter information, solve a problem, or answer a question
Small groups	Designing questions for a database, preparing presentations
Large Groups	Learning how to use a computer tool; observing presentation

Teaching, Learning, and the Curriculum

As you learn more about integrating computers into the teaching/learning process in later chapters, you will find that a teacher is a mentor and instructional designer who helps students focus on problem-solving activities. A teacher works with children who have many different learning styles and backgrounds and who bring to class many different levels of skill and knowledge. To use computers to help students solve problems that will lead them to construct their own knowledge about a content area, you need to know exactly how to design instruction that guides them through this process. To design effective instruction, you need to know some teaching models.

Models of teaching

While you are learning to be a teacher, you learn many different kinds of instructional models. Models of teaching that are most useful for planning computer-supported instruction are in the information processing family (Joyce, Weil, & Calhoun, 2000; Woolfolk, 2000; Bransford, Brown, & Cocking, 1999). As you continue to read this text, you will recognize that all the models for computer-supported lessons fit into larger, common models of teaching that most teachers learn and use throughout their careers.

What Is an Instructional Model?

An **instructional model** is based on research that has been done on how people best learn certain kinds of information. The model is a series of steps or techniques for presenting information in a way that helps learners remember and use it. Although there are many models, we will look at just one example, the inductive-thinking model. It consists of three strategies with nine steps and is used to teach concepts. In a practical sense, concepts are ideas and their associated examples. Examples of concept lessons include: the parts of speech, the classification of (rocks, plants, animals, kinds of governments, kinds of literature). The bulleted items below list the steps for using the inductive-thinking model to teach a concept lesson.

Inductive-thinking model

- Strategy One: Concept Formation
    - Phase One: Enumerating and Listing Examples
    - Phase Two: Grouping Examples
    - Phase Three: Labeling, Categorizing Examples (Classification)
- Strategy Two: Interpreting Data
    - Phase Four: Identifying Critical Relationships
    - Phase Five: Exploring Relationships
    - Phase Six: Making Inferences
- Strategy Three: Applying Principles
    - Phase Seven: Predicting Consequences, Explaining Unfamiliar Phenomena, Hypothesizing
    - Phase Eight: Explaining and/or Supporting the Predictions and Hypothesis
    - Phase Nine: Verifying the Prediction (Joyce et al., 2000, p. 140)

instructional model
A series of steps or techniques for presenting information in a way that helps learners remember and use it effectively.

When executed well, this teaching model helps students learn concepts efficiently and thoroughly. Your question might be, "What do computers have to do with this teaching model?" The answer is that computers provide tools that enhance many steps in the inductive-thinking process. They either provide or process information in such

TABLE 1.2 ■ Using Computers with the Inductive-Thinking Model

Inductive-Thinking Model	Computer Tool
Strategy 1	
Concept formation	
Phase One: Enumerating and listing	Internet for research; word processor
Phase Two: Grouping examples	Visualization tools (Inspiration, presentation software)
Phase Three: Labeling, categorizing examples (classification)	Visualization tools (Inspiration, presentation software)
Strategy 2	
Interpretating Data	
Phase Four: Identifying critical relationships	Visualization tools (Inspiration, presentation software)
Phase Five: Exploring relationships	Database; spreadsheet
Phase Six: Making inferences	Database, spreadsheet
Strategy 3	
Applying principles	
Phase Seven: Predicting consequences, explaining unfamiliar phenomena, hypothesizing	
Phase Eight: Explaining and/or supporting the predictions and hypotheses	Presentation software; word processor
Phase Nine: Verifying the prediction	Internet for research

a way that students gain a deeper understanding of the concepts they are studying. Table 1.2 revisits the steps of the inductive-thinking model. Note the computer tools associated with each phase of the model.

Later chapters in this book answer questions such as, How would I use the Internet to help students enumerate and list concepts? How would I use visualization software to help students identify critical relationships? How would I use spreadsheets or databases to help students explore relationships? How would I use presentation software to help students explain and/or support their predictions and hypotheses? The inductive-thinking model is just one of many teaching models. As you learn more about computer tools and how to use them, you will begin to anticipate when they are useful. The models you will learn about in this book span the K–12 grade levels and apply to all content areas.

> Using computer tools to support teaching models

Assessment and Evaluation

Assessment and evaluation are significant elements of the instructional planning process. In fact, when teachers design instruction, one of the first questions they ask is, "What should my students know and be able to do when they have finished this lesson?" Fortunately, just as there are models for teaching effective lessons, there are also models for evaluating them. One very common lesson evaluation model is called Bloom's Taxonomy (Bloom, 1956). Benjamin Bloom describes his taxonomy as "levels of thought." Table 1.3 lists the levels of Bloom's Taxonomy in the first column. Skills in the beginning of the list are called lower-order thinking skills. They increase in complexity as you read down the list. The final three skills listed in column one are called higher-order thinking skills. For students to exercise higher-order thinking skills, they must have acquired supporting information at the lower levels of the taxonomy.

The center column of Table 1.3 supplies some words that describe the performance of students who master information at that level. Compare these words with the phrases of the inductive-thinking model and notice the similarities. The third column of Table 1.3 lists some computer tools teachers use to help students attain the levels of knowledge and performance listed in the first column. After looking at Tables 1.2 and 1.3, you should see some similarities. The models for teaching and evaluating fit together and use the same computer tools to accomplish the same ends.

Your goal for any lesson or unit that you teach will be to help your students attain thinking levels as high on Bloom's Taxonomy as they are capable of achieving. Later chapters reference Bloom's Taxonomy as a way of creating a perspective and context for the use of computers in the teaching and learning process. For now, don't worry that you don't know everything about all of the computer tools listed in Table 1.3. The table is another way to demonstrate how and where computers fit into the teaching/learning process. Details will come later on.

> The connection between higher- and lower-order thinking skills

Productivity and Professional Practice

The computers in your school will influence how you do your administrative work. You may be required to maintain a web site for your class where you update assignment information and report to parents. You will be asked to communicate more with parents because there are electronic tools available for communication, such as email. It is likely that you will use electronic attendance reporting systems. In addition, you

TABLE 1.3 ■ Bloom's Taxonomy with Relevant Computer Tools

Level of Thought	Description	Computer Tool
Knowledge	Name, locate, tell, list, repeat, point to, describe	Drill and Practice Software
Comprehension	Define, summarize, infer, project	Visualization Software; tutorials
Application	Use, solve, adapt, relate, perform	Internet research; Databases; Spreadsheets; Simulations
Analysis	Compare, classify, screen, examine, test for	Presentation Software; Visualization Software, Simulations, Databases, Spreadsheets
Synthesis	Create, develop, generate, build, compile, design	Presentation Software; Word Processor
Evaluation	Judge, reject, criticize, rate, rank	Presentation Software; Word Processor; Internet Research

may have to learn how to use an Integrated Learning System (ILS). These systems contain libraries of software that tutor and drill students in basic language arts and mathematics skills. They track student progress and provide a variety of reports.

Another administrative use teachers may now find invaluable is the growing number of standardized test scores stored electronically. Student test scores (e.g., Iowa Test of Basic Skills) in many districts are reported and maintained as electronic databases. This format gives teachers the ability to do more than just look up how a single student scored on "math computation," for example. If teachers know how to use a database or spreadsheet, they can perform **queries** to answer questions such as:

- Is there a group of students in my class that is performing poorly on capitalization?
- Does my class really need to review punctuation before we learn how to write paragraphs?
- Which math concepts do I need to review with my class before I start on first-degree equations?
- Which students scored below the fortieth percentile in both spelling and punctuation?

Using data that school districts routinely collect in this manner is called *data-driven decision making*. In the past, although school districts collected reams of data about their students, it was impossible to do much more with it than give students and their parents test scores and compare district scores to national scores. Now, with electronic databases, teachers and administrators can use the data to make instructional decisions in single classrooms, buildings, and entire districts. In a later chapter you will learn how to teach with spreadsheets and databases. In the process of learning that, you will learn how to use them well enough to help you make instructional decisions for your classroom.

> Data-driven decision making

Another way computers are helping teachers is in distance education. Over the course of your career, your state will ask you to take classes to stay current in your field. At some time in your life, it is likely that you will take a class taught entirely over the Internet, television, or a combination of delivery technologies. You may also teach one yourself or monitor students who are taking one. Some people are reluctant to try such courses in spite of the fact that "distance courses" allow them to make their own schedule and save the time that it takes to drive to and from a class. Research demonstrates that distance classes can be as effective as traditional classes. Roblyer and Edwards (2000) say that many studies done over a forty-year period indicate there is no significant difference in instruction using distance technologies and traditional instruction. They further indicate that research has shown that the delivery system isn't the determining factor in the success of a course, but rather it is the quality of the course materials that determines its success (p. 197). We will go into more detail about distance classes when you study the Internet in a later chapter. For the time being, however, be aware that distance education is a growing and thriving area in the field of educational technology.

> Distance education

Social, Ethical, Legal, and Human Issues

Finally, as important as knowing which keys to press to get a spreadsheet to work, how to fix a jammed printer, or how to construct an effective technology-supported lesson, you will become a role model for your students about the human side of technology.

query
A way of asking a database or spreadsheet for specific information or patterns of information.

Using expensive computer
resources effectively

You will have to make sure that all of your students have equal access to the computers in your room or laboratory, that the aggressive and/or skilled ones do not monopolize them while others who have fewer skills are intimidated. Furthermore, because computers are still not as common as pencils, you will do the educational triage that funnels scarce computing resources to the students who need them the most. It will be your responsibility to ensure that those from diverse backgrounds will get the same chance to learn and use the premier tool of the information age.

It is possible that the child who will **hack** your school network—or the Pentagon, for that matter—is sitting at a desk in your classroom. To do this the *hacker* uses special programs to figure out passwords that ordinarily protect the computer from such intrusions. Some hackers are not malicious, they do it for the same reason other people climb mountains—because the challenge is there. Nevertheless, the activity is illegal and wrong. Other hackers break into computers to get information or to disrupt email or other organizational functions. It is important for students to understand that electronic crimes are as punishable as physical crimes, and that people who are caught are punished. It could be your model and your teaching that changes adventurous students before they go too far.

You can almost be sure that at least one of your students will send an inappropriate email to someone. Your school may have guidelines for computer usage that students (and, often, their parents) will have to read and sign, but you will have front-line responsibility for seeing that the guidelines are followed. Again, your reaction to situations and the guidance you give will help students understand that there is right and wrong in the electronic world, and that wrongdoers are accountable.

You will want to research and discuss copyright issues with your students. Because electronic plagiarism is so easy, you will want to design tasks for your students that will minimize the possibility of their using information, graphics, video, and audio without both transforming it and giving appropriate credit to the owner of the material. This is so important we will spend some time on copyright issues as we study the Internet and its uses.

Preparing Students for the World of Work

Another perspective on using computers in school classrooms involves our need to prepare students for the world of work. The tools that they use to analyze information in schools are the tools they will use when they enter the job market. Bill Gates in *Business @ the Speed of Light* (1999) lists the characteristics of successful business in the information age. In the following list are those items directly related to the technology tools students should know how to use. In side notes the associated tools for each item are listed.

- Insist that communication flow through the organization using email so that you can act on new information with reflex-like speed.
- Study sales data online and find patterns and share insights easily. Understand overall trends and personalize service for individual customers.
- Use digital tools to create cross-departmental virtual teams that can share knowledge and build on each other's ideas in real time, worldwide. Used digital systems to capture corporate history for use by anyone.

hack
Break into a computer or network without permission.

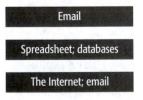

Email

Spreadsheet; databases

The Internet; email

- Convert every paper process to a digital process, eliminating administrative bottlenecks and freeing knowledge workers for more important tasks.
- Create a digital feedback loop to improve the efficiency of physical processes and improve the quality of the products and services created. Every employee should be able to easily track all the key metrics.
- Use digital tools to help customers solve problems for themselves, and reserve personal contact to respond to complex, high-value customer needs.

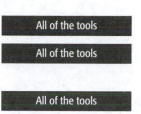

All of the tools

All of the tools

All of the tools

■ THREE KINDS OF COMPUTER USE

This book is primarily about using computer tools to support the teaching/learning process. Nevertheless, it is important that we touch briefly upon all of the possibilities for helping your students learn with computers. There are three major possibilities:

- Teaching your students about computers
- Using a computer as a teacher
- Using computer tools to assist your students to acquire and learn information and to develop higher-order thinking skills

Because of the nature of computing in K–12 schools, you will probably be involved in teaching at least *some* children *some* computer skills for reasons which you will learn in a few paragraphs. In addition, with the right software and the right population of students, you will also use the computer as a teacher. These activities are relatively easy for a teacher to think through and do successfully. For this reason, we will touch on them only briefly. The challenge comes in designing lessons that use computer tools effectively. This topic will be the focus of the remaining chapters in this book.

Teaching about Computers: Computer Literacy

As more children grow up with computers in their homes, teachers will spend less time teaching students about computers. For the time being, however, many students still come to school without basic computer skills.

There are certain things that students need to know about computers both as a life skill and before they can use them as a cognitive tool. They need to know the names for different parts of a computer so they can discuss computer problems with other people. They also need to know some basic troubleshooting techniques to try when a computer or one of its peripherals will not work. In addition, they need to understand how to save and retrieve files successfully. Finally, they need to know the fundamentals of the tool software they use, such as cutting and pasting, working with images, writing formulas in spreadsheets, sending and receiving email and attachments, and doing sorts and queries in databases. Your students will have acquired some of their skills from other teachers, but unless your school has a district-wide scope and sequence for teaching skills to students, it is unlikely that your class will be uniformly computer literate.

Basic skills for computers use

peripheral
Printers, scanners, probes, zip drives, cameras, and other devices that provide input to or output from a computer.

Digital divide

Those who do not come to school with basic computer skills are probably victims of the *digital divide* (U.S. Department of Commerce, 2000). The digital divide is a popular term for the cultural barrier that faces people who do not have access to technology and the Internet—or the ability to use them effectively if they are available. According to the U.S. Department of Commerce, the digital divide exists because of one or more factors, including geography, ethnicity, education, and economics. Statistics from this report indicate that although many of your students will be acquainted with computers, you will still have a significant number of students who are not. Some of the most dramatic statistics in the report indicate that household income is the most important indicator of whether or not there are computers in your students' homes. As you look at Figure 1.1, think about the demographics of your community. How many students will come to you knowing how to save and retrieve a file or use a word processor or presentation software?

Computer literacy, though certainly not as important as reading, can be viewed in a similar fashion. Other learning is based upon it. In order for students to learn history, mathematics, science, or language arts, they need to be able to read. In order for students to use the cognitive tools that computers provide to facilitate learning in history, mathematics, science, or language arts, they must have some rudimentary computer skills. Alert and skillful teachers will discover which students are not computer literate and will assist them in learning the necessary skills to use the tool.

For this reason, if you are just becoming literate in some or all of the computer tools this book presents, it is important that you do two things:

1. Be reflective as you learn new computer skills during this course. Ask yourself what was not clear to you. Note any tricks or tips that you discover during the learning process so you can share them with other beginners.

Be a reflective learner

2. Watch how the person who is teaching you computer skills demonstrates and explains each concept. Be aware of your own reactions, as well as the reactions of

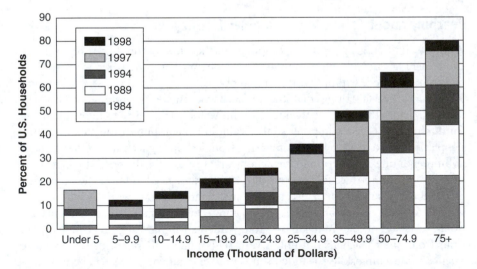

FIGURE 1.1 ■ U.S. Department of Commerce Research on Percentage of Home Computers

other students in your class. If you have an opportunity, watch someone else teach computer skills to children at the level you intend to teach.

How people react to learning new skills varies with their learning style and degree of intimidation. Remember that people learn by doing. When you are showing others how to use a computer, let *them* have the mouse in their hand and their fingers on the keyboard. Talk them through processes, explaining as you go.

It is important to teach students to operate the software they will be using, even though doing this takes valuable class time. Computer skills are **prerequisite knowledge** that will help students learn faster and better using your technology-supported lessons. Do not overload students with computer skills they do not know as you teach them new content. Just as it is impossible to learn to do long division before learning how to add and subtract, if students do not know the key presses they need to complete a complex, computer-supported lesson, you will be wasting their time.

The **cognitive load** involved in learning new computer skills and new content at the same time makes it impossible for students to learn either very well. In a classic study, G. A. Miller (1965) determined that our working memory (where information resides before it goes to long-term memory) only allows us to hold "7 ± 2" chunks of information in our minds at one time. According to Gagne, Yekovich, & Yekovich (1993), "Because of the limited capacity of WM (working memory), it is difficult to perform several mental tasks at once. . . . Usually people are comfortable doing only one cognitively demanding task at a time."

The first time you make an assignment that uses a computer tool, use an LCD projector to demonstrate to the whole class the computer skills they will need by modeling a simple activity for them. Then give students some computer time and some practice activities to help them learn or remember. As the school year progresses, you will have to do this less and less.

Using the Computer as a Teacher for Your Students

Introduction   Instructional software was education's first genuine attempt to put computers to work in classrooms. The idea that the computer is a teacher grew out of Skinnerian research that suggests immediate feedback, along with rewards, motivates learners and improves knowledge retention. During the 1960s and 1970s, educators and software developers worked very hard to adapt the computer to be a teacher. This effort resulted in large collections of instructional software that ran on mainframes, such as Control Data's PLATO system developed by William Norris. He believed that computers could replace teachers for the delivery of instruction (Roblyer & Edwards, 2000). This genre of software has shown some success in specific areas of education (which we will discuss shortly), but it has not lived up to its early promise. Instructional software that is effective usually is quite expensive and/or very narrow in scope. In other words, educators do not need to fear that a computer will replace them. However, educators do need to know how to judge whether instructional software is effective or not and when its use is appropriate.

Kinds of instructional software titles   There are three kinds of instructional software. They are usually identified as tutorials, drill-and-practice, or simulations.

History of computer-based instruction (CBI)

prerequisite knowledge
Knowledge that students must have in order to assimilate and learn new information.

cognitive load
How many chunks of information a person can think about at one time.

Tutorials vary widely
in quality

Tutorials.   Tutorials cover a specific topic. They explain a subject. Often they contain elements that allow students to explore information, practice using the information they have explored, and take a test when they have finished exploring and practicing. One derogatory name for poor tutorial software is "electronic page turner." Page upon page of text interspersed with graphics and a question every page or so is the worst kind of tutorial software. It offers hardly more for a learner than a book (if anything) and is not nearly as portable. Better tutorials are written in a nonlinear fashion using **hypertext** and **hypermedia** so that learners may follow themes or strands of thought. Well-written tutorials, as well as drill-and-practice programs, are especially useful with exceptional students. "For students who require small steps and many repetitions to learn a new concept, computers are the perfect, patient tutors, repeating steps and lessons as many times as necessary" (Woolfolk, 2000).

Drill and practice
helps students with
factual knowledge

Drill and Practice.   Before students use this software they should have already had some related instruction. Drill-and-practice software contains questions or problems which students answer and on which they receive feedback. This kind of software can be quite helpful for specific learning problems. It is helpful when students need to learn basic facts or skills before they can move on to higher-order conceptual thinking. In a typical drill and practice session, the computer gives the student a problem, the student suggests a solution, and the computer indicates whether the suggested solution is correct. Sometimes, better drill-and-practice software allows students to ask for hints or gives an explanation with the solution. Some software titles allow students to challenge themselves with a timer. Drill on math facts, as well as spelling and other skills associated with language arts, are examples of typical content that drill-and-practice programs address. The main idea for teachers to remember is that drill-and-practice software is not written to introduce concepts. Teachers introduce new concepts and assign activities to reinforce what has been taught. After an adequate introduction, drill-and-practice software is *one* useful way to help students interact with content.

Simulations stimulate
higher-order thinking

Simulations and Modeling.   Simulations and models, if they are well written and really do represent the real world, are the most complex and helpful of the three kinds of instructional software. Because of the computer's ability to do complex calculations quickly, programmers can build models of reality. Sometimes these models contain graphics that help students visualize what is being simulated. Others are purely numerical. "Some scholars assert that simulations and computer-based models are the most powerful resources for the advancement and application of mathematics and science since the origins of mathematical modeling during the Renaissance" (Bransford, Brown, & Cocking, 2000, p. 201). Examples of simulation software include SimCity (and the rest of the Sim series), Oregon Trail, and Geometer's Sketchpad.

Simulations provide "what if" sessions for students. In Oregon Trail, for example, students can ask "what if" questions such as:

■ What if I spend all of my money on food at the beginning of the trip?
■ What if I save my money and depend on hunting?
■ Should I cross the river or get to my destination by going the long way?

---

hypertext
New windows of text that expand on a topic when the user clicks a "hotlink" word or icon.

hypermedia
New windows that show related graphics, sound, or video when the user clicks a "hotlink" word or icon.

Models are different than simulations because students build them with real-world data. Models are built with computer-based visualization and analysis tools into which students may import real-world information. Once students have imported real-world information, they may then ask "what if" questions or view alternate representations of the data. Examples of concepts students have successfully studied with modeling tools include: acceleration, light, sound, climate, population ecology, history, genetics, Newtonian mechanics, velocity, and water quality (Bransford et al., 2000, p. 204).

The complexity of a simulation or model has to do with the number of parameters or variables that a student can set. The likeness to reality that the simulation produces has to do with the accuracy of the mathematical formulas behind the **user interface.** Oregon Trail, used mostly in upper elementary grades, has only a few parameters for users to set. Geometer's Sketch Pad, on the other hand, has many more. Simulations are different than tutorials and drill-and-practice software in two major ways:

■ Simulations require higher-order thinking skills: analysis, judgment, and synthesis.
■ Good simulations are rare. Teachers can't say, "I think I will go to a software catalogue and pick out a simulation on this week's social studies (or science, or language arts) unit," and expect to find a good one that applies to their grade level and specific curriculum. After careful research you may find one or a few (depending on the content area) simulations that will help you during a school year.

To see how simulations work, you can explore some that exist on the Internet. One site supported by the Shodor Education Foundation (1996) contains tools for both modeling and simulation on astronomy, environmental issues, fractals, mathematics, and biomedical problems. You will find the address of this site in the Annotated Resources section at the end of this chapter.

The Computer as a Teacher   Computers can be used to deliver lessons if they are used wisely. First, the software must match the curricular goal. This restricts the number of titles available for many topics, especially beyond the elementary grades. While there are many programs that teach early math and reading concepts, an English teacher might have a hard time finding a piece of software related to a particular short story or novel. A social science teacher may likewise find nothing on the colonial period in America that a book cannot do just as well. Teachers of mathematics have a larger choice of drill-and-practice programs on topics ranging through calculus. Science teachers will find some isolated software on topics that match their curriculum, but still cannot depend on software to teach more than perhaps 10 percent of their science curriculum. Students with cognitive disabilities historically have benefited the most from instructional software because of the nature of the computer itself: patient repetition of facts.

Second, the software must be used appropriately. Drill-and-practice and simulation software provides practice with facts and ideas after a teacher has presented them. Tutorials provide a back-up or review for a teacher presentation but are rarely good enough to teach a concept without a teacher's help. Third, if an existing book, classroom activity, or worksheet can do the job as well as a software title, then it is more cost effective to use what is available.

Simulations reflect the real world

user interface
How the screen displays information and provides opportunities for the user to navigate through the program to find more information to modify or display.

Instructional software covers a limited amount of information

Instructional software must be used appropriately

Using a Computer as a Cognitive Tool

This third use of computers in the teaching/learning process is full of even more possibilities for teaching and learning. Computers provide new and effective ways for students to gather, analyze, and present information. The computer tools provide motivation, incentive, and even feedback to students doing tasks that lie at all levels of Bloom's Taxonomy (Jonassen, 2000). Computer tools support three components of the information processing tasks that students use to acquire facts and skills: gather, analyze, and display/present information.

Data analysis tools

Gathering Information   Achieving information literacy is key to the economic well-being of our students. As our school system developed, it was based on what nineteenth-century students in industrial America needed: skills in reading, writing, and arithmetic. The information age has not so much changed the need for those basic skills, but has added another: information literacy. "Learning how to learn is fundamental to economic and personal success" (Carr, 1998, p. 1).

Information literacy is a key to success in the twenty-first century

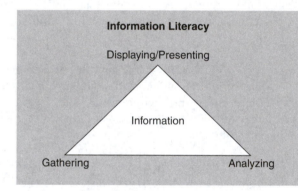

The Internet is the premier tool of our era for gathering information. Internet browsers (Explorer, Netscape), associated search engines (e.g., Google, Lycos), and email clients (e.g., Hotmail, Eudora, Pegasus) are all specialized tools for finding information or communicating on the Internet. Gathering information on the Internet includes knowing how to find, retrieve, and use text, audio, and video files as well as how to communicate with others.

Gathering information reflectively

However, there is much more to the information-collection process than just using the tools. In addition to knowing how to get information, students need to know what to do with it once they have it. They need the skills to decide whether it is fact or opinion. If the information is fact, they need to know how to determine whether the facts are accurate. They also need to know how to cite information and understand copyright issues.

Displaying and Presenting Information   When people think of using computers to present information, what often comes to mind is the Powerpoint presentation. A finished

Powerpoint presentation is the proverbial tip of the iceberg in terms of student learning. The power of presentation software for students lies in the planning process they must use to make the presentation. The act of using presentation software teaches students concepts and processes as they visualize the relationships among ideas.

Presentation software helps students understand relationships among ideas

In order to do a presentation, students first write an outline, then create a **concept map.** Drawing a concept map, either on paper or in a computer application such as Inspiration, helps students acquire facts and also helps them see relationships that exist among the facts.

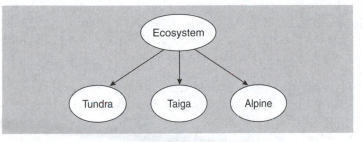

Next, students write a **storyboard.** In this phase of the preparation, they think about how to effectively display the information from their concept maps. They decide which ideas should be emphasized, and how. They decide where to make hyperlinks between screens to reflect the structure of the information they are presenting. Only after they have written the storyboard do they begin to create the actual presentation.

The nonlinear nature of online presentations is one of the reasons student authors learn so much as they develop a presentation. In an electronic report, students can make hyperlinks from page to page. They do not have to think "from first to last," as they would in writing a traditional report; instead they think about the logical connections among ideas. Rather than being simply a fun way to prepare a speech, presentation software provides effective and meaningful tasks to help students learn facts (at the lower end of Bloom's Taxonomy) and relationships (at the higher end of the taxonomy).

Word processing is another way of presenting information. The word processor is a powerful tool because it:

Word processing software expands each student's collection of writing and editing tools

- Provides high-quality output for children with coordination problems who cannot write well with a pen
- Permits students to edit their work and change it without having to re-copy a whole paper or report
- Provides students another way to check their spelling, punctuation, and grammar
- Has reading index indicators to help students judge the level of their writing
- Provides students with the ability to create tables easily and quickly
- Allows students to import graphics, charts, and graphs to illustrate and amplify their writing

concept map
Sketch of the relationship (possibly hierarchical) among concepts or topics.

storyboard
Author's tool for planning screen elements, possible user interactions, and the sequence and flow between screens.

Looking at the list above, it is clear that the word processor makes the act of writing easier, makes the result look better, provides some feedback to the student that only a teacher could otherwise give, and adds variety to the ways that students can present information in a report.

Data analysis tools

Analyzing Information   Tools for analyzing information include databases and spreadsheets. In the past when students gathered information, they often collected it from textbooks, encyclopedias, and magazines. The facts that they gathered had been pre-analyzed for them and their job was to learn the facts and memorize the conclusions of the author who provided the information. When students wrote reports, they would sometimes read several authors who might have interpreted the facts differently. In this case, the students then were asked to weigh the merits of the arguments and judge which arguments seemed to make the most sense. Rarely, however, did the students start with just the facts, analyze them, make their own judgments, and then go to the experts for information. Databases and spreadsheets make this process possible for academic topics.

Computer tools allow students to make their own judgments

Databases and spreadsheets allow students to input raw data and find patterns in it from which they can make predictions, draw inferences, and describe unknowns. Databases and spreadsheets are alike in two ways. First, they both provide **sorts** and queries. For example, a user could perform a sort to find the tallest animal and a query to find all animals that are carnivorous and nocturnal. A second similarity between databases and spreadsheets is that users can do calculations using both. However, databases are built to analyze text and spreadsheets are most useful for numbers. You will learn much more about the different strengths of databases and spreadsheets in later chapters. The key point to remember now is that students are working with raw data when they use databases and spreadsheets to analyze information. They are not working with someone else's analysis of the raw data. In this sense and in line with the constructivist perspective on education, students first construct their own knowledge, then with that background they consult experts so they can make their own judgments about the topic at hand. The ability to analyze data is another element of information literacy.

■ SUMMARY

Educational technology is a broad field, with potential for high impact on teaching and learning. It is more than computers, more than computer tutorials, drill and practice, simulations, or tools. Proper use of educational technology requires an understanding of the computer and its associated software and peripherals and how they all support the teaching and learning process. That support of the teaching and learning process takes several avenues, which are summarized in Table 1.4.

The focus of this book will be to demonstrate instructional models for tool software that is found on most computers. Tool software is effective for two reasons. First, it provides learners practice with information across the levels of Bloom's Taxonomy. Second, it is the software of the "real world." As students learn to use tool software to solve problems, they are not only learning both the information and the skills they need in their classroom, but also the skills that will serve them well when they reach the world of work.

sorts
Sorts put information in order (a-to-z or 0 to 100, for example).

TABLE 1.4 ■ Technology in the Teaching and Learning Process

Topic	Example
Technology operations and concepts	• Knowing the basics of computer operation and maintenance • Knowing how to use the Internet, word processor, database, spreadsheet, and presentation software
Planning and designing learning environments and experiences	• Constructivist learning environment • Problem-based learning
Teaching, learning, and the curriculum	• Models of teaching that nurture and use information processing skills such as problem-based learning and constructivism
Assessment and evaluation	• Develop goals and objectives based on a learning taxonomy like Benjamin Bloom's
Productivity and professional practice	• Increase communication with parents • Distance learning • Use of Integrated learning systems to track student performance
Social, ethical, legal, and human issues	• Understanding the ethical use of computers • Being careful to recognize the effects of the digital divide

■ REFERENCES ■

Bloom, B. S. (1954). *Taxonomy of educational objectives handbook I: Cognitive domain.* New York: David McKay Company, Inc.

Bransford, J. D., Brown, A. L., & Cocking, R. R. (Eds.). (1999). *How people learn: Brain, mind, experience, and school.* Washington, DC: National Academy Press.

Carr, J. A. (1998). Information literacy and teacher education. ERIC (ED4242331) http://www.ed.gov/databases/ERIC_Digests/ed424321.html.

Gagne, E., Yekovich, C., & Yekovich, F. (1993). *The cognitive psychology of school learning.* New York: HarperCollins.

International Society for Technology in Education, NETS Project. (2000). National educational technology standards for students. Eugene, OR: Author. www.ISTE.org.

Jonassen, D. (2000). *Computers as mindtools for schools.* Upper Saddle River: Merrill.

Joyce, B., Weil, M., & Calhoun, E. (2000). *Models of teaching.* Boston: Allyn and Bacon.

Miller, G. A. (1956). The magical number seven, plus or minus two: Some limits on our capacity for processing information. *Psychological Review, 63,* 81–97.

Reiser, R., & Dempsey, J. (2002). *Instructional design and technology.* Upper Saddle River: Prentice-Hall.

Roblyer, M. D., & Edwards, J. (2000). *Integrating educational technology into teaching.* Upper Saddle River: Prentice-Hall.

Schacter, J. (1999). The impact of education technology on student achievement: What the most current research has to say. Santa Monica: Milken Exchange on Education Technology, Milken Family Foundation. http://www.mff.org/edtech.

Shodor Education Foundation. (1996). Master tools. http://www.shodor.org/master.

Thomas, J., Mergendoller, J., & Michaelson, A. (1999). *Project-based learning handbook.* Novato: Buck Institute for Education.

U.S. Department of Commerce. (2000). Falling through the Net: Defining the digital divide. Washington, DC: Author. www.ntia.doc.gov/ntiahome/fttn99/contents.html.

Woolfolk, A. (2000). *Educational psychology,* 8th ed. Boston: Allyn and Bacon.

■ ANNOTATED RESOURCES ■

www.ISTE.org

Standards

On this site, you will find ISTE standards for both students and teachers. In addition, you will find a rich library of lesson plans, books about specific areas of educational technology, news of events, and professional conferences for K–12 teachers.

www.ntia.doc.gov/ntiahome/fttn99/contents.html

Digital divide

At this site, you will find many more charts and accompanying text that define the digital divide. If you understand the demographics of the schools in the area where you will be teaching, you could study this information with your future job site in mind.

Anderson, L. W., & Krathwohl, D. *A taxonomy of teaching and learning: A revision of Bloom's taxonomy of educational objectives.* In press.

Bloom's Taxonomy updated

Anderson, L. Rethinking Bloom's Taxonomy: Implications for testing and assessment. ERIC (ED435630). Found on the Allyn and Bacon website under the identifiers "Bloom's Taxonomy" and "Scoring Rubrics."

Benjamin Bloom's Taxonomy is in the process of being updated in an interesting table of two dimensions rather than Bloom's original single dimension. The top row of the table is very similar to Bloom's "levels of thought." The second dimension, the left-most column, details kinds of knowledge. So, for example, one cell of the table might be "remembering factual knowledge." The next might be "remembering conceptual knowledge." The complete rubric is published in Woolfolk (2000) with the permission of Anderson and Krathwohl.

The impact of education technology on student achievement: What most current research has to say. www.milkenexchange.org.

Milken research report

The complete copy of this eleven-page report may be viewed or downloaded in its entirety from the Milken web site. Although some dates in the publication seem old, I share the frustration of anyone who has tried to find a large body of solid, recent empirical research on the effect of computers in the teaching environment. This is a young field and the greatest work in the area is yet to be done.

www.shodor.org/master

> This web site is a fascinating place to visit. The site has many working simulations that are appropriate for middle school through grade 12. Names of the simulations at this site include GalaxSee, SimSurface, Environmental Models, Fractal Modeling Tools, GnuPlot, BioMedical Modeling, and The Pit and the Pendulum. On this page there are further links to "Models in Medicine and the BioSciences" and an "Environmental Sciences" page. Each of these pages has more interactive modeling and simulation problems.

`· Simulations`

The digital divide and its implications for language arts. ERIC (ED442138).

> This article not only discusses the digital divide but also provides five Internet sites with more information, along with references to journal articles.

`Digital divide`

Hanza, M. K., & Aalhalbi, B. (1999). SITE 99. Society for Information Technology and Teacher Education International Conference. ERIC (ED432220).

> This article speaks to the use of computers to motivate students as well as to support learning at all levels of Bloom's Taxonomy. It expands on the use of computers in the curriculum, discussing their use to enhance creativity.

`Teaching in the information age`

Duschene, S. (1998). Teaching functional skills through technology: Using assistive technology and multimedia tools to develop career awareness for students with cognitive disabilities. ERIC (ED4413111).

> This 97-page discussion tracks a 7-week career awareness exercise for four cognitively disabled fifth grade students, showing how computer tools and peripherals assisted these students with a positive learning experience. It will provide you with an overview of how to develop a computer-supported unit.

`Computers and cognitively disabled students`

Cooper, P. A. Paradigm shifts in designed instruction: From behaviorism to cognitivism to constructivism. *Educational Technology,* v. 13(5), 12–18 May, 1993.

> Constructivism and technology work very well together. This article follows the history, development, and implementation of constructivism. The author places constructivism in the larger context of approaches to designing instruction. It is not easy reading, but for the persevering reading Cooper provides a concrete and detailed comparison and contrast of the three educational philosophies.

`Constructivism and the classroom`

The science of learning. *Educational Leadership.* November, 2000.

> This edition is devoted to the science of learning. Two articles especially describe the application of constructivist principles to the classroom: "The Brain-Compatible Curriculum" and "Brain-Based Instruction in Action." These articles are well written and very readable.

`Brain-based learning`

An Introduction to Computers for Teaching

OBJECTIVES

- Give examples of how computer tools are integrated into the teaching/learning process.
- Analyze an example of computer tools integrated into the teaching/learning process using a general instructional model.
- Name content areas for which each of the tools is most useful.
- Name commonly taught cognitive processes or skills associated with each tool.

Role of the teacher

Good teachers know how to design lessons that help students remember what they learn. Teachers in a learner-centered classroom are not primarily lecturers and presenters, but rather knowledge engineers. They design presentation strategies that play to the strengths of how their students learn best. The purpose of computers for educators has not been primarily for computation but for the presentation of information to students.

Throughout this book, we will take virtual field trips. We will visit classrooms where teachers and students are using computer tools, and after the field trip, you will read observations on the lesson that you observed. You will learn the strategies that the teacher used to set up the lesson and why they were used. Before we start talking about "a general teaching model," we will take our first two field trips.

FIELD TRIP 2.1

A Technology-Supported High School Classroom

Teaching in a mainstreamed classroom

This mainstreamed classroom provides instruction to children of many abilities, some who cannot read the text and understand what they have read, and others who read very well and score high on standardized tests. Ms. Anthony has struggled with the problem every year for the eight years that she has taught. In the beginning, she taught to the readers and let the non-readers drift, so long as they did not disrupt the rest of the class. Then, feeling guilty, she taught to the non-readers and let the readers drift, which didn't work either. Readers can be just as disruptive as non-readers when they are not challenged.

Ms. Anthony learned about text-reading software in a summer workshop and decided to try to solve the reading problem that kept her and her students from the content that she loved and wanted to teach. After two or three tries, she figured out how to use technology effectively to involve all of her students in learning and doing science.

Her fourth and most successful technology-supported unit was the astronomy chapter in the science book. In this unit, like the others she taught, she provided the students with several activities. One activity required the students to read the textbook for information that she wanted them to know. If they chose, students could scan the text of the assignment into the computer, transfer it to text-reading software, sit, and listen while the computer displayed the text on the screen as it read that same text back to the students. She gave all of her students training in this process and then allowed them to either use the process or read to themselves silently. Along with the reading assignment, Ms. Anthony gave students an assignment involving an electronic database. While she was preparing for this unit, she found a NASA database of objects in and near our solar system. The database provided her with the name, mass, density, atmosphere (if any), distance from the center of the Milky Way, and several other fields of information for the students to peruse. Before she provided her students with the electronic database, she removed the name of each object and substituted a letter.

> **Text-reading software**

> **Electronic database**

> **Developing an assignment**

She then set up a problem for them. Working in teams, the students became NASA scientists who had successfully launched a probe that had sent the information contained in the database back to Mission Control on Earth. Using sort and query functions, the students worked with the database to name as many objects as they could, given information from their assigned reading and other information they could glean from the library and the Internet. Their goal was to draw a map of the part of the galaxy represented by the database and to write a report describing the objects on the map. Ms. Anthony hoped the students would recognize their solar system and the earth.

She was pleased with the results. Her assignment had something for everyone. Because of the text-reading software, the non-readers had an opportunity to get the information they so often missed because they could not read. Those students who enjoyed problem solving had an opportunity to not only solve problems with the database but also unobtrusively model the process for their less skillful teammates. Students who were more graphically inclined were able to model their graphical skills by making maps, while other students who enjoyed writing used the word processor to model their writing skills. Everyone was involved. No one missed information because of a skill deficiency.

Our second field trip in this chapter will take us to an elementary language arts classroom where students are learning how to organize sentences into paragraphs and paragraphs into compositions.

> **Teaching writing**

FIELD TRIP 2.2

A Technology-Supported Elementary Classroom

Mr. Robbins has found the concept of organization to be one of the most difficult language arts topics that he teaches. During the first ten years that he taught, he showed children how to outline. Although this technique works for some children, many others believe that outlining is busywork and do not see the connection between outlining and a finished composition. Still others simply never understand the hierarchy of importance that topics take on in an outline.

> **Concept mapping**

After attending a workshop on concept mapping, Mr. Robbins began teaching children how to map concepts in preparation for writing a composition. In the workshop he learned how to use a piece of software called Inspiration to actually do the mapping. The great feature of the software is that it not only allows students to make concept maps, but converts concept maps to outlines and outlines to concept maps. The children then cut and paste the final outline into a word processor where they filled in the outline they had created.

Concept maps are graphical outlines. In the workshop that Mr. Robbins' school district provided for him, he learned to capitalize on having students do both an outline and concept map. Because the outlining and concept mapping were done on a computer and could be viewed quickly and easily (as either an outline or a map—the software made the change), students could look at their topics in several different ways before they actually began writing. They could write an outline first and turn it into a concept map by just clicking on a menu item. Alternatively, they could start with a concept map first and then turn it into an outline, again by simply clicking on a menu item. From there, they could cut and paste their outline into a word processor and begin fleshing it out. While they were working with the concept map and outline in Inspiration they began to see that when they did their concept maps they would often think of many different and sometimes unrelated ideas.

Seeing relationships

When they turned these concept maps into outlines they could tell that some ideas just did not fit or that they were in the wrong place. They could easily fix their errors in logic by cutting and pasting. When they clicked back from their outlines to their concept maps, they found that they could generate more ideas and rearrange them quickly. They began seeing the outline and concept map as tools to help them think, not as wasted effort that they would have to repeat once they began writing with a word processor.

Using computers to enhance learning requires thought and planning

You can see that using computers in a classroom is a complex process that requires some training as well as much thought and planning. The first few times you use a computer to support a topic that you teach, it will be more work, not less. It will not be anything like having students sit in front of a computer and absorb knowledge from software that someone else wrote.

How computers help students

With respect to student learning, you can draw two conclusions. First, in some cases computer tools help students with skills they lack, such as reading and/or computational skills. When they use computer tools this way they are not held back in a content area because of their lack of skill with reading, writing, or numbers. Second, students using computers are able to think at a higher level on Bloom's Taxonomy than they would without the computer. The computer does the low level tasks, giving students the mental space to analyze and synthesize information.

How teachers use computers

With respect to teaching, you can also draw some conclusions. Students and teachers must have a goal with an interesting problem or several problems to solve. The solution to the problem may require more than one kind of computer tool. And, finally, computer skills are not taught for their own sake but as a means to an end. Curricular objectives are always the goal. Computers support those objectives.

Table 2.1 lists the most useful and available software commonly used for solving problems or completing projects at different grade levels and in different content areas. Each type of software will be discussed in more detail later in this book. Just familiarize yourself with these tables now. As you read this book, you will learn more about each item as you acquire more understanding about the tools themselves and the instructional situations in which they are used.

Most tool software is applicable at most grade levels and content areas. There is a notable exception. Notice that instructional software heads the list of useful software

TABLE 2.1 ■ Useful Tools

Useful Tools—Grades K–3	Useful Tools—Grades 4–12
For English Instructional software Word processor for young children Hypermedia/Presentation software Internet	**For English** Word processor Database Presentation software Internet Instructional software
For Science Instructional software Internet Databases Hypermedia/presentation software Word processor	**For Science** Spreadsheet Internet Database Presentation software Instructional software Word processor
For Social Studies Instructional software Databases Presentation software Internet Word processor	**For Social Studies** Spreadsheet Internet Databases Presentation software Instructional software
For Mathematics Instructional software Calculator Word processor Internet	**For Mathematics** Word processor Spreadsheet Calculator Instructional software Internet
For Foreign Language Internet Instructional software Presentation software	**For Foreign Language** Internet Instructional software Presentation software
Music Notation software The Midi	**Music** Database Presentation software Notation software The Midi

Common uses of software by grade level

for grades K–3. Instructional software is especially useful for students who are learning the facts that they need to help them reason and think at higher levels. Drill-and-practice software for mathematics and spelling are good examples. Software titles that teach such items as making change or doing fractions are two other examples.

■ INSTRUCTIONAL MODELS AND COMPUTERS

When a teacher is new to integrating computers into the teaching/learning process, it is difficult to know which elements of instruction the technology improves upon, which it neither helps nor hinders, and which it actually impedes. Instructional time is such a precious commodity and computers are so scarce and expensive that the first thing a teacher should try to understand is what they are good for. A case in point would be drill-and-practice software. A computer is an expensive set of flash cards when it is used merely to generate spelling or multiplication problems and give quick feedback. A card can do this function as well. Similarly, computer tutorials which are simply electronic page-turners are an extravagance for students who can read and turn their own pages in a textbook.

On the other hand, for students using a large electronic database to investigate the relationships among creatures in a biome, the computer is unmatched in its ability to elicit analytical and synthetic thinking on the part of the user (Bransford, Brown, & Cocking, 1999, p. 203). Similarly, editing on a computer is faster, easier, and suits the attention span and physical writing skills of children better than a pencil (Roblyer, 2000, p. 117). Tables 2.2 and 2.3 list many of the learning activities or models for which each tool is best suited. These learning activities are models because they are shells into which teachers of any grade level or content area can fit their own curriculum. They are models because they describe an instructional process.

Constructing Technology-Supported Lessons

There is a systematic way to construct technology-supported lessons. Once you decide on goals for your lesson and choose the problems you want to teach, then you decide on the models and supporting tools that fit the problem. The models are named in Table 2.2 and 2.3 and explained by the rest of the chapters in this book. It is not necessary to memorize the information in Tables 2.2 and 2.3, but you do need to read

TABLE 2.2 ■ Lesson Construction Models for Software Tools

Tool	Learning Activities (Models)
Word processor	The newspaper
	The research report
	Rewrite (style, content)
	Revision editing
	Journaling; lab reports; notetaking; group investigations
	Composition
	Creative writing
	Substitution exercises [Supply the missing (words, sentences, paragraphs); Remove the extra (words, sentences, paragraphs)]
	Ordering; sorting
	Outlining; logical sequencing
	Grammar; thesaurus; spell checker
	Following directions; writing directions

TABLE 2.3 ■ More Tools and Their Uses

Tool	Uses
Databases	Describing an unknown
	Making a prediction
	Making a decision
Spreadsheets	Solve story problems
	Teach what-if thinking
	Teach estimation
	Show relationships
Presentation software	Classify and describe knowledge
	Illustrate steps in procedures or processes
	Expose students to information in many different contexts (text, video, graphics, animation, and audio)
	Provide students an opportunity to construct knowledge in unique ways and different contexts
Internet & Email	Talk to the expert; data collection; newspaper; simulation; role playing; electronic debate; classroom discussion; research; communication; presentations

them carefully. As soon as you understand more about how each tool works and how some of them work together, the information there will feel automatic to you.

Figure 2.1 is a summary of the process the teachers in our field trips used as they thought about the information they had to teach and the best way of teaching it. Notice that the lesson has steps, no matter what the content of the lesson is.

✔ CHECKING YOUR UNDERSTANDING

2.1

Analyze the ways Mr. Robbins and Ms. Anthony used the computers in their classrooms. To do this, use Tables 2.2 and 2.3. Identify the tools that these teachers used and the instructional model or models the teachers used with each tool.

2.2

Analyze the learning outcomes of Mr. Robbins's and Ms. Anthony's students with Bloom's Taxonomy, Table 1.3. Find each learning outcome or product that resulted from the lesson and place it at one of the levels of the table.

2.3

Below you will find an outline to use as a guide for planning a computer-supported lesson. Pick a topic that you know very well and design a lesson for students at a level you think you might teach.

    I.   Name the unit for which you want to use computer support.

        A. State your goals for this unit.

        B. Name all of the tools that could be used (Tables 2.1) for this unit.

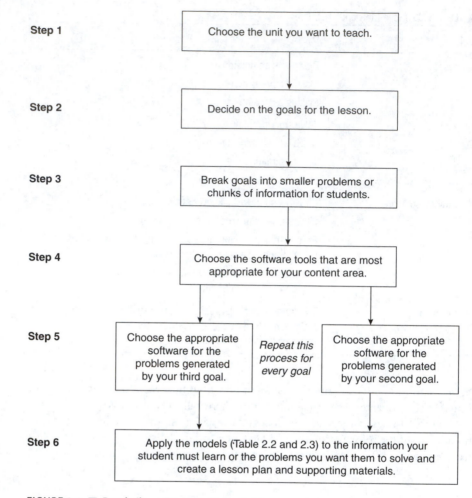

FIGURE 2.1 ■ Developing a Computer-Supported Lesson

    II. Add detail to your *first* goal:
        A. Concepts students are to learn.
        B. Problem they will solve.
        C. Computer tools (Tables 2.1) and associated models (Tables 2.2 and 2.3) your students will use.
        D. Possible ways to use the tool to teach the content or solve the problem described in II. A.
        E. What products do you want your students to produce or skills they should demonstrate as they work on this goal? Use Bloom's table to classify your student's products or skills.
    III. Add detail to your *second* goal: Repeat steps in section II until you have described your approach to accomplishing your goals.

■ SUMMARY

Using computers to teach involves looking at content first and identifying computer tools whose function facilitates student interaction with the material. In our field trips we learned that computer tools have a wide range of applicability—from helping students read, to helping them reason. Although understanding how computer tools apply to teaching content seems complicated, it can be approached in an organized and ultimately intuitive fashion.

For the remainder of this book we will explore this organization (the models of Tables 2.2 and 2.3). First you will learn how to match models to information that you must teach. Then you will learn that each model associated with each tool is composed of a series of steps. You will learn to apply these steps to build lessons for your students. In addition, you will learn some ways to determine if you achieved your goal—a satisfactory learning outcome for your students.

■ REFERENCES ■

Bransford, J. D., Brown, A. L., & Cocking, R. R., (Eds.). (1999). How people learn: Brain, mind, experience, and school. Washington, DC: National Academy Press.

Roblyer, M. D., & Edwards, J. (2000). *Integrating educational technology into teaching.* Upper Saddle River: Prentice-Hall.

■ ANNOTATED RESOURCES ■

Seng-Seok-Hoon (1998), Enhancing Learning: Computers and Early Childhood Education. EDRS IR019590.

Those who specialize in early childhood education will find this article helpful. It is a summary of research about computer use with preschoolers. The references will lead the reader to further research.

Computers and preschoolers

Lloyd, M. (1998). The problem cycle. *Learning and Leading with Technology,* (26), 3 pp. 6–13.

This article will give you some perspectives and ideas. As you continue your reading in this book, you will learn that integrating computers into the teaching/learning process will depend on your skill in identifying and writing problems in a context that motivates and challenges students.

Writing problems

Guerard, Elizabeth B. Texas district links pay raises to tech proficiency. *eSchool News,* September 6, 2001. *http://www.eschoolnews.org/news/showStory.cfm?ArticleID=2987*

If you would like to see how what you have just read about the uses of computers in classrooms relates to the skills that you must have when you become a teacher,

Computers and the real world

go to this online article. The author talks about how teacher skills will be measured. She includes four levels:

Level One:

- An understanding of operating systems
- An understanding of Microsoft Word
- An understanding of electronic gradebooks
- An understanding of how to use email
- An understanding of the Internet
- Completion of a Level One practicum

Level Two:

- The ability to use multimedia and desktop publishing programs
- The ability to use one of the following: spreadsheets, Inspiration, or TimeLiner
- A completed lesson plan with a teacher-generated technology product incorporating desktop publishing, multimedia, and one of the following: spreadsheets, Inspiration, or Timeliner

Level Three:

- The ability to use and create web pages
- An understanding of peripherals, database, and file-management utilities
- A completed unit plan with a teacher-generated and student-generated component

Level Four (optional):

- A teacher-created web page for student and parent access, published to the district intranet and the Internet
- The ability to mail-merge documents
- An understanding of photo editing
- The advanced use of database, spreadsheet, multimedia, and desktop publishing
- A completed six-week plan for the integration of technology into all aspects of the curriculum for one subject area

A teacher's proficiency at any level is measured with a product and is graded by a committee of teachers using a rubric. To understand more about the philosophy behind this program, go to the Internet site and read the whole article.

CHAPTER 3

Information Retrieval

OBJECTIVES

- Describe the history of the Internet.
- Use a research model and the Internet to write a report.
- Know how to judge the quality of information on the Internet.
- Know rules of copyright for Internet materials.
- Know two ways courses are delivered at a distance.
- Judge the quality of distance courses.

To use the Internet effectively, you (and your students) will need to be able to do the following:

- Find the address bar in a browser, enter an address, and go to a site
- Download text, graphics, and plug-ins from an Internet site
- Bookmark Internet sites for later reference
- Navigate through Internet sites
- Use the refresh button
- Download and save text, graphics, audio, and video files
- Display downloaded files in appropriate applications

■ A SHORT HISTORY OF THE INTERNET

The vision for describing the Internet was articulated long before we had the technology to implement it. The first public description of the Internet is credited to

Vannevar Bush, a U.S. government employee, in an article in the *Atlantic Monthly* in 1945. He said:

The memex

Consider a future device for individual use, which is a sort of mechanized private file and library. It needs a name, and to coin one at random, "memex" will do. A memex is a device in which an individual stores all his books, records, and communications, and which is mechanized so that it may be consulted with exceeding speed and flexibility. It is an enlarged intimate supplement to his memory.

It consists of a desk, and while it can presumably be operated from a distance, it is primarily the piece of furniture at which he works. On the top are slanting translucent screens, on which material can be projected for convenient reading. There is a keyboard, and sets of buttons and levers. Otherwise, it looks like an ordinary desk.

Vannevar Bush did more than just dream about this device. He helped fund it. As director of the U.S. Office of Scientific Research and Development during World War II, he employed more than 6,000 scientists and coordinated the development of the atomic bomb. Coordinating that many scientists from the military and universities around the country required an extensive communication system. This need helped Bush envision the memex.

The military–university partnership developed by Bush and the funding structure that he created led to the initial funding of the Internet by the Defense Advanced Research Projects Agency (DARPA). Bush's vision was moved forward by J. C. R. Licklider who refined Bush's memex into a vision of his own. In an article entitled "Man-Computer Symbiosis" published in 1960, Licklider said,

The vision becomes DARPANET

It seems reasonable to envision, for a time 10 or 15 years hence, a "thinking center" that will incorporate the functions of present-day libraries together with anticipated advances in information storage and retrieval.

The picture readily enlarges itself into a network of such centers, connected to one another by wide-band communication lines and to individual users by leased-wire services. In such a system, the speed of the computers would be balanced, and the cost of gigantic memories and the sophisticated programs would be divided by the number of users.

Within two years of writing this article, Licklider was hired by DARPA to actually build a network linking the Department of Defense computers at the Pentagon, Cheyenne Mountain, and Strategic Air Command Headquarters. Because funding for research to develop the Internet came from DARPA, it was originally called "DARPANET" or the "ARPANET" (Stewart, 2000).

It took several years for the technology to catch up with Licklider's vision. Researchers from Massachusetts Institute of Technology (MIT) and University of California, Los Angeles (UCLA) divided the tasks and in September of 1969, UCLA became the first **node** on the ARPANET. The Stanford Research Institute (SRI) became the second node, and the first message was sent from one of the scientist's laboratories (Leonard Kleinrock's laboratory) at UCLA to SRI soon after the second node was

The first message

established. That same year two more nodes were added, one at the University of California Santa Barbara and one at the University of Utah.

By the end of 1969, the Internet existed. In 1972 Robert Kahn, one of the researchers who worked on the development of ARPANET gave the first public demonstration of the new network technology. In that same year the first, tremendously popular application was written for the new network—email. Its development by J. R. Tomlinson was motivated by the researchers themselves. They were constantly working on improvements to ARPANET and needed to communicate with each other. (Leiner, Cerf, Clark, Kahn, Kleinrock, Lynch, Roberts, & Wolff, 2000).

> The first email application

■ THE MODERN INTERNET

The modern Internet is far different from the text-based Internet that people used until the early 1990s. The "toolbox" that holds the many tools the Internet provides is the web browser, the two most popular being Explorer and Netscape. The browsers are **graphically based**, but as the Internet matures and **bandwidth** increases, the information that we receive over the Internet will gradually include more video and audio as well.

To use a browser, type in the Internet address of the site of interest, press Enter, and if all goes well, within a few seconds (or a minute if your bandwidth is low and the page to which you are going has many graphics) you will see the page to which you have pointed your browser. From there, you may choose to go to other pages at the site by clicking on buttons or highlighted text. If you do not already know how to execute this process, you should find out from a reference book or your instructor.

All browsers do the same things. They allow you to go to different Internet sites, search for, view, and download information. Although the two different browsers do the same things, there are subtle differences between the two that cause them to run better at some sites than others. When this is the case, the site will often tell you by saying something like "Before you click on this button, you should know that this link will run better in Netscape than in Explorer" (or vice versa). Since you know that this will happen if you spend much time browsing the Internet, it is a good practice to make sure that both browsers are available on your machine and the computers in your classroom or lab to begin with. Nothing is more frustrating than to go to a great site and learn that your browser will not handle it. To get to your great site you will have to spend a half hour downloading and installing new browser software or, worse, wait for your school's technology coordinator or a technician to come and install it for you.

Attached to browsers are "plug-ins." Plug-ins are small programs that help a browser do something such as play a video or audio segment, display a graphic, or display text in some special way. Your browser will come with a set of basic plug-ins that will do all of this for you. As new technologies develop or old ones improve, new plug-ins appear with them. Consequently, when you go to a site and want to see or do something special, your computer may ask you if you want to download a special plug-in that will make something at that site work. Usually plug-ins are self-extracting and installing, and you don't have to do much to make them work. There is always the

> The web browser

node
A computer that stores or sends information it receives until a user on a personal computer can retrieve the information. Email travels to its address through many nodes on the Internet.

graphically based
The modern browser supports pictures as well as text. This has not always been true. Older machines in some schools do not handle some graphics well. If Internet pages in your school display slowly, consider switching off the display of graphics.

bandwidth
The amount of information that can pass through the cable that carries Internet information to a computer. Text does not take much bandwidth; graphics, audio, and video do. Bandwidth in schools is often a problem. As students download graphics, audio, or video, access slows for everyone on the system.

exception, however. Then you have to delete and start over. Sometimes they never work, and you do not get to see or do the special activity for which the plug-in was written. Examples of plug-ins are QuickTime, RealPlayer, Shockwave Flash, LiveAudio, and Video for Windows.

Issues in Internet research

While browsers display information on your computer, using your browser's "save" or "save as" function on the file menu allows you to download almost anything that you can see for future reference. This is where students genuinely need guidance from teachers. Questions that should come up include,

- "Is this information or graphic worth downloading?
- Once it is downloaded, how should it be used?
- What copyright issues should be addressed?
- How should this information be referenced?

We will answer these questions in the next section of this chapter.

■ USING THE INTERNET FOR RESEARCH

How the Internet complicates the information-gathering process

As a student, you are familiar with doing research and writing reports or presenting the results of your research. Chances are, you have been doing research since the third or fourth grade. Although having access to the Internet does not change the basic research model, it does complicate the process for three reasons:

- The quality of the information on the Internet is highly variable;
- The information is not limited to text and pictures/charts as printed in books. It is also formatted as animation, audio, and video;
- Most textual information can be copied directly from the Internet to a student's disk and from there into a word processor.

A research model

Defining a research process with clear rules and expectations will help students be aware of some of the challenges of Internet based-research. While there are many research models and some are more appropriate to certain content areas than others, for the purposes of our discussion we will use the "NetSavvy Skills Framework" by Jukes (2000). The five steps in this model include: ask, access, analyze, apply, and assess.

Asking Questions

Begin with a problem

Asking a question and/or defining a problem is the key to a successful research project. No amount of technology can take the place of this first critical step. The assignment must be meaningful and its scope appropriate. A good research assignment will provide an opportunity for students to gather facts, look at them critically, analyze them, and make judgments about how those facts relate to each other and to the world that they know and live in. A good research assignment starts with a clearly stated question or problem.

Some projects take advantage of Internet-based resources that the Internet offers better than others do. To really use the resources of the Internet to motivate your students as well as give them a starting point for their project, you should focus the project on some initial piece of information. From that point, your students then can use other sites to interpret the initial information or problem. For example, you could use a web site such as:

Examples of kinds of Internet sites that help articulate a problem

- A virtual museum
- A social issue discussed in an online newspaper
- An online magazine or journal
- An online science project or experiment
- A data collection project that you will learn more about in Chapter 5

From that initial scrap of information, you may develop the question and help your students understand the scope of the project. For example, you could send your students to an online art museum to begin a research project on how art reflects the prevailing philosophy of historical periods.

One reason that it is so important for students begin with a question is the ease with which they get off task. There are many interesting topics on the Internet, and it is easy to click on one hyperlink after the next. Because real learning requires an effort to relate new knowledge to old knowledge, learners who browse the Internet do not often learn the information they are passing through (Jonassen, 2000).

Real learning comes from processing information, not just viewing it

Accessing Information

Search Engines   Knowing that information on any topic you can think of is probably somewhere on the Internet is one thing. Knowing how to find it is entirely another. To find information on the Internet, you use a search engine. You access Internet search engines from your browser by typing in an address. There are many different search engines to choose from. Each has its strengths and weaknesses. Examples of search engines are found in Table 3.1.

Search engines usually do not index the whole Internet

An example of strengths and weaknesses of search engines was documented by Grimes and Brand (2000) when they compared Fast Search to Google. According to the authors, Google seems to find the most relevant links and Fast Search uncovers links

TABLE 3.1 ■ Search Engines

For Adults		Suitable for Children	
Google	www.google.com/	Searchopolis	www.searchopolis.com
Ditto	www.ditto.com/	Ask Jeeves for Kids	www.ajkids.com
Fast Search	www.alltheweb.com/	Ivy's Search Engine Resources for Kids	www.ivyjoy.com/rayne/kidssearch.html
Hot Bot	hotbot.lycos.com/	Surfing the Net with Kids	www.surfnetkids.com
Ask Jeeves	www.askjeeves.com/		
Excite	www.excite.com/		

that other engines overlook. If you do not find what you want with one search engine, use another search engine. There is a special site, a kind of search engine review page at http://searchenginewatch.com/reports/index.html. Here you can find a list of commonly used search engines, their sizes, and other pertinent information. You may wonder what "size" means. Search engines do not always search the whole Web. The owner of the search engine may only index a quarter or a half of the Internet. That is why using more than one search engine is helpful if you do not reach your target on the first try.

Using search engines with children is different than using search engines yourself. Search engines for adults do not discriminate among the links they deliver. When children are doing searches on their own and your school has no filtering process (no proxy server), then they should use search engines made for young people. These search engines generally will only return selected information appropriate for children. Table 3.1 clearly differentiates search engines that are appropriate for children.

Searching and the time your students spend on it is a process you must plan. You want your children to learn search skills, and your students must gather information to complete their reports, presentations, database, or spreadsheet assignments; however, computer resources are often an issue. There are usually not enough computers in a classroom or in the library to provide students an ideal amount of time to conduct a full search on a topic, download the information they find, and convert it to the format they need. A successful search with limited resources can be conducted at least two different ways.

First, you can divide the research topic into subcategories and assign those categories to groups of students who work together to compose their searches (which you will learn about in the next section). For example, if you have five computers in your classroom, you can divide your class into five groups and your research project into five subtopics. Each group can work together to conduct searches, choose and download relevant information, and label it in a common folder that all students in the class can see and access. If you have one computer in your classroom, you can still divide your class into groups to do the research and make your computer one center among several others. Then as the children rotate through the centers, they will get the research done. Using this model, children use a common body of information from which to write their research project or presentation so you will not evaluate them on the quality of their research but rather the skill with which they use the information they have.

A second method for using Internet searches to gather information requires the teacher to do part of the research and the students to individualize or customize with their own research. The teacher finds sites ahead of time, bookmarks them in the browser on the computers to which the class has access, and then gives the students time to go to the bookmarked pages and gather information. Then, in any remaining time, students may do their own searches. As you bookmark sites for your students, consider the following questions:

■ Are there "biases, error, or misleading omissions in the document" (Branch, Kim, & Koenecke, 1999)?
■ Is there advertising that is not appropriate for students?
■ Is the information dated?
■ Is the reading level appropriate?

Marginal notes:

Search engine review page

Children should use age-appropriate search engines

To be effective, you should plan the search process carefully

Divide a topic into subtopics and assign each topic to a subgroup

Find some sites ahead of time and let the children customize the search in the remaining time

- Is there unsuitable vocabulary, ethnic, or gender stereotyping?
- Is the information clearly presented with appropriate headings and subheadings (Branch et al., 2000)?

If you decide that you will bookmark sites for students, you can still include sites that you would consider bad because of biases, errors, or misleading omissions, and challenge your students to find the information that they should not use. This is one good step to prepare them for the time when they can do their own searches on the open Internet.

Conducting Effective Searches   Searching is a skill for which there are helpful rules and tips. Not all search engines use exactly the same rules, but if the rules vary much from the rules in Table 3.2, there are usually instructions. Many children's search engines format these rules as menus so that children do not have to remember the symbols. Searchopolis, for example, not only provides menus that allow for menu-based searching, but also allows students to select the grade level of the text of articles in the list it returns.

Search rules

Analyze

Information Literacy   Although we all try to teach children to be critical of the information that they gather, no matter where they get it, it is becoming increasingly im-

TABLE 3.2 ■ Conducting Effective Searches

Symbol	Example
+ (plus sign)	+ "Civil War" + "revolutionary war" + "War of 1812"
This sign marks search terms that must appear on each web page. When a term is not preceded by a plus sign, the engine considers it a request, not a requirement.	The search above would return a list of pages where all three of these wars are mentioned. The quotes tell the search engine to treat what is inside of them as a single search term.
- (minus sign)	+reptiles +amphibians -Arachnids
This sign marks words that you *do not* want to be present on any of the pages that the search returns.	This search limits sites to pages about just reptiles and amphibians but not arachnids
AND	"short story writers" AND playwrights
Using AND between two search terms prompts the engine to return a list of web pages that contain both terms.	
OR	Llamas OR alpacas
OR between two or more search terms returns a list of pages that contains at least one of the search terms.	The search engine would produce a list of pages containing one or the other terms but not both.

portant to teach them how to be critical readers because of the huge variation in quality of information they will find on the Internet. In the days when print was king, most (not all) widely circulated text had some claim to legitimacy because a panel of editors or scholars had reviewed it. Now, any individual may post an opinion for all three billion people in the world without consulting anyone. Consequently, one step in the research model is to authenticate and evaluate information.

Authenticating information

Authentication is the process of deciding whether the information is accurate or not. To do this, the student must answer some questions, such as:

- Who wrote this? Is this person an expert or a layman?
- Is the information based on facts or is it an opinion?
- Is this person trying to convince readers about an ethical or moral issue?
- Is this person trying to sell something?
- Can I find two other corroborating articles or pieces of information?

This process is called triangulation. Students should be careful about this step. If the original information came from the president for the "Society for the Preservation of White Pine Trees," and the two corroborating pieces of information came from the vice president and secretary of the same organization, then the triangulation is a failure.

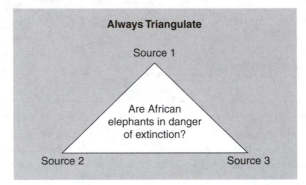

This step is quite time consuming but also key to teaching children how to negotiate the real-world questions that living in an information-based society poses for them. Remember that students may use other sources of information—books, encyclopedias, people—in conjunction with their Internet searches.

Apply   Once students have acquired information, they analyze it and make judgments about it. The analysis and judgments usually are presented in a product: a report, presentation, chart, or graph. As you proceed through this book you will find that there are intermediate steps between acquiring information and presenting the final product. You will learn that students may find information on the Internet and use a database, a spreadsheet, or presentation software to do the actual analysis.

By applying information to solve a problem and draw a conclusion, children connect it to what they already know and consequently learn it

Assess   Once students have completed a research project and had the opportunity to have their product evaluated either by peers or by their teacher, they should reflect on the research process itself. During this part of the project, they define what they have learned, how they learned it, and how the process they used could be modified (Jukes, 2000). This part of the process may be part of a class discussion or a journal entry. In an information-based society, knowing how we learn is nearly as important as what we learn.

The WebQuest

The WebQuest is a slightly different way of approaching Internet research than the research model we have just explored. It is an "inquiry-oriented activity in which some or all of the information that learners interact with comes from resources on the Internet, optionally supplemented with **videoconferencing**" (Dodge, 2000). In the case of a WebQuest the videoconference could be from the class doing the WebQuest to an expert or to another class on a similar quest. Dodge was one of the first to define and formally use the WebQuest. He indicates that there are two kinds of WebQuests, short-term and long-term. The goal of a WebQuest is to challenge students to use higher-order thinking skills (analysis, synthesis, and evaluation) as they interact with information. Before you read further, you should look at a sample WebQuest on the Internet to see how they are constructed. Just do an Internet search for WebQuest to find one. Also, you can check the annotated sources section of this chapter, where you will see references to more WebQuests in different content areas if you would like to look at other examples.

Now that you have worked with a real WebQuest, we will spend some time thinking about the theoretical underpinnings of WebQuests and learning the steps teachers use to build them—that is, the *model*. WebQuests fit under the umbrella of constructivism because they include the following elements of the constructivist perspective:

- Multiple representations of content
- Student construction of content
- Complex learning environment
- Social negotiation and shared responsibility as a part of learning (WebQuests are often done as group projects.)

In other words, the question posed to the students cannot be answered simply by collecting and spitting back information. A WebQuest requires students to "transform information into something else. . . ." (March, 1998). Furthermore, WebQuests are an example of problem-based learning because they are "inquiry-oriented" and based on a "do-able, engaging task" (Dodge, 1998).

The steps for building a WebQuest include the following:

- Introduction
- Task
- Process for completing the task
- Resources (marked web sites) for completing the task
- Evaluation

videoconferencing
Participants use the Internet to send audio and video of themselves to other people.

Using the online WebQuest(s) you reviewed as your model, think about your options for completing each step in the process of WebQuest creation. Thinking about the introduction and the task you should remember, first of all, that the WebQuest that you write should be carefully connected to the rest of your curriculum (March, 1998). It should build on what your students know and should include information and skills that are included in competencies required by your district or state. Once you are sure that your quest is connected to the curriculum, then you design a problem. Examples of some classes of problems include:

- Contemporary problems (human rights, ecology, politics)
- Evaluating history (wars, tragedies, discoveries, exploration, the development of great ideas)
- Understanding common activities (finding a job, taking a trip)
- Using the imagination (journeys to distant places and times, including places where people can't go physically like inside of the human body or into space) (Yoder, 1999)

Note that WebQuest problems are written like a story, not an assignment. The teacher who authors a WebQuest should write to make the problem interesting with much descriptive detail. Typically the problems are fuzzy, meaning that there is not one correct answer.

Once the students understand the problem, they usually require help completing the associated tasks to solve the problem. Timelines help because they benchmark the activities and products that the WebQuest requires. It is also helpful to give students the **scoring rubric** that will be used to grade their work on the WebQuest. To see a sample scoring rubric for a WebQuest, go to http://edweb.sdsu.edu/webquest/webquestrubric.html.

Another important part of the teacher's work is to provide students with relevant resources. These may be found on the web, in print, or they may be people with whom students correspond, have a videoconference, or meet in person. If you author your WebQuest on the web itself, you may include the resources as hyperlinks on your site. This is very efficient for students who then do not have to type in addresses to get to the information that they need. If you cannot put your quest on the web, then a list of links on paper will work. Be sure to include sources that do not always agree with each other or do not give the students a complete answer to the problem in one reading. The goal of the WebQuest, aside from providing an opportunity for students to learn many facts, is to give them an opportunity to analyze, synthesize, and evaluate multiple, incomplete, and conflicting sources of information.

In order to evaluate students' work with the WebQuest, they must produce some kind of product. Examples of kinds of products include:

- A searchable database in which the categories in each field were created by the learners
- A microworld that represents a physical space that users can navigate through

scoring rubric
Tool for grading assignments that do not end in an answer that is either right or wrong, used to help students understand how to complete the process properly and provide standards by which they can judge a finished product.

- An interactive story or case study created by learners
- A document that describes an analysis of a controversial situation, takes a stand, and invites users to add to or disagree with that stand
- A simulated person who can be interviewed. The questions and answers would be generated by learners who have deeply studied the person being simulated. (Dodge, 1997)

You can see that the WebQuest is a very structured Internet-supported research project. There are many WebQuests already written by teachers and available on the Internet. Before your write one of your own, you might consider using one that has already been written and tested if you can find one that fits your curriculum. The first time you try the WebQuest with your students you might also consider doing a short one more focused on facts just to help both you and your students learn the process.

Copyright Issues and the Internet

Recognizing copyright issues should be a part of the curriculum that students learn by doing. In the course of any research project, students will use other authors' works. Students should use this information according to copyright guidelines and should cite authors, artists, musicians, and videographers appropriately. Knowing the rules is a matter of referring to guidelines, and proper citation is a matter of looking at templates for each kind of citation.

Copyright Guidelines   Everything is copyrighted whether or not it has a copyright notice (Templeton, 2000). Fortunately for educators, however, there are special guidelines for the use of information by teachers and students based on "brevity, spontaneity, cumulative effect, and copyright attribution" (Bakker, 2000, p. 39). If educators and students follow these guidelines, they do not have to ask for advance permission from copyright holders to use text or other media in writing or presentations. Some general rules apply. First, students may only use copyrighted materials for a course that they are taking and only to display them in class or at school-related activities. Teachers may use copyrighted materials for a course taught face-to-face or in distance instruction.

Furthermore, teachers may only use these materials for two years, after which they must write for permission. Guidelines for specific media are found in Table 3.3.

Beyond these general guidelines there are some special cautions about altering artwork and music. Furthermore, a notice should appear at the beginning of a **multimedia** presentation alerting viewers that the piece was created using the "Fair Use Guidelines for Educational Multimedia." Bakker (2000) suggests that teachers create a template of this announcement for their students to use.

> **multimedia**
> Information presented in more than one format, possibly including text, graphics, video, audio, and animation.

Proper Citation of Multimedia Materials   Teaching students to cite their sources is important. Ethics entailed in fair use guidelines require it, and in engaging in the process

TABLE 3.3 ■ Copyright Guidelines

Type of Media	Limitation
Motion media	Up to 10 percent or three minutes, whichever is less
Text material	Up to 10 percent or 1,000 words, whichever is less
Poems	An entire poem of less than 250 words, but no more than three poems by one poet or five poems by different poets from a single anthology
Long poems	250 words plus no more than three excerpts by one poet or five excerpts by different poets from a single anthology
Music, lyrics, and music video	Up to 10 percent but no more than 30 seconds of music. If the work is altered, the melody must be recognizable.
Illustrations and photographs	No more than five images by one person and no more than 10 percent from a single published work
Numerical data sets	10 percent or 2,500 fields or cells, whichever is less

From Bakker, C. (2000). *Multimedia Schools, 7*(3), 39–41.

your students will acquire a skill they will use for a lifetime. Following is a general citation model (Grabe & Grabe, 2000):

Author/editor. (Year). Title (edition) [Type of medium]. Producer (optional). Available: Protocol (e.g., ftp, http): Site/Path//file. [Access date].

An example of this format looks like the reference below:

Ekham, L. (1999). Tips for promoting collaboration and interactivity in online distance learning. State College of Education, University of West Georgia, USA. Available: http://computed.coe.wayne.edu/Vol5/Ekhaml.html. [Retrieved from the World Wide Web on 8/28/00].

The reason that the access date is included is because of the transient nature of information on the Internet. Date of access gives a reader some idea of how efficient it might be to try to find a piece of information. The older the retrieval date, the less likely the information still resides at the quoted Internet address.

Bloom's Taxonomy and Internet Research

Student research on the Internet is a complex process that promotes thinking at many levels of the taxonomy. In a sense, the unreliability of the accuracy of information on the Internet is helpful. Students no longer can copy information as they once did from encyclopedias and hand it in either untransformed or only modestly modified or paraphrased. In addition, strict adherence to copyright laws also prevents students from using just one author to provide them with information. Although teachers must always be alert to the students who cut and paste information from sites they find on the Internet, students who follow the rules work at almost all levels of the taxonomy (Table 3.4).

TABLE 3.4 ■ Bloom's Taxonomy and Internet Research

Level of Thought	Description	Internet Research Activity
Knowledge	Name, locate, tell, list, repeat, point to	As the students read articles and triangulate to determine the accuracy of facts, they learn the facts.
Comprehension	Define, summarize, infer, project, describe	In order to avoid plagiarism, students must summarize information and relay it in their own words.
Application	Use, solve, adapt, relate, perform	
Analysis	Compare, classify, screen, examine, test for	During the process of triangulation, students must examine, compare, and test information and ideas for accuracy and logic.
Synthesis	Create, develop, generate, build, compile, design	When students write their report they create a new piece of work compiling ideas and facts as well as generating conclusions.
Evaluation	Judge, reject, criticize, rate, rank	When students write a conclusion for their report they judge among competing ideas and draw a conclusion.

■ LISTSERVS

Being on a computer listserv is like being on a mailing list. Listservs are focused discussions on a specific topic. When a member of a list emails information on the topic at hand, the rest of the members of the list receive that email and may respond to it if they have something pertinent to say.

Listservs are like mailing lists

Mailing lists are not all the same size. Some lists have hundreds of members who have communicated for several years, whereas other lists are for small, local discussions devoted to a topic that lasts only a few months. Since the software and computing resources for managing a list are neither complex nor expensive, school districts or universities may maintain such lists for instructors who want the advantages of the mailing list format for class discussion.

Large, public mailing lists are another source of information available on the Internet, especially if you or your students have a question for which you cannot find an answer. As a user, you may subscribe to a list and unsubscribe from a list as well. The only software you need for using a list is your email software. However, there are some conventions and procedures you should be aware of if you decide you want to subscribe to a mailing list.

Each list has two different addresses, an administrative address and a submission address. If you want to join a list, remove yourself from a list, or suspend receipt of mail from the list while you are on vacation, you send messages to the administrative address of the list. If you want to submit email related to the discussion at hand, you send your messages to the submission address.

To join a list you should create a message addressed to the administrative address of the list, leave the subject line blank, and in the body of the messages type: subscribe listname (your) firstname lastname. If I were to join the Community Learning Network (CLN) list (a list of educational lists), I would send an email to the administrative address of the list with a blank subject head and the following message: subscribe CLN_UPDate Carolyn Thorsen. Once I have done this, I will begin receiving all of the email that the members of the list send. I will also receive a list of instructions from the administrator of the list that will tell me how to suspend receipt of email while I am gone, and other options. It is important to keep this information. To remove my name from a list I have to create an email addressed to the administrative address saying: unsubscribe listname.

There are many lists for educators. There are indexes of listservs to help you find a listserv you need. A good example of a list of listservs is the Community Learning Network maintained by a Canadian educational organization. To give you an idea of the variety of lists available that are of interest to educators, the mailing lists posted by this organization beginning with the letter "e" are in Table 3.5.

The CLN is an especially good location for finding educational listservs. The lists themselves are reviewed for content. In addition, if you subscribe to the CLN list itself, the organization sends weekly bulletins detailing new lists that appear on the Internet. Because lists are public, anyone can submit a comment. Unless you are sure of the contributors to a list, it is wise to subscribe to a list and monitor it for a while before you allow your students access to the list. Another way of working with a list in a K–12 classroom is to subscribe to the list yourself and email appropriate entries to your students by forwarding them.

✔ CHECKING YOUR UNDERSTANDING

3.1

Problem 1

To become a good searcher you must know a little about your tools—search engines, for example. For this exercise, search "Information Literacy" in each of the search engines listed in Table 3.4. Answer the following questions:

- Which search engine gives you the most hits?
- Which search engine gives you the most *relevant* hits?
- Which search engine gave you the best hit?

Now repeat the previous exercise using "Plagiarism" and "WebQuest" as your search terms and answer the three questions above about each term. Choose and read what you believe are the best articles. List the criteria you used to determine which articles are best.

Problem 2

Develop a topic for a research project for a class that you teach or will teach someday. Using Table 3.3, construct a list of at least twenty search terms that you would use to gather information on this topic. A search term or key word is a combination of words and symbols found in Table 3.3. Write down the search terms and conduct the search for each term using one of the search engines listed for adults.

TABLE 3.5 ■ Educationally Appropriate Mailing Lists Beginning with the Letter "E"

earth	euthanasia	egypt	england	equity
earthquakes	evangelism	elections	english	ergonomics
eating	events	electrical	enlightenment	estates
ecology	evolution	electromagnetics	entertainerment	ethics
economics	exercise	electronics	entertaining	Ethiopia
economy	exhibitors	email	entertainment	ethnicity
ecosystems	existentialism	emergencies	entomology	ethnography
editing	exobiology	emergency	entrepreneur	ethnology
editorials	expatriates	emigrants	environment	Eritrea
editors	exploration	employees	environmental	eugenics
export	extraterrestrial	employment	epilepsy	Eurasia
ezines	engineering	energy	epson	Europe

Community Learning Network, http://www.cln.org/lists/home.html.

Record how many hits you get for each search term. Record how much usable information you obtained from each search. Now repeat your search using one of the children's search engines. Again, record the number of hits and the quality of information that you receive. Write a short paper on your experience with searching using the two different kinds of search engines.

■ DISTANCE LEARNING

Distance learning is a rapidly growing area in education that serves students who cannot attend school in a traditional manner. Most distance courses are delivered using one of two delivery technologies: Interactive television (IT) and the Internet. These technologies allow students dispersed over a wide geographical area to get instruction. There are a number of reasons for using one or the other of these technologies. Small, rural districts find them useful because they provide courses that students would otherwise be unable to take, such as AP (advanced placement) classes and foreign language classes. They are also useful for students who cannot be in a traditional classroom because of job or family responsibilities. These two technologies are alike in that they serve populations that are not served by the traditional classroom. They are different because students in an interactive television class must "attend" at a specified time, whereas Internet-based coursework can be completed by a student working alone, at any time of the day (or night).

Interactive Television

Interactive television is delivered using a variety of technologies—microwave, satellite, fiber optic cable, cable, and digital telephone lines. The instructor and even part of the class may be in one location while the rest of the class is in several different locations. Each location can see the other location, though few systems allow participants to see all locations at once. In a typical configuration, the instructor talks to a class, which meets simultaneously in several different geographical locations. The instructor can see one other location on a monitor but hear comments from all of the locations. To display information to the class, instructors have various display devices that make their job easier. For example, they can switch the video output, allowing students to see the instructor's computer screen rather than the instructor. Students can still hear the instructor explain what is on the computer screen. When student attention needs to be focused on notes being written on a large pad of paper, the instructor clicks another button to switch to a camera positioned over the pad. These cameras are called document cameras. Sometimes the instructor can split the video so that both the pad of paper and the instructor appear on the screen for the students. This allows students to both see the pad of paper being used as a chalkboard and to see their instructor at the same time. Instructors also may use video output to a VCR, allowing their students to view a video as well.

Teaching techniques

You may one day teach using such an arrangement. A well-designed instructor station that provides the tools described in the last paragraph is not difficult to learn to use. It is disconcerting at first not to have face-to-face contact with all of your students. You must make a conscious effort to include everyone—to keep switching the video that you see to different sites so that all of your students feel like they are a part of the class. Getting students from different sites to interact with each other and with the rest of the class takes an extra awareness and special planning on the part of the instructor. Increasingly, school districts have this technology available, and knowing how to use this kind of classroom is an advantage when you seek employment.

Internet-Based Courses

Teaching courses using the Internet as a delivery tool is more properly called "computer-mediated distance instruction" (Palloff, 1999, p. 6). This delivery method is by far less expensive to implement than interactive television, but places a great deal of responsibility on the learner. Successful students in online classes have some common characteristics: they are introverted, highly motivated self-starters (Palloff, 1999, p. 8).

Characteristics of successful students

Instructors who deliver their courses on the Internet often rely on sophisticated software that provides a virtual classroom. Examples of such environments include CourseInfo's Blackboard and WebCT. These environments include areas where students can access:

A virtual classroom

- Assignments
- Announcements
- Course materials
- A syllabus
- Pages for student and instructor introductions
- External web links for students to explore
- A **chat room**
- A discussion board area for "mail-in" discussions—the course may have multiple discussion boards running concurrently within the discussion board area
- An email system that allows students and instructors to send email to individuals or groups

chat room
A computer site where two or more participants conduct a conversation with text messages in "real-time."

- A test construction area where instructors may create multiple choice questions, multiple answer questions, matching questions, short answer questions, and essay questions
- A test delivery area where students may take tests and receive immediate feedback online
- A grade book area where instructors post grades and see all recorded grades, and students may see their own grade

In other words, the software that resides on the Internet provides a complete virtual classroom.

In spite of these support mechanisms, students in online courses may still have problems—technical problems and learning style problems (Ko & Rossen, 2001, p. 195). Concerning technical problems, for students to be successful they must have some prior training in the basics of computer use: email, attachments, Internet addressing, and navigating through software. They must also have access to technical support during the course in case their computer or their software fails. Institutions that deliver computer-mediated instruction should have a technical support hot line to help students through these difficulties. If you or a student at your school decides to take such a course, the first question to ask your provider is how much technical support they will give you.

`Technical support`

Learning style problems are a different matter. The medium favors verbal rather than visual or kinesthetic learners (Ko & Rossen, p. 196). Students miss the visual feedback that a teacher standing in front of them gives. In addition, the communication is disjointed. If the student is stuck on step 4 of a math problem, s/he may not know how to proceed until the instructor answers email the next day. Being an online student requires both patience and trust (Palloff & Pratt, p. 38).

`Learning style problems`

Being an online teacher requires organization above all. It requires knowledge of teaching models and a willingness to use them. As an online teacher you would find yourself spending a great deal of time sending or receiving email answering your students questions. Often instructors set up a telephone conversation at least once during a course and to give students their telephone number as well. Some distance instructors set up Internet-based chat sessions with students, though some students object because the reason they took the course in the first place was because they could not be in a certain place at a certain time. If you ever consider accepting an assignment teaching a computer-mediated course, be aware that you will spend more time preparing and teaching the course than you would if you taught a traditional face-to-face course (Mielke, 1999).

`Teaching online`

Summary of Key Elements of Distance Instruction

Whether you are using interactive television or computer-mediated instruction as a teacher, student, or as a counselor to students who are taking a distance course, there are some critical elements for success. Garrels (1997) describes five critical elements for successful teaching and learning at a distance:

- Instructor enthusiasm. This requires animation and comfort in front of the cameras, or with the technology utilized. Faculty support and interest are critical to the success of distance learning endeavors.

- Organization. Teaching materials must be prepared in advance; timing, variation, and smooth transitions must be planned. Instructors should allocate from three to five hours of preparation for each hour of distance instruction. Great attention to detail is required long before the actual classroom activity occurs.
- Strong commitment to student interaction. Whatever the modality used to teach at a distance, the instructor must encourage and facilitate ongoing communication between the students and the instructor.
- Familiarity with the technology used in the class format
- Critical support personnel

One question people often ask is, "Do students learn the same amount of information online as in a traditionally delivered course?" Studies find that students taking courses delivered by distance education do perform as well or better on assignments, class activities, and exams as students in traditional classrooms (Rintala, 1998).

■ SUMMARY

The Internet is a vast repository of information that varies in quality. The U.S. government funded its development to provide for rapid and reliable communications and data transfer among scientists and the military. Today's Internet has become a powerful teaching tool because of the amount and variety of information which resides there and because it provides for the rapid exchange of information. In order to find this information students must learn to use search engines and search strategies. The one important caveat for all to remember is that the variation in the quality of information places the burden on the student to be information literate—to know which information is the most usable and to use triangulation for testing the accuracy of information.

The Internet has also opened up a new format for learning called the virtual classroom. Students who cannot attend class because they are ill, have family responsibilities, or live in rural or remote areas now have the opportunity to take courses and in some cases earn certificates or degrees over the Internet. Being a teacher or student in a distance class requires a new set of skills and a different mindset. Students must be motivated self-starters. Students taking computer mediated distance instruction must have a basic set of computer competencies as well as the ability to learn with less visual and kinesthetic input than they receive in a traditional classroom.

■ REFERENCES ■

Bakker, C. (2000). Saying "yes" instead of "no": Promoting the fair use guidelines for educational multimedia. *Multimedia Schools.* May/June, Vol. 7(3), pp. 39–41.

Branch, R. M., Kim, D., & Koenecke, L. (1997). Evaluating online educational materials for use in instruction. ERIC (ED430564).

Dodge, B. (1997). "Some thoughts about WebQuests." http://edweb.sdsu.edu/courses/edtec596/about_webquests.html. [Retrieved from the Internet on April 2, 2001].

Dodge, B. (1998). Webquests: A strategy for scaffolding higher level learning. Presented at the National Educational Computing Conference, San Diego. Available: http://edweb.sdsu.edu/webquest/necc98.htm. [Retrieved from the World Wide Web on April 4, 2001].

Ekham, L. (1999). Tips for promoting collaboration and interactivity in online distance learning. State College of Education, University of West Georgia, USA. Available: http://computed.coe.wayne.edu/Vol5/Ekhaml.html. [Retrieved from the World Wide Web on 8/28/00].

Garrels, M. (1997). Dynamic relationships: Five critical elements for teaching at a distance. Faculty development papers. Available online at: Indiana Higher Education Telecommunication System http://www.ihets.org/distance-ed/fpapers/1997/garrels.html [Retrieved from the World Wide Web on 9/15/01].

Grabe, M., & Grabe, C. (2000). *Integrating the Internet for meaningful learning.* Boston: Houghton Mifflin Company.

Grimes, Brand (2000). The best of the web. *PC World.* August, 2000, p. 108.

Jonassen, D. (2000). *Computers as mindtools for schools: Engaging critical thinking.* Upper Saddle River: Prentice-Hall.

Juel, P. Q. (2000). Information literacy: A process approach to effective research. Unpublished master's thesis, Boise State University, Boise, Idaho.

Jukes, I., Dosaj, A., & McCain, I. (2000). It's not the Internet, it's the information: Net savvy for the information highway (presentation handout). Thornburg Center for Professional Development. [Retrieved October 1, 2000, from the World Wide Web. http://www.thecommittedsardine.net/handouts/in.tiiti.pdf.

Ko, S., & Rossen, S. (2001). *Teaching online: A practical guide.* Boston: Houghton Mifflin.

Leiner, B., Cerf, V., Clark, D., Kahn, R., Kleinrock, L., Lynch, J., Roberts, L., & Wolff, S. (2000). A Brief History of the Internet by the men who built it. http://www.isoc.org/internet/history/brief.shtml. [Retrieved February 12, 2001 from the World Wide Web].

Licklider, J. C. R. (1960). Man-computer symbiosis, *IRE* (now IEEE) Transactions on Human Factors in Electronics, vol. HFE-1, pp. 4–11, March 1960.

March, T. (1998). Why Webquests? An introduction. http://ozline.com/webquests/intro.html. [Retrieved from the World Wide Web on April 5, 2001].

Mielke, D. (1999). Effective teaching in distance education. ERIC (ED436528).

Palloff, R., & Pratt, K. (1999). *Building learning communities in cyberspace: Effective strategies for the online classroom.* San Francisco: Jossey-Bass Inc.

Rintala, J. (1998). Computer technology in higher education: An experiment, not a solution. *Quest,* 50(4), 366–378.

Stewart, William (2000). Living Internet. http://livinginternet.com. [Retrieved February 15, 2001 from the World Wide Web].

Templeton, B. (2001). 10 Big myths about copyright explained. http://www.templetons.com/brad/copymyths.html. [Retrieved from the World Wide Web January 12, 2001].

Yoder, M. (1999). The Student WebQuest. *Leading and learning with technology.* Eugene, OR, International Society for Technology in Education, v. 27, n. 6.

■ ANNOTATED RESOURCES ■

Research

ERIC: Branch, R. M., Kim, D., & Koenecke, L., Evaluating online educational materials for use in instruction, ERIC (ED430564).

The full text of this article is available on ERIC. The citations used represent only a small part of the article. Because there is so much instructional software on the Internet, the authors have provided a checklist of items for teachers to use as they decide if Internet-based instructional software is appropriate for their students.

Evaluating Web pages

Schrock, K. Evaluation of World Wide Web sites. ERIC (ED436187).

This article leads to eleven articles on this topic. Of special interest is a section entitled, "What are the Important Aspects of Teaching Web Site Evaluation to Students?" Some articles in this section include: "It must be true: I found it on the Internet," "Misinformation on the Internet: Applying evaluation skills to online information," and "An Internet research model (Relevant and meaningful Internet articles for the K–12 classroom)."

Research models

There are other research models besides the one presented in this book. Each has a slightly different emphasis and slightly different guidelines. You could read them all and develop a research model of your own that best fits the age, skills, and needs of your class.

Http://www.big6.com

The "Big 6 Research Model" has six steps: task definition, information seeking strategies, location and access, use of information, synthesis, and evaluation. The site provides detailed information on how to implement this model in a classroom. K–3 teachers, look for the link "the super three" under resources for an age-appropriate model.

http://ctap.fcoe.k12.ca.us/ctap/Info.Lit/strategies.html

This information literacy model has seven steps: identifies a need or problem, seeks applicable resources, gathers information, analyzes information, interprets and synthesizes information, communicates information, and evaluates process and product. Each of these main topics is supported by explanatory information.

http://www.asis.org/Bulletin/Feb-99/Kuhlthau.html

Kuhlthau's research model: Kuhlthau takes a slightly different approach. She identifies six stages: initiation, selection, exploration, formulation, collection, and presentation. This model focuses on barriers to the success of this process and how to overcome them.

http://www2.widener.edu/Wolfgram-MemorialLibrary/webevaluation/examples.htm

Web pitfalls

To see examples of different kinds of pitfalls on the web, go to this site.

http:// www.cln.org/lists/home.html

Listservs

Community Learning Network. This site is a list of lists. It is especially helpful because it is edited for educational content. As a teacher I would be reluctant to recommend that students themselves join a list, because lists are open to the public and the quality of discussion varies. On the other hand, as a teacher, I would join a list myself to learn about the latest issues, arguments, and information on a topic of interest.

Lu, Mei-Yu. Online resources for K–12 teachers: Children's and adolescent literature. Indiana, 1999. ERIC (ED436009).

The Internet provides information about more than technology. It is also a rich source of ideas and lesson plans. This article indexes online resources for K–12 teachers of children's and adolescent literature. Topics include:

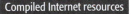
Online reading resources

- Literature-based lesson plans
- Aids to materials selection
- Professional development resources

Harry, D. & Melbourne, L. Using the Internet to enrich teaching and learning. ERIC (ED433218).

This publication provides a 10-page list of resources for science teachers at all grade levels. Topics include:

Online science resources

- Facilitating productive interactions
- Finding new sources of information
- Seeking assistance
- Staying informed
- Extending classroom instruction
- Doing research
- Getting involved in projects
- Enrich personal experience

This is an excellent collection of science resources which not only provides sites but also provides examples of methodologies for using the Internet in the science classroom.

Universal access

Teachers must be sensitive to those with disabilities when they give assignments that require Internet use. This 10-page document entitled, "Universal design: Ensuring access to the general education curriculum," discusses issues teachers should be aware of as they work with disabled students. ERIC (ED43366b).

Distance learning

To learn more about how Internet courses provide more interaction among students and between students and teachers than in traditional correspondence courses, read: "Tips for promoting collaboration and interactivity in online distance learning" by Leticia Ekham. The site is found at http://computed.coe.wayne.edu/vol5/Ekhaml.html.

Feyton, M., Ducher, Y., Park, C., & Meros, J. (2002). *Teaching ESL/EFL with the Internet: Catching the Wave.* Merrill/Prentice Hall.

This is a practical approach full of daily lesson plans and activities for the ESL/EFL teacher. ISBN-13-088540-1.

ESL/EFL

Keating, M., Wiles, J., & Piazza, M. (2002). *LearningWebs: Curriculum Journeys on the Internet.* Merrill/Prentice Hall.

This book has many ideas for using the Internet as well as a comprehensive listing of sites with information from "Aardvark" to "Zebras." To give you a flavor for some of the topics in between, topics include weather, rainforests, world literature, wedding customs, subtraction, and Vikings.

Compiled Internet resources

Email and Discussion Boards

OBJECTIVES

- Describe the elements of email software using appropriate terminology.
- Describe basic models for teaching email-supported lessons.
- Judge the quality of student work based on email-supported lesson models.
- Describe the elements of Internet conferencing.
- Provide models of teaching for Internet conferencing-supported lessons.
- Judge the quality of student work based on Internet conferencing-supported lessons.

This chapter is about teaching models that use email. This seemingly simple technology, which many of us take for granted, has much potential for improving student communication and writing skills (Russell, 2001). Effective use of email technology depends on the teacher's skill in applying an appropriate teaching model and using the intrinsic motivation that writing for an audience supplies for students. To get the most out of reading this chapter you should be able to:

- Address and send an email
- Add entries to an address book
- Find entries in an address
- Make a distribution list (nicknames) and save it
- Use a distribution list (nicknames) to send the same email to several different people
- Make folders (mailboxes) for filing the email messages you receive
- Make rules (filters) for screening or directing your email to special folders
- Add an attachment to an email message

- Open an attachment (text or graphic) to an email message
- Save an attachment to an email message in a file on your hard drive or a floppy disk
- Know how to forward a message

■ EMAIL

Email software allows users to communicate with each other **asynchronously.** If you want your students to communicate with students in another school, district, state, or country, email is an ideal medium for two reasons. First because it is asynchronous, email enables you to avoid scheduling conflicts that are caused by different daily schedules, school vacation schedules, and time zones—problems that are inherent in some other technologies such as telephone conferencing. A second important advantage of email is motivation. Students write better when they know they are writing for an audience (Gordon, 1999; Harrington, Holik, & Hurt, 1998; Lambert, 1999; Stoicheva, 2000). If the students are not initially motivated, they become motivated. The scenario in the next few paragraphs is real writing from real seventh grade students.

Scenario. Seventh grade students are engaged in an electronic debate (email is the tool). School 1 is debating School 2 on the topic of whether people are responsible for their actions if they are under the influence of drugs or alcohol. The two classes have just read a novel in which the main character had to make this decision. The "Barbarians" is the name of one group of four students involved in the debate. The "Piranhas" is the name of the other group of four students.

School 1

"Dear Barbarians,

We desagree. For the first time the punishment should have got and 2 week in community service. The fine was to expensive since she returned the bracelet and worked most of it the fine should only be $200."

School 2

"Dear Piranhas,

Again, we disagree completely. And for one, Kit didn't return the bracelet; she got caught. Also, her community services were fine because she needed to learn. She should have been given the full time because if they let her off easy this time, she might think she could get off the hook again. Also, in the end the community services helped her figure her problem out.

P.S.

Your writing was confusing and difficult to understand. We usually check our work before we send it."

email software
A program such as Eudora, Pegasus, or Microsoft Outlook used for writing and sending messages.

asynchronous communication
The parties involved are not all present at the same time. Messages sent are not received or acted upon until later; examples are U.S. mail and email. In contrast, a phone conversation is synchronous.

After that postscript, the Piranhas did check their writing before they sent it. They were embarrassed. The Barbarians learned the effect of sloppiness as well. When they sent their admonition back to the Piranhas, they checked it many times so they would not leave an opening for their opponents to level a similar accusation.

The question now is, "How does one set up an effective lesson that uses the email, a list serve, or a discussion board?" To begin to answer that question we will take our next field trip. Be aware that during our field trips, events do not always occur the way the teacher expects them to. Unexpected circumstances pop up when you are using computers in the teaching process. It is as important to know what to do when things go wrong as it is to know the correct way to lay out a technology-supported lesson. With that introduction, let us begin with our next field trip.

FIELD TRIP 4.1

Solving a Problem

Ms. Anderson's fifth-grade social studies class was buzzing with excitement. Ms. Anderson had recently begun a unit on the geography of their state and the students had a problem to solve. When they began the unit, Ms. Anderson had told them that when they finished the unit they would know how to read maps, know about other communities in their state, and know how to write to people they did not know. Although there was some mild interest in map reading and distant children, Ms. Anderson's objectives were not what caused the excitement among the students. It was the problem. Ms. Anderson presented the problem to her students this way.

Setting up a problem

"We are going to learn about another community in our state by talking with children in that community in a class just like this one. To talk to these children we are going to use email. Here is the problem: I am not going to tell you the name of these students' community and their teacher is not going to tell them the name of our community. Instead, you are going to have to ask them questions about where they live and what they do; they are going to ask you questions as well, because they have the same problem to solve that you do. You can ask them questions about what the land looks like, the population of the community, recreation opportunities—anything that you can think of to give you clues about where they might be. When you get answers back, you will want to get a map out as well as your textbook on state geography and history, and compare those answers to the information in your books and maps.

Explaining the process

You are going to work in groups of four. Every other day your group will write five questions for the children at the mystery school. They will also work in groups of four to write questions for you. Each day that we send questions, a different person in your group will email the questions your group has to the group you are working with at the mystery school—but first, another person in your group will proofread the questions. So, Susan, John, Sam, and Maria, you are in the "Orange" group. Adam, Yolanda, Ed, and Holly, you are. . . . Now, just to get ourselves started, this first day let's write our five questions as a whole class. Then each group can go to the computers and send the questions together. One person can type them in while the others watch and check for typos. Also, remember what you have learned about **netiquette** (Box 4.1). You will want to make a good impression on the students in the mystery community. If you have forgotten how to send email, take a notebook with you and write down notes about the key presses that you have forgotten so you will be able to send the questions when it is your turn. Before we begin writing questions together, let's look at the big map of our state on the wall and think about the possibilities."

At this point, Ms. Anderson began teaching the content that she needs to teach about her state's geography and history. She made sure her students knew where their own community is on the map,

BOX 4.1 NETIQUETTE

Netiquette is the name for the rules of online politeness. They are:

1. Use meaningful subject lines.
2. Do not type with all caps (they are hard to read and are the Internet version of shouting).
3. Quote only the parts of a previous email that you need to make your reply clear.
4. Send virus-free attachments.
5. Make sure that you know the size of your attachment before you send it, and check with the recipient to be sure it is OK to send an attachment of that size.
6. Do not pass around e-hoaxes, such as false virus alerts.
7. Do not pass around chain letters.
8. If you use signature files, keep them small and add only contact information. (Stewart, 2000)

pronounced the names of other communities, and asked students to talk about communities they have visited. She reviewed the features of a topographical map that indicate elevation, longitude, and latitude. Using an LCD projector (see Box 4.2) (a device that projects a computer image to a screen) attached to her computer, she even took the students on a virtual airplane trip around their own community using encyclopedia software provided by her school district. Students were able to compare the topography of the paper map to the more dynamic topography of the virtual airplane trip. Then she began soliciting questions from the students and writing them on the board. As students suggested questions, she modeled the writing and thinking process by helping them pick just the right words, adding commas where they were needed and explaining why, and making sure that each question had a question mark at the end. She mentioned several times that when people communicate with someone that they cannot see and do not know, the only impression the other person gets is based on how expressive and how correct the writing is. When she finished the discussion, tours, and admonitions, students divided into their groups, went to their computers, typed in their questions, and sent them, knowing that the day after that they would get their first communication from the unknown.

Ms. Anderson had carefully thought through the organization of the activity. Students spent fifteen minutes in their groups every other day analyzing the previous set of responses and using those responses to generate more questions. At the beginning of each day, she had a student volunteer print the responses from the other school so they would be ready for the class at the appropriate time. She typically does this because any number of things can go wrong if she waits until the actual lesson time session to print responses to questions. Whenever anything goes wrong, it takes time away from instruction that she cannot afford to lose.

What can go wrong? The printer may run out of paper or it may jam. The network may be down so that the printer will not work. The other school may not have sent answers to the questions for one reason or another. If her student volunteer works on the printouts first thing in the morning, then if there is a problem she will be able to adjust and not lose that precious fifteen minutes of lesson time tinkering with the printer or making something up to fill in the gap. If all goes well, she collects the printouts for each group, previews them for appropriateness, and sets them in her out-basket where they will be ready when she needs them.

How does she solve the problems? The first two, running out of paper and printer jams, are simple. They just take time, which she has if she tackles the job first thing in the morning. If the network is down, she emails, calls, or visits the network administrator to find out the seriousness of the problem and then either makes other plans or has the volunteer print out later. If responses from the other school have not shown up, she checks her email because the teacher in the remote community is usually careful to inform her about glitches which happen occasionally. It is usual for either class to have an assembly or a fire drill at least once during the three weeks they have planned for the cooperative project. If the exchanges take place every other day, it is more likely that these occasional interruptions will not disturb the flow of work, since there are two chances for a class to get its responses back. There are, however, days when no responses arrive. (Teachers can plan for different spring breaks, but snow days and flu

Solving problems

epidemics just happen). Communication between the two cooperating teachers is essential in this case. Nothing kills a project like this faster than not keeping the schedule that the two of you have planned and not then communicating about it.

A more difficult problem than not having all of the responses show up is having just some of the responses show up, such as four groups get their responses but the fifth does not. This can happen because the child at the other end thinks he/she has sent the response and has not. On an every-other-day schedule, there is usually time to inform the other teacher of the missed responses. If, however, it appears that the responses are not going to arrive in time for the lesson, the teacher should write the responses so that her students can get on with the business of learning.

In the end, when the two schools finally guessed each other's locations, students in each pair of groups introduced themselves to each other and sent pictures. Ms. Anderson's students, who each had a copy of all the questions and answers that they received from the mystery school, wrote a report about that region of the state. They included not only the information that they received from the other school, but information from their books, maps, and encyclopedias as well.

Student products

> **BOX 4.2 COMPUTER PROJECTION DEVICES**
>
> A key piece of equipment to know how to use is a computer display device. Currently, there are two popular devices for classroom use: the large television monitor and the LCD projector. A large television monitor with computer-to-video conversion hardware and software is the most affordable. Most schools have televisions, on carts for their classrooms. Cable runs from the computer to the television, and special software is installed on the computer to adapt the video signal that it produces to a video signal the television can understand. The advantage of the television/computer display is the price. Most conversion software and hardware costs less than $150. The disadvantage is the readability of the screen. Letters are ragged, and the last rows of students in a 30-person class cannot see the screen well. LCD projectors attach directly to the computer and need no special software to make them work. The better projectors are light, portable, and project well enough to be used in an undarkened room. They often come with built-in speakers as well, supporting video as well as audio. The disadvantage is their cost, which is significantly more that the cost of the computer-to-video conversion kits for televisions.

Because we are looking at email as a tool that challenges students to work at all intellectual levels, we will now look at Ms. Anderson's assignment using Bloom's Taxonomy as a backdrop (Table 4.1). You can see that in this example, no level of the taxonomy was neglected, although this will not always be true for every tool and every lesson. It is most important that you are aware of the levels of learning that your lesson does cover. Then, if some levels of the taxonomy are excluded because you have used an electronic tool for its ability to work at other levels of the taxonomy effectively, you must design other worksheets or exercises to fill the gaps.

Not all assignments cover all levels of the taxonomy

■ DISCUSSION BOARDS

discussion board
Electronic forum where people can write ("post") comments and read other people's responses. Sometimes access is limited by user names and passwords.

Our next look at asynchronous communication is the **discussion board,** which provides more structure for students than email does. If your school has a server set up to manage discussion boards, you can engage your class in an electronic discussion. All the students will be able to see each other's questions and responses.

TABLE 4.1 ■ Bloom's Taxonomy and a Simple Email-Supported Geography Lesson

Level of Thought	Description	Email Activity
Knowledge	Name, locate, tell, list, repeat, point to	Locating geographical features and towns on a map.
Comprehension	Define, summarize, infer, project, describe	Students summarize the information they have received from another school to help them write a report.
Application	Use, solve, adapt, relate, perform	Using information they receive from another school, students find a place on the map.
Analysis	Compare, classify, screen, examine, test for	Students compare information that they have received from the mystery school to information they have collected.
Synthesis	Create, develop, generate, build, compile, design	Students add information from encyclopedias or other sources to the information they have received from their mystery class.
Evaluation	Judge, reject, criticize, rate, rank	When information they have received from the mystery class conflicts with their own research from other sources, students must judge which information is correct.

To help you understand the kind of interface students are working with in the next field trip, look at Figures 4.1 and 4.2. These two screen shots are from a discussion board built with a Microsoft FrontPage **wizard.** The wizard used to build this discussion board consisted of eight dialogue boxes. The teacher creating it was prompted to

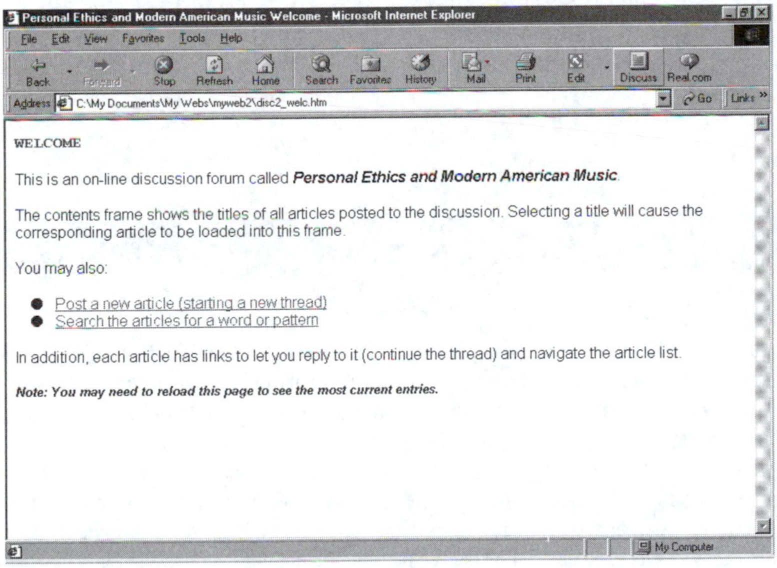

wizard
Software feature that prompts users through the steps of a task so they need not know all the technical details.

FIGURE 4.1 ■ Welcome Screen

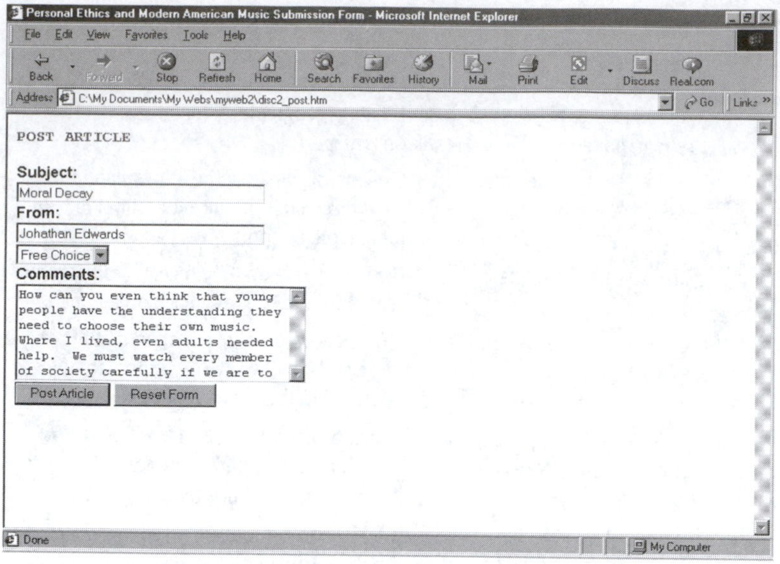

FIGURE 4.2 ■ Posting a New Article

enter a name for the discussion, to define "categorizes" for the students' responses, and to select and arrange the items. The discussion board took the teacher less than fifteen minutes to create.

The welcome screen states the topic of the discussion and gives students directions on how to proceed. Students post a new article to the board by choosing a subject, indicating their identity, choosing a category, and making their comments, as illustrated in Figure 4.2. Figure 4.3 shows the expanded category box. By setting up categories, the teacher gives students cues that will guide the discussion.

Let us take another field trip 4, to see how a discussion board can support a role-playing assignment.

FIELD TRIP 4.2

Role Playing

John Sanders's junior literature class was nearing the end of its first semester. The students had studied the early Puritan writers, the writers of the revolution, the early Romantic poets, and the short story writers and novelists of the mid-1800s. To any given ethical or moral question, all of these writers bring the habits of mind and philosophies of the era in which they lived. Mr. Sanders knew it was time to summarize and teach students the difference between the Puritan, Colonial, and Romantic periods in American writing and wanted to do more than just give a lecture and have students write a comparison/contrast paper. He does this every year, and every year it is the same. One or two gifted students come up with something original, almost everyone else hands in nothing more than slightly embellished lists that are

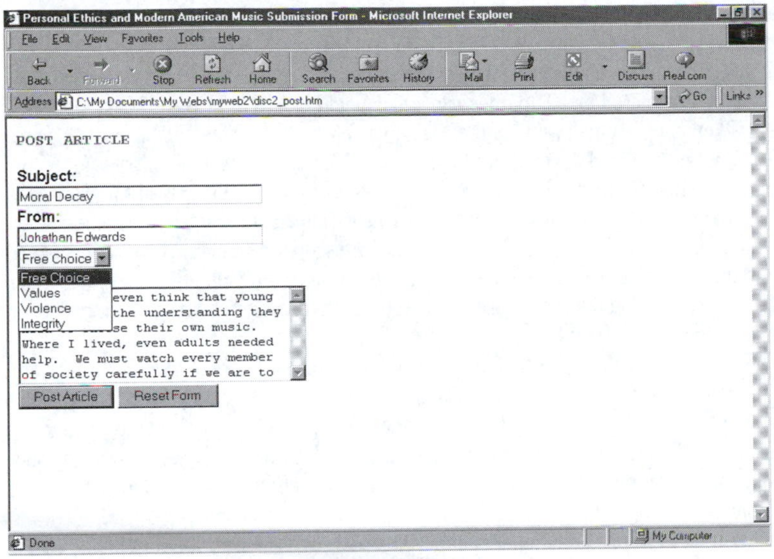

FIGURE 4.3 ■ Category Box

really converted lecture notes, and a few just don't get the point and hand in disorganized papers that don't answer the question.

This year, Mr. Sanders is approaching this assignment differently. Instead of assigning the comparison/contrast paper "cold" with only his lecture for preparation, he has provided an electronic role-playing assignment he believes will give his students enough writing and thinking practice to improve the quality of their comparison/contrast papers. He believes the hook that will capture his students' attention for this role-playing assignment will be an interesting problem. The logistics of the assignment are not trivial. It is a lot of work to think things through. First, he defines his instructional objective: All students will be able write a reflective paper comparing and contrasting themes in early American literature.

Next Mr. Sanders writes the problem. It reads like this:

> Due to a science experiment involving a time machine gone awry, the authors Jonathan Edwards, James Fenimore Cooper, and Mark Twain are transported to a research laboratory somewhere in North America. Although somewhat confused at first, all of them are adjusting to their new lives and have decided to accept the inevitable. Researchers are slowly acclimating them to modern society. They all live in a small dormitory at the lab where they share a kitchen and living room. One night while flipping through the channels on their big screen TV, Jim Cooper discovers MTV and stays, fascinated by the costumes, music, and violence. Jonathan Edwards, horrified, insists that the machine be turned off. When Cooper refuses, Edwards threatens to smash the television and Twain intervenes. Cooper turns the volume to mute, and a lively debate about violence, bad words, modesty, and other pertinent topics ensues.

After Mr. Sanders has defined his instructional objective and written the problem, he began thinking about how he would organize this lesson. At first glance, the project seemed like a huge organizational nightmare. He planned to have each student secretly play the part of one of the time-shocked authors. Having secret identities would let students avoid the stereotypes about themselves and their abilities that inevitably build over the course of the semester. But *he* still wanted to know who sent each message in case someone tried to use anonymity as a license to behave badly. He also wanted to make sure that the discussion was organized, so the students would be sure to cover the most important

The content and instructional problem

The problem for the students

Organizing the lesson

themes. He planned to check out the LCD projector one day and review the highlights and best exchanges in all of the discussions with the whole class before they write their paper.

Deciding on the tool

After all of this, Mr. Sanders finally got around to thinking about which electronic tool would help him the most. First, he considered email. In one way, email would be easiest. He and his students are email aces. They had exchanged email with another class in an electronic debate and talked with an expert on Mark Twain using email and did not have too many problems. However, Mr. Sanders just could not figure out how to work out two items: anonymity and keeping all the threads of the discussion straight. When a person uses email, the address is obvious, especially the addresses at his school. Also, it would be almost impossible to keep all of the threads of the discussion straight. The students would not able to consistently make up the name of a theme and type it into the "subject" area of the email. Taking a big leap, he decided that the tool to use is the web-based discussion board that he had taken an in-service on just the previous month.

Presenting the problem to students

Having made up his mind about the goal of the assignment, the structure of the assignment, and the tool he will use, Mr. Sanders spoke to his class like this:

"Your goal as you execute this assignment is to take the role that has been assigned to you and become that person in the discussion. Take the position on the issue that you think your historical counterpart would take. If you are Jonathan Edwards, you will begin the debate. If you are James Fenimore Cooper, you will speak second, and if you are Mark Twain, you will speak third.

Explaining the process

"Remember that these were all passionate people who had strong beliefs about right and wrong and the world in which they lived. If you can, try to use the language they would use and the arguments that you think they might have used. Do not hesitate to be creative and to extrapolate (use things you know about them to say things you think they might say). Once you have written your first exchange, then you must add to the discussion every other day. Reply to the points the other members of your group make as well as make points of your own. Remember that you must not reveal your identity to anyone in the class. The only way others will be able to communicate with you is through your writing, so you will have to make an extra effort to make your work readable. Choose your words carefully. If something in one of your opponents' replies is unclear to you, say so. You can't argue with a statement that you don't understand. I will monitor your discussions so that I can understand your thinking. If your group starts spinning its wheels or there is a problem, I will help. Before we start, let's go to the lab—I have reserved it for this hour to show you how a discussion board works. After that, we will rotate through the computers in our classroom. Starting tomorrow for the next two weeks, you will get an opportunity to read your groups' messages and send one yourself every other day."

Now let us apply Bloom's Taxonomy to Mr. Sanders' assignments (See Table 4.2). What range of intellectual skills did the students use as they argued with each other about ethics as they played their roles as early American writers? You can see from the table that one level of thought was not addressed, but that students did activities associated with both the upper and lower levels of the taxonomy.

■ A MORE ELABORATE USE OF EMAIL

Ms. Anderson's fifth graders' use of email for their geography project, the Mystery School, was simple group-to-group communication. In the next field trip we will look at a more complex use of email in which individual students will work in groups to solve a problem.

TABLE 4.2 ■ Bloom's Taxonomy and an Electronic Discussion Board Assignment

Level of Thought	Description	Discussion Board Activity
Knowledge	Name, locate, tell, list, repeat, point to	In order to argue effectively students have to look up facts about the writers or find them in the author's works.
Comprehension	Define, summarize, infer, project, describe	Students have to summarize author's views for the different categories of the discussion board.
Application	Use, solve, adapt, relate, perform	
Analysis	Compare classify, screen, examine, test for	Students have to compare the viewpoints of the different writers.
Synthesis	Create, develop, generate, build, compile, design	Students develop a debate strategy to convince their opponents and teacher that they have the strongest argument.
Evaluation	Judge, reject, criticize, rate, rank	Using viewpoints other than their own personal point-of-view, students had to judge the validity of another's arguments

FIELD TRIP 4.3

Using Email for a Math Project

Mr. Grant, a high school math teacher, knows that the National Council of Teachers of Mathematics (NCTM) has suggested that students improve their problem-solving skills. He has tried to incorporate more problem-solving into his classes, but sooner or later, the whole process bogs down. At first students work well in groups, but as the year wears on, it seems that it is always the same students who contribute the most while others hang back and let the aggressive students talk. By the time the first semester ends and the second semester begins, the aggressive, talkative students are solving the problems. The listeners might as well be listening to them stand up and lecture at the whiteboard for the amount of effort they are putting into their problem-solving sessions. Last year's test scores reflected this dichotomy, and Mr. Grant wants to do something about it. He has devised an electronic problem-solving activity using email to stimulate participation by each member of a problem-solving group.

The instructional shortcoming

Mr. Grant prepared his students for their next problem-solving exercise by explaining that they will do it electronically, still in groups, but using email as the vehicle for communication. He presented the change in format positively, not mentioning that it was an effort to get those who will not participate in oral discussions to participate in written discussions. Instead, Mr. Grant explained that it is important for everyone in class to become comfortable with the language of problem solving, and be able to articulate in writing the process and procedures that they are applying.

Getting ready to begin the exercise

Mr. Grant has five computers in his classroom and twenty-eight algebra students. He shuffled a deck of thee-by-five-inch cards with students' names written on each and made five piles of cards: three piles with six cards and two piles with five cards. Then he read aloud the names of the members of each group as the students wrote down the names of the people in their groups. The groups then huddled for ten minutes and exchanged email addresses. This first day of the assignment, Mr. Grant did not present the problem. Instead, he taught their first lesson on linear equations.

distribution list
Email function that allows users to send out the same message to a group of people rather than sending it out to one person at a time. Some email software calls this function *"nicknames."*

rule or **filter**
Instructions to categorize incoming and outgoing email.

Following general instructions he gave them, in the part of the class period that is set aside for doing end-of-section problems, each member of each group took a turn at their assigned computer. The students had been told to type a **distribution list** using the email addresses they collected earlier during the class period and including Mr. Grant's address. After creating a distribution list, each student sent one test message using the list. Next, each student created a folder ("mailbox") called "Chocolate Problem" to hold all of the email exchanges that would occur during this assignment. Finally, each student made a **rule (filter)** to route any incoming email message with "chocolate problem" in the subject line to that folder.

The next day students again went to their assigned computer to see if they had received the test email messages from the other members of their group and if the email messages had gone to their Chocolate Problems folder.

This did not go smoothly. Mr. Grant had hoped to introduce the actual problem during that class period, but instead he spent his entire time during the study period helping students fix incorrect email addresses, incomplete distribution lists, and rules that did not work. Tired and a little frustrated, he reflected that in ten years he would not have to do this. These skills will be so much a part of the culture it will not be an issue anymore. For the time being, however, if he wants to attempt an assignment like this, he knows he will spend some time teaching technology skills.

On Thursday, three days after Mr. Grant told the class about the new way of approaching their biweekly problem, the class was ready. Every member of every group got messages from every other member of the group, and they all went directly to each students' Chocolate Problem folders. This was a problem-solving experience in itself! And now the problem:

Setting up the problem

Mr. Grant began, "If you will focus on the overhead now, I am going to give you your problem. You don't have to write it down because I have emailed it to each of you. Here it is:

Augustus is trying to make chocolate milk. So far he has made a 10 percent chocolate milk solution (this means that the solution is 10 percent chocolate and 90 percent milk). He has also made a 25 percent chocolate milk solution. Unfortunately, the 10 percent solution is too weak, and the 25 percent solution is way too chocolaty. He has a whole lot of the 10 percent solution, but he only has thirty gallons of the 25 percent solution. How many gallons of 20 percent solution should he add to the 25 percent solution to make a mixture that is 15 percent chocolate (which Augustus is sure will be absolutely perfect)?" (Herr & Johnson, 1994)

Mr. Grant continued, "Since we haven't tried solving a problem like this before, I want to give you some rules.

- First, as you might have guessed, I don't want you to discuss this out loud. If you get an idea, you should write it down for the rest of your group.
- Second, the same rule applies about this problem as for the others: If your group solves the problem, do not tell others your solution. You may be cutting off discussion that will show us a different way to solve the problem.

The process

- Third, and most important: You must contribute one comment (no more) to the discussion every day. Your comment may be either a relevant question or a relevant answer. Here is an example of a relevant question: Why did you decide to use the guess and check method instead of looking for a pattern? A relevant answer does not have to be a correct answer, just something that moves the discussion forward and adds a new perspective to the problem.
- Finally, you will get a grade for this assignment. As you remember, I am on your distribution list, so every assignment that you send to the other members of the group will come to me as well. This is how I will grade your work." Mr. Grant displayed a table on his overhead (Table 4.3).
- You will schedule your contributions so that one day you will go to the computer, read, and print out your email. You will spend a day reflecting on the contributions of the other members of your group. The next day you will provide either a question or a comment."

TABLE 4.3 ■ Scoring Rubric for Problem-Solving Assignment

Questions	Point value
Question is directly related to the information in another person's comments.	15
Question uncovers a logic flaw in someone else's question or answer.	25
Comments	
Comment restates what the group already knows.	10
Comment restates what the group already knows in a unique way.	15
Comments restate what you know and adds information.	25
Charts	
Improves a diagram or chart that someone else has already submitted.	15
Provides a diagram or chart that helps explain the problem.	25
The Solution	
Solves the problem	25 points for the person who solves the problem 20 points for each member of the group who has contributed at least one 25-point question, comment, or diagram to the discussion.

So that is how Mr. Grant began his assignment. The problem itself was complex because it involved two problem-solving strategies: guess-and-check and subproblems (Herr, p. 361). Every day he skimmed his students' work. He kept students' scores in a spreadsheet and at the end of the week cut and pasted the students' scores into email so they could get a feel for the quality of their contributions.

He was generous for this first electronic assignment because neither he nor his students knew what to expect. He used the scoring rubric he had handed out the first day. He had planned to extract some of the best questions and responses each day to show the class examples of good work. But he decided that would give students too many answers and compromise the effectiveness of the assignment. Instead, at the end of the assignment when the problem had been solved, he printed out especially good comments, questions, diagrams, and exchanges, and transferred the printout to an overhead so he could show his students what they did right. It would have been much easier if he had a computer projector for his room. As it was, he would have had to check out a projector and move one of the student computers or his computer to hook up to the projector. When he looked at the trade-off in time he decided printing out and making transparencies backed up by email to individual students was a more efficient use of his time. Checking out the LCD projector and setting it up would be using technology for the sake of technology, something he did not have time for.

End of lesson summary

Using technology is not always appropriate

TABLE 4.4 ■ Bloom's Taxonomy and a Problem-Solving Lesson

Level of Thought	Description	Problem-Solving Activity
Knowledge	Name, locate, tell, list, repeat, point to	
Comprehension	Define, summarize, infer, project, describe	Student is given points for re-stating what the group already knows.
Application	Use, solve, adapt, relate, perform	Student solves the problem.
Analysis	Compare, classify, screen, examine, test for	Students test other students' solutions.
Synthesis	Create, develop, generate, build, compile, design	Students create a chart or diagram
Evaluation	Judge, reject, criticize, rate, rank	Students judge the adequacy of others' solutions.

Now that you have had an opportunity to observe a sophisticated use of email in a classroom—one that uses the functions available with most email software, we will again analyze the lesson with Bloom's Taxonomy (Table 4.4). Note that students do not deal with the first level of the taxonomy at all, but are quite engaged in the higher levels of the taxonomy.

✔ CHECKING YOUR UNDERSTANDING

`4.1`

Having now read three examples of email-supported instruction, it is time for you to think of a lesson of your own. Do not worry about technical details. Concentrate on the design of the lesson. As with any technology-supported assignment, your concerns are what students need to know and finding a technology that will help them learn faster or better. Write it in the form of a story, much like the field trips you have read. Make sure that your story touches on the following:

- The reason for the technology supported lesson
- Student objectives
- The information you want your students to learn
- The problem you will ask them to solve
- Problems that you anticipate as you execute the lesson
- The technology that will be available to you
- Management of your classroom (Will you use groups? If you do, how will they work?)
- Amount of time the lesson/unit will take
- How you will evaluate your students' performance

After you write your lesson, make a table with the levels of Bloom's Taxonomy like the tables in this chapter. Place the activities in your lesson in the appropriate cells of your new table.

■ ASYNCHRONOUS COMMUNICATION: TOOLS AND METHODS

You have just explored three different ways of using email in three different content areas for three different student grade levels. You should look beyond the content and grade level presented in each of the field trips to the pedagogy. In the upcoming discussion, we will explore some of the technical details of these assignments, but you should have some instructional content and problems of your own to think about as you read. Also as you read, keep your response to "Checking Your Understanding 4.1" in the back of your mind. Knowing more about technical details may require you to change your response.

Email

Since the first email message was sent in 1972, the complexity of email software has increased. The very first email software allowed the user to type in an email address and send a message. Now email software includes many features, including address books, distribution lists, folders (mailboxes), rules (filters), and attachments. We are going to cover all these as we go into some detail that explains how Ms. Anderson, Mr. Sanders, and Mr. Grant managed their lessons.

> Common email features

There are at least two good email programs that you can download for free from the Internet: Eudora and Pegasus. Both are quite functional and you can find both download sites by doing an Internet search on their names. Although your school provides you with email software at work, you may want to use one of these at home, or you may want to recommend these to your students for their use at home. Besides using email software that resides locally on your computer, you can also use web mail that is supported by your Internet service provider or provided free on the net along with an account. To use free web mail, you must be willing to put up with advertisements. People access web mail software by typing an Internet address into their Internet browser, pressing Enter and going to the web mail site the address points to. One popular example of web mail is Microsoft's hotmail. This service is accessible from the Microsoft home page.

> Free email software

Address books do not have direct instructional use, but an address book would certainly have helped Mr. Grant set up his project much faster. Do you remember how he asked his students to huddle for ten minutes and exchange email addresses? Some students wrote the addresses incorrectly and others typed them incorrectly. It took Mr. Grant two days to fix all of the problems. If, on the other hand, Mr. Grant had created a class address book and copied it to the email directories of the computers in his classroom, things would have gone much more smoothly. Then, as his students were making their distribution lists, they could type in the names of the classmates in their groups and the correct email addresses would have been inserted automatically.

> Address books

Individual versus Group Email Projects   When teachers began using email in their classrooms, one common strategy was to pair students in their class with students in another, remote class and promote pen pal exchanges. The activity seems simple enough,

> Common problems with one-on-one email exchanges

but it is time-consuming and filled with many possibilities for failure. Children in their first blush of excitement would write the introductory message and then run out of things to say. That in itself is disconcerting if you have planned on a year's worth of highly motivated exchanges between your seventh graders and their pen pals in the Ukraine. The solution is to carefully monitor every set of exchanges and to assign a topic for the exchange. This takes time and whether you will achieve your instructional objective as the result of the exchanges is uncertain. And then, how do you deal with your student who sends the barest minimum on each exchange to Alexy on the other side of the world who writes volumes and is terribly interested. If you have only one such student in your class you might be able to fill the gap, but if you have six or seven, something or someone will go by the wayside.

Absences are another difficult problem with one-on-one exchanges. Recall that Ms. Anderson checked every day that all of the groups in the other school had responded. She only had five groups. What if she were worried about twenty or thirty individuals instead? What if a child in the Ukraine were to come down with the flu and be out of school for two weeks? Or what if the same were to happen to one of your students? The task of "ghost writing" messages for twenty children is a chore, even once a week. In other words, if you decide you are going to undertake a project involving one-on-one exchanges, you should have a well-defined instructional objective, a limited scope of exchanges, standards that your students understand ahead of time, and back-up plans—along with the extra time that it takes to execute them. For more information on one-on-one exchanges and some references to successful exchanges, see Harris (1998) "Curriculum-Based Telecollaboration."

Distribution Lists   Another email feature that has instructional use is the distribution list. Distribution lists allow users to email the same message to a group of individuals effortlessly. Furthermore, users may save distribution lists and use them repeatedly in the case of group discussions. Generally, electronic group discussions are more effective instructional vehicles than discussions between individuals; hence, the need for distribution lists.

> More on distribution lists

The distribution lists that Mr. Grant used in his problem-solving lesson were based on one strategy of group work: many students contribute to the solution of a common problem and the teacher monitors each student's performance. Mr. Grant's students set up a group in their address books called "Chocolate Problem." They typed in the email addresses of the members of that group, including Mr. Grant. Once they had done this, to send a message to all the members of the groups they simply typed "Chocolate Problem" into the "To:" line of their emails.

Why didn't Ms. Anderson use distribution lists with her fifth graders? Fifth graders are capable of working in electronic groups and setting up distribution lists. What were the mechanics of the process she set up? First, Ms. Anderson was not interested in monitoring individual contributions to the discussion. She used her email project to generate interest and provide motivation. She felt that students would be interested enough in solving the problem that they would not need to be graded on their contributions to the group. The mechanics of the groups were different as well. Her groups and the groups at the other school sent one group message and received their messages as a group as well. In other words, each exchange consisted of only one message and one reply to all members of a group. To support this approach, she asked each of the groups to give themselves a name. Then she went to the school email administrator and asked her to create sign-ons and passwords for each group using that name. The teacher in the cooperating school did the same. Consequently, each group only had to remember and correctly enter one address—the address of its cooperating group.

Folders and Rules   Email software also allows users to create folders (mailboxes) much as they create them to store other work on the computer. These folders are quite helpful for organizing assignments. Mr. Grant's class stored their email in a folder called "Chocolate Problem." Folders are quite handy when students are receiving email from several sources or about several different assignments or problems. Furthermore, the computer can direct email about the assignment to these folders with rules (filters).

Rules perform a routing function based on a variety of different criteria. Figure 4.4 (Harris, 1990–2000), is an example of a typical rule entry screen using the Pegasus software. As you observe the screen shot of the Pegasus rule-making dialogue box, you see elements common to most rule-making engines. The idea behind the function is that when the computer receives an incoming message, it looks for specific text in whatever area of the message the user specifies. In Figure 4.4, the user is in the process of selecting the action the computer is to perform when it receives a message with "debate" in the subject line. Notice the list of possibilities in the drop-down list at the bottom.

Moving and deleting files are the two most common reasons for creating rules. If you receive many messages from a list, for example, and you don't want them cluttering up the really important email that you must read on a daily basis, then make a rule that sends them to a folder that you can open and read when you have the time. Like Mr. Grant, you can teach your students to make rules that separate their email into

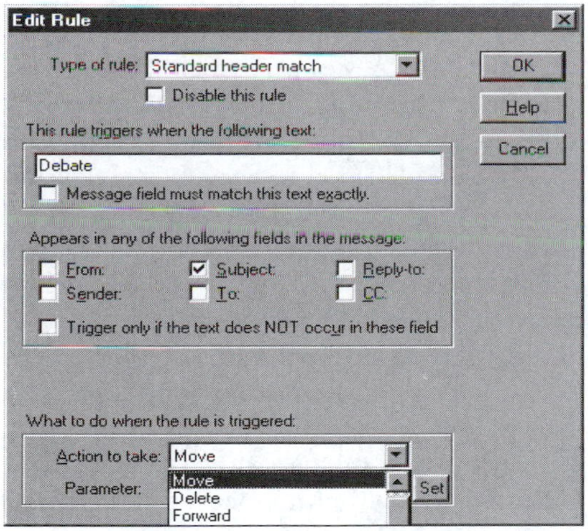

FIGURE 4.4 ■ Examples of "Rules" Screen

folders for each project that involves email. Now, let's go back to the rule making process in Figure 4.4. If the computer sees an incoming message with the subject line "debate," then it treats the message as the user prescribed in the drop-down list box at the bottom of the screen. In Figure 4.4, the user has selected "Move", and specified where to move the email that has "debate" in the subject line header. The user will choose the project folder, and from now until the user disables the rule, all new messages with a subject line "debate" will be routed immediately to the project folder, where the user can open and read the messages.

Teaching students to
use rules

It is a little tricky to get students to see the point in all of this, especially the first time they try to use rules. The concept can go wrong in two ways. Either students enter the rule incorrectly or just ignore you and do not enter a rule at all. Then their email starts accumulating, and they lose messages while claiming they were never sent. After you have asked your students to enter a rule, it is a good idea to check it and make sure it is working.

Students who do not observe the subject line requirement present a more difficult problem to solve. If someone misspells the subject line or forgets to enter the required subject line, then the recipients get a message that will not obey the rule. Peer pressure is helpful here. Make sure that your students feel free to tell other students when they send messages that do not obey the rules.

In spite of the disruption that a misspelled subject header causes when students are trying to use rules, students learn a valuable real-world lesson. If a spelling error causes major disruption with their classmates, students are more careful. As you lose time as a result of problems that computers and other technologies cause, you must gauge the value of this extra time in terms of the real-world lessons students learn. Yes, your class may have lost time on linear equations or the geography of South America, but your students may also have learned the value of a correctly spelled word and the importance of attention to detail.

Attachments   Attachments are a final feature of email that Mr. Grant's students used heavily during their problem-solving assignment. One step in the process of setting up a problem involves drawing a diagram of the problem or making a table. Since Mr. Grant's students are quite familiar with spreadsheets, they made their tables for the problem-solving exercise with a spreadsheet, attached it to their email, and every member of the group received the attachment. Other members of the group could then open the table with spreadsheet software, read it, modify it, comment on it, and send it back to the group in another attachment. Any file may be attached to an email message: graphic, database, spreadsheet, word processor, or presentation. The only caveat is that the receiver of the attachment must have software that will read the attached file. This is extremely important. When you are thinking about sending attachments to classes in other parts of the country, save your work in common file formats. Table 4.5 describes some typical file formats readable by software that is found on most computers.

Ms. Anderson's group did not use attachments until the very end of the activity, when each member of each group attached a short, word-processed biography of him- or herself along with a scanned picture. When the activity was finished, Ms. Anderson made sure that the biographies and their accompanying graphics were deleted from the students' email directories since these files take up a lot of space (because of the

TABLE 4.5 ■ Common File Formats

Kind of Document	Common File Formats
Graphic	.jpg; .gif
Audio	.wav
Video	.mpg; .avi
Text	.txt; .rtf
Spreadsheet or database files	Unless you know that your recipient uses the same kind of spreadsheet or database software that you do, export your data as a comma or tab-delimited text file. You will learn how to do this in a later chapter.

graphics). If enough of these files are left in the class email directory on the server, she knows the network administrator will call on her to remove them.

Web Boards

If your school supports one, web-based discussion boards are wonderful alternatives to email. They are not difficult to set up and maintain and are much easier to use for discussions. You may remember that Mr. Sanders used a web discussion board format for the review in his American literature class. There are several products on the market that perform this function. Two that have been very stable over the last several years are WebBoard and Microsoft FrontPage.

Web conferencing software

Most web discussion boards are very similar. Notice in Figure 4.5 that the contents column allows the user to access any previous message (the titles of which are

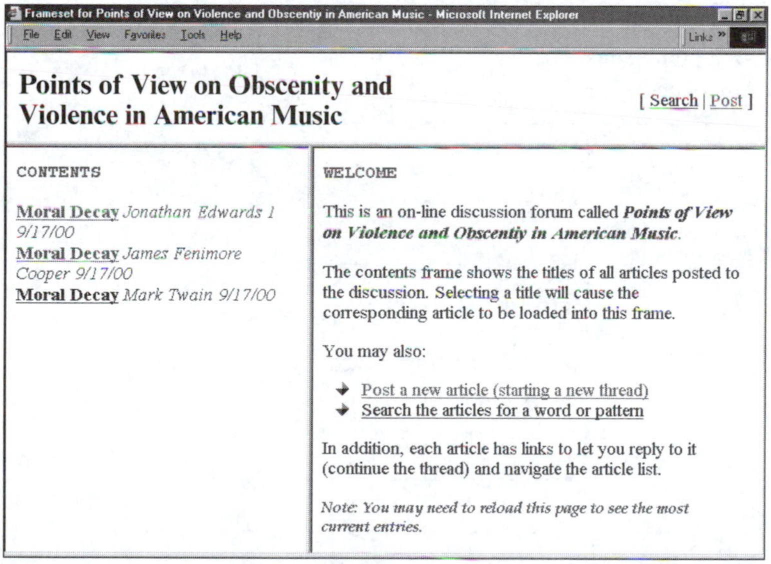

FIGURE 4.5 ■ Introductory Screen after Several Exchanges

Setting up a discussion

underlined, followed by the authors' names and the posting date. From this screen, students can do three things: read previously posted messages, search for text in any of the previously posted messages, and post a new message. Because the students in Mr. Sanders' class each had an alias, we see the names of the authors they played rather than the students. Only Mr. Sanders knew who the authors really were. In order to set the discussion up like this, Mr. Sanders had to ask the network administrator to provide sign-ons and passwords for each student. He also asked the network administrator to set up a separate discussion space for each group of students so that the whole class would not be contributing to the same discussion board. This means that each group went to a different Internet address to activate its discussion space.

Keeping Track in a Discussion: Three Ways

First let us look at the process of posting a new message. Figure 4.6 illustrates the screen just before Jonathan Edwards hits the Post Article button. As with email, the message has a subject line, but notice the untitled box below the "From" entry. In order to guide learners' discussion, the teacher may set up categories, called *strands,* ahead of time. The strands here encompass the themes Mr. Sanders expects students to address from their character's historical and cultural perspective: values, violence, free choice, and obscenity. Here we see that "Jonathan Edwards" has posted a comment that he classifies as being in the category of free choice. In Figures 4.7 and 4.8 both Cooper and Twain reply.

Keeping track of messages

Notice that on the left side of the screen, students can keep track of replies because they are indented under the message that prompted them. If you compare this capability of a web discussion board to having to sort through messages all dumped into the same folder during an email discussion, you can see the advantages. The web board

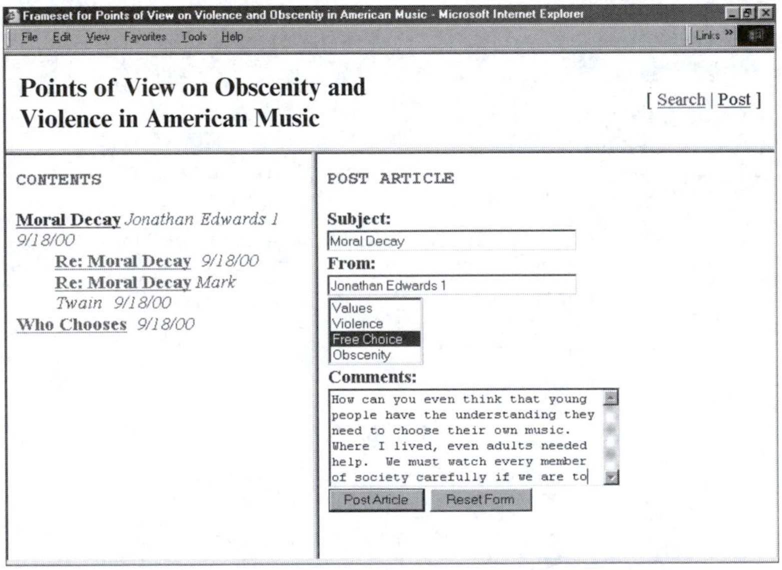

FIGURE 4.6 ■ Jonathan Edwards Chooses His Category and Writes His Message

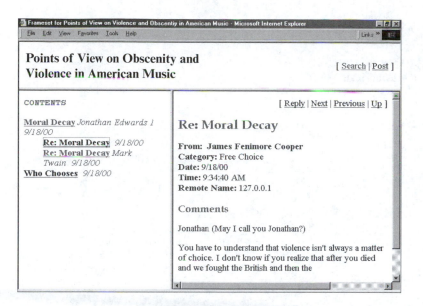

FIGURE 4.7 ■ James Fenimore Cooper's First Response Window

gives members of a discussion group two ways to keep track of and categorize messages: using categories and separating messages into a lead message and its replies.

Web board software gives users a third method of categorizing messages. If a group member wants to start a discussion on a new topic then rather than reply to a

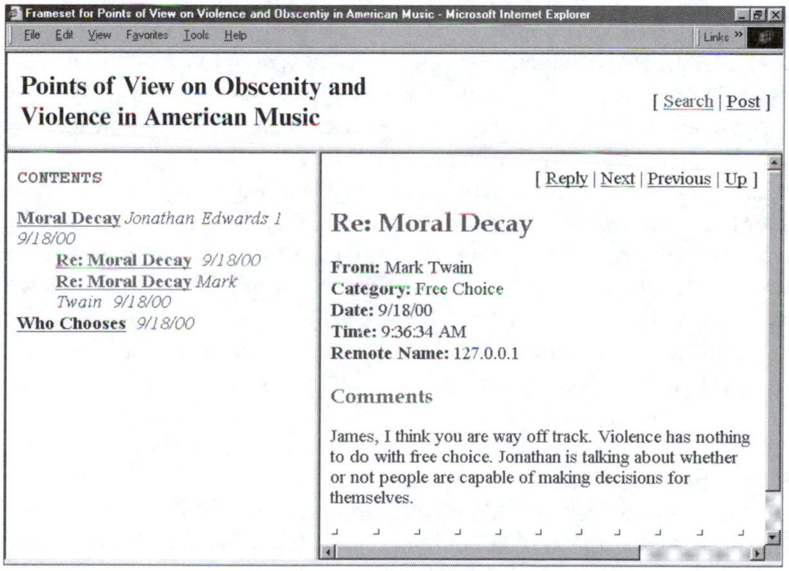

FIGURE 4.8 ■ First Part of Mark Twain's First Response Window

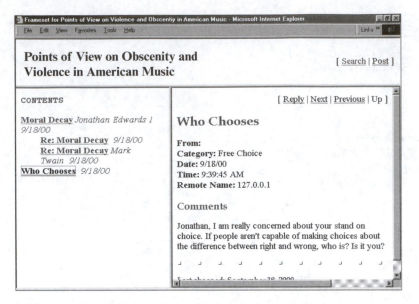

FIGURE 4.9 ■ Mark Twain Begins Another Strand

New strands

previously posted message, the participant may choose to start a new strand. This is what Mark Twain does when he starts worrying about who gets to set the standards in Figure 4.9. When Edwards replies to this challenge, his reply will be indented just like the replies in the strand in Figures 4.7 and 4.8.

Search Function

One final, useful feature of web discussion software is the search function. If a discussion is active and continues for two or three weeks, a large number of messages will accumulate. Again, emphasizing that the software (discussion board) and the method (a discussion) are not the objective of the lesson, but rather some final, thoughtful project such as a paper, speech, or speech accompanied with a computer presentation, it is helpful for the participants of a web board discussion group to have access to the messages that have been sent. It is even more helpful if the hundred or so messages are organized and searchable. If, for example, the student who played the role of Mark Twain were trying to get her thoughts together on everyone's comments about "choice," she could go to the search screen (Figure 4.10) and set up a search. The particular discussion board she is using lists the results of her search in Figure 4.11. The items are listed by name, are clickable, dated, and each is given a score that provides some indication of relevance to the topic. This student can now follow this theme through the messages and synthesize the information and make judgments about it. She is working at a very high level on Bloom's Taxonomy. Contrast this to the alternative: listening to Mr. Sanders lecture for an hour, discussing a few questions here and there, and doing a 5- or 10-minute role play involving three students with five minutes at the end of the lecture for students to ask questions.

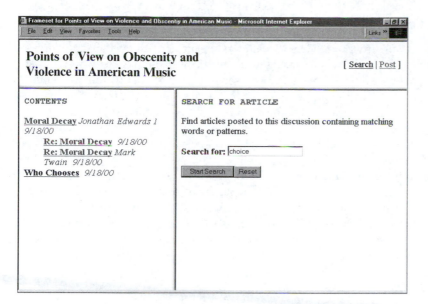

FIGURE 4.10 ■ Setting Up a Search

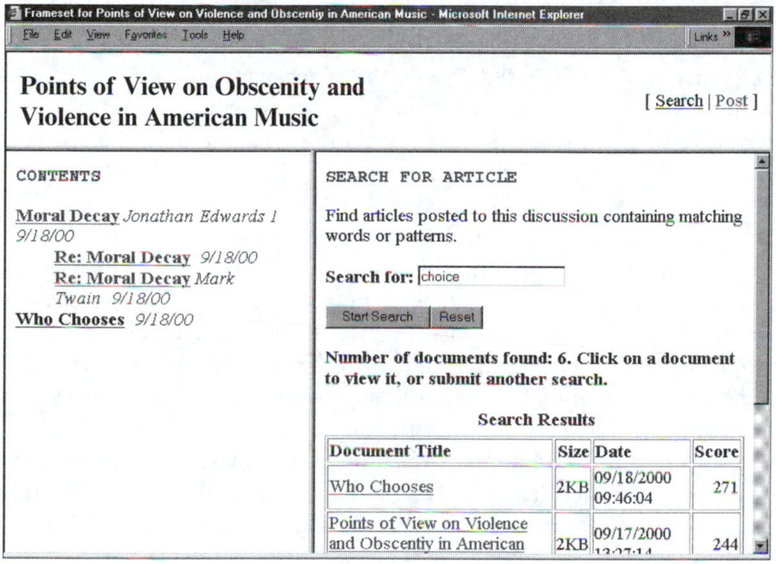

FIGURE 4.11 ■ Search Results

Discussion Monitoring

Web discussion software provides Mr. Sanders one further, behind-the-scenes oppor-tunity that we have not yet discussed. Aware that there are pranksters in his class who would love to use their anonymity to add some spice to the discussion, Mr. Sanders read all of the new entries to the discussion every day. And sure enough, the very first week, one student chose to test the rules on obscenity. Mr. Sanders simply left the mes-sage headers in the discussion so that he would not disable all of the existing links and replaced the offending messages with "This message has been removed." He reminded the student about rules and etiquette. Remember that Mr. Sanders warned his students ahead of time that he would be reading their email. The warning, though not ab-solutely necessary in a legal sense, is courteous and shows respect for students (Har-ris, 1999). There were no more problems. Mr. Sanders continued to read the messages and assisted students when their discussions stalled. Sometimes he would go to a member of a discussion group that seemed to have run out of words and plant a sug-gestion that got the group going again. He felt free to do this since he wasn't grading the students.

Planning and Evaluating Asynchronous Communication Projects

Although we have not taken a field trip to classrooms doing activities based upon each of the models in Table 4.6, we have talked about the major planning strategies as well as possibilities for failure involved in using email and discussion boards. Almost all of the activities in Table 4.6 are possible, using either of the two technologies that we have discussed, either simple email or a discussion board.

Although we have touched on evaluation (Table 4.4), it is time to say more. The kinds of activities that we have been exploring are not ends in themselves, but rather a means to help students acquire information and achieve curricular objectives. It seems odd to evaluate this learning process. An analogy might be watching a child's eyes as s/he reads paragraphs in a book while preparing for a test. The real evaluation of a com-munication-supported activity is the end product (test, paper, presentation), not the method of acquiring information. However, there are times when a teacher needs or wants to evaluate students' activities. For this situation, Table 4.7 is a general rubric that is applicable to most Internet communication supported activities. If you compare Table 4.7 to Table 4.4, you can see that Mr. Grant modified it to suit the needs of his con-tent area. He really did not care as much about spelling and grammar as he did about the problem-solving process and getting everyone to participate. Table 4.8 gives you some general ideas that you will almost certainly have to modify depending upon your objectives.

As you decide how asynchronous computer communication may help you achieve your instructional objectives, you will begin to recognize some tasks that you must complete whether you decide to conduct a role playing activity, a simulation, or use email to connect your students to an expert. Box 4.3 has some steps that you should always think through before you start.

TABLE 4.6 ■ Uses of Email and Web Conferencing

Name of Activity	Description of Activity	Advantages = "+" Disadvantages = "–"
Student-to-student communication in different parts of the world	Students studying geography, culture, or science journal for or otherwise communicate with a student from a different culture in a distant location.	+ Some individual students learn a great deal from the exchanges; – Hard to keep going; difficult to match to the curriculum
Classroom-to-classroom exchanges	These kinds of activities often center on collecting and sharing data. Classes along the same river may collect water samples, for example.	+ Easier to organize and manage than one-to-one exchanges. – The teacher(s) of the other class(es) must be committed to the project.
Peer tutoring	Older or more experienced students work with younger or struggling students	+ One more way to get help (if it works) to students who need it. – Difficult to find an older student with the time and interest in a long-term tutoring relationship; students who are struggling often have difficulty reading and writing well enough to make email work for them to participate in this activity.
Exchanging email with an expert	Teachers may seek out and find an expert in a topic their class is studying: a writer, scientist, or professional, for example. The class works together to formulate questions that the expert answers. This may be a one-time exchange or several exchanges may take place.	+ Easy to organize; class is highly motivated if the expert is famous. – The expert may have trouble speaking in a language your kids understand. You may have trouble finding an expert with enough time to help you.
Group investigation and brain-storming	Students are placed in groups and asked to solve a problem.	+ Students not only help each other learn content but also model their problem-solving skills for each other; students must write well to communicate well. – The groups' email must be read and monitored on a daily basis for two reasons: to provide help when students run out of words and ideas and to check for offensive postings.
Simulations	Discoveries, voyages, expeditions, and battles can be simulated. i.e., the Oregon Trail, the Battle of Gettysburg	+ Very motivational for students; students learn a great deal of content doing research so that they can respond appropriately to the events that the simulation requires them to respond to. – Preparation for simulations is extensive. The timing and amount of student response to the simulation must be carefully choreographed. Students must have reference materials and some background. There must be a goal or product to measure student performance.
Role playing	Any modern or historical situation in which there is a clash of culture, ideas, or philosophy provides a topic for role playing activities	+ Easy to set up. Students are motivated and like the activity. May be used as preparation for papers or tests. – If each student in the group doesn't take his/her role seriously, the rest of the students in the group miss a point of view; postings should be checked daily.

TABLE 4.7 ■ General Scoring Rubric for Student Messages

1	2	3
Evaluation of the Entire Discussion		
Contributes 3 messages	Contributes 5 messages	Contributes 7 messages
Some messages have spelling and grammar errors	All messages have been spell checked	All messages are grammatical; all messages have been spell checked
Individual Messages		
Comments unrelated to discussion topic or repeat previous messages	Comments related to discussion; repeats another student's message but with different words	Comment adds at least one new perspective
Student neither finds a logical flaw nor adds perspective; does not address the issue	Student finds a logical flaw in another student's message but offers no alternative.	Student response correctly argues another student's message

---

BOX 4.3   STEPS FOR PREPARING ASYNCHRONOUS COMMUNICATION-SUPPORTED INSTRUCTION

1. Decide on your instructional objective.
2. Decide on and construct your evaluation for the activity.
3. Decide whether the students will work alone, in groups, or as a class.
4. Decide how long you want to spend on the lesson.
5. Choose a model (Table 4.7).
6. Choose a tool (email/discussion board).
7. Think through all of the technical features of the tool.

   a. If you are using email, how will you give students email addresses?
      i. Plan to create distribution lists, if necessary.
   b. If you are using web conferencing, how will you set up your discussions—one discussion group or multiple?
      i. Provide student sign-ons to the web discussion group.
      ii. Create appropriate strands (categories) for your discussion group.

8. Write a compelling, challenging problem for students with appealing context (write a story).
9. Locate/write and assemble supporting materials for students.
10. If students haven't been trained in the use of the technology you will use, train them.
11. On the first day of the unit or lesson, explain the objectives and tell students how they will be evaluated. If possible, show students examples of previously executed projects so that they will know what is expected. At this point in the history of the use of computers in classrooms, students often have no models on which to base their performance.

✔ CHECKING YOUR UNDERSTANDING

4.2

1. Look in the "Annotated Resources" section of this chapter for Internet sites with email- or discussion board-supported lessons other teachers have created. Find a lesson plan that addresses the content area and grade level in which you teach or wish to teach. Compare this lesson plan to the steps listed above. If the lesson plan does not address one of the steps above, decide how you would execute that step.

2. Prepare and teach a lesson to a group of your peers on how to use an email client or web board. Because your peers probably have these skills already, they should role-play students at the age that you specify. The purpose of this activity is for you to get used to teaching technology skills to other people. As you complete this activity, you will find that you take for granted many steps that must be explained and demonstrated to naive users.

3. Using the steps outlined in Box 4.3, plan a complete activity for a grade level and topic of your choice. Evaluate your activity against Bloom's Taxonomy.

■ SUMMARY

In this chapter we have been looking into classrooms to see some of the more common uses of email and email-based discussion. We have looked at their advantages and disadvantages and seen some success and a little failure too. The three field trips that we took describe only a few of the possibilities.

■ REFERENCES ■

Gordon, C. (1999). Students as authentic researchers: A new prescription for the high school research assignment. ERIC (EJ603683).

Harrington, M., Holik, M., & Hurt, P. (1998). Improving writing through the use of varied strategies. ERIC (ED420874).

Harris, D. (1990–2000). *Pegasus mail: Version 3.1 for Win 32* (Tenth Anniversary Edition).

Harris, J. (1998). Curriculum-based telecollaboration: Using activity structures to design student projects. Learning and Leading with Technology, 26(1), 7–15.

Harris, J. (1998). Virtual architecture: Designing and directing curriculum-based telecomputing. Eugene, OR: International Society of Technology in Education.

Harris, J., & Jones, G. (1999). A descriptive study of telementoring among students, subject matter experts, and teachers: Message flow and function patterns. Journal of Research on Computing in Education, 32(1), 36–51.

Herr, T., & Johnson, K. (1994). Problem solving strategies: Crossing the river with dogs. Emeryville, CA: Key Curriculum Press.

Lambert, G. (1999). Helping twelfth grade honors English students improve writing skills through conferencing. ERIC (ED427344).

Russell, M. (2001). The Secretary's conference on educational technology: Measuring impacts and shaping the future. http://www.ed.gov/ Technology/techconf/2000/report.html [Retrieved February 1, 2001 from the World Wide Web].

Stewart, B. (2001). Common sense netiquette rules. http://msn.zdnet.com/m . . . / 0%2C14261%C2564953-hud00025hm3%2C00.htm. [Retrieved February 20, 2000 from the World Wide Web].

Stoicheva, M. (2000). The digital divide and its implications for language arts. ERIC (ED442138).

■ ANNOTATED RESOURCES ■

Chan, M. "No talking please; just chatting: Collaborative writing with computers." ERIC (ED415836)

Using chat with ESL students

This reading is appropriate for ESL or foreign language teachers at the secondary level who are looking for methodologies for improving written communication skills.

Telecollaborators Wanted, *Leading and Learning with Technology,* Vol. 28 No. 8, p. 46

Finding a partner for email collaboration

This article describes a clearing house where you can find teachers who are interested in participating in telecollaborative projects.

Structuring Internet-Enriched Learning Spaces for Understanding and Action, *Leading and Learning with Technology,* December/January 2000–1 Vol. 28 No. 4.

Writing Internet-supported lessons

This article will help you focus on lesson design using the kinds of Internet-based communication discussed in this chapter. There is an excellent chart listing activities, their structures, and the kinds of learning they support. In addition there are links to sites that support many of the listed activities.

Presentation Software

OBJECTIVES

- Describe a lesson that uses presentation software.
- List the steps for preparing a presentation.
- Name software used for creating presentations.
- State the reasons why presentation software helps students learn.
- List five ways information may be represented with presentation software.
- Match the steps for creating a presentation to levels of Bloom's Taxonomy.

You can read far enough into Chapters 5 and 7 to learn the basics of presentation software assignments, and then go to Chapter 6 to read about screen design techniques that will help you develop your own skills as you practice with presentation software. Then, when you start thinking about how to implement a presentation software-based assignment in your classroom, you can go back and read about idea mapping and storyboarding in Chapter 7, to learn how to maximize student learning. After you glean what you can on first reading, practice a while and read these chapters again. You will understand more the second time and will be able to hone your skills for using presentation software to improve the teaching/learning process in your classroom. Skills that are needed for using presentation software are listed below.

- Make a button and link to another page.
- Make a hot word and link to another page.
- Make a text box.
- Change fonts in a text box.
- Change levels in a list.

- Change foreground and background colors.
- Scale graphic objects.
- Digitize graphics, sound, and video.
- Scan documents and images.
- Capture computer screens.
- Import a graphic.
- Import or insert an object (image, sound, etc.).
- Use a paint program to create graphics composed of lines, rectangles, ovals, and so on.
- Use a graphics program to enhance scanned images.
- Understand the advantages and disadvantages of different file graphics formats.
- Insert a new slide (card, page).

We start this chapter with a field trip. Probably the first thing you want to know about presentation software is what a classroom looks like when it is getting ready to start a hypermedia project. You will read about Jeff, who has learned the skills for making presentations with computers but has never been asked to use the software to complete an assignment.

Although this example involves a tenth-grade biology class, those who teach in the early grades can benefit from this snapshot of a classroom as much as middle or high school teachers. Younger students work with less information, but the methods for working with information and presentation software are similar. The same is true of content areas. If you are an English, language arts, or social studies teacher, you should think about topics that you teach and draw some conclusions about how an assignment like this would look with your content and your students. Here are some questions the field trip should help you to answer:

Useful for all grade levels, content

- What does an assignment that uses presentation software look like?
- How would you introduce such a unit to students?

Jeff's biology class is just starting a new unit on plant and animal cells. The teacher, Mrs. Hansen, told the students they will have a test over the new unit in three weeks. Then she told them about the activities that will help them prepare for the test.

FIELD TRIP 5.1

Learning about Cells

Jeff, who is wincing at the thought of writing definitions in his lab notebook and answering end-of-chapter questions, imagines himself using a ruler to measure the stack of worksheets for the unit. He hopes the class will at least get to use the microscopes to see some cells. That would make the thought of all of the other work nearly bearable. Instead, the teacher surprises him. She says, "No definitions this time, no end-of-chapter questions, and no worksheets." Jeff, suddenly interested, wonders cynically if she has something even worse in store.

Explaining the activities

She says, "We are going to use the computers a new way for this unit. You will write an electronic report called *A Hypermedia Guide to Cells.* We will divide our time among talks and demonstrations by me, reading the text, doing and documenting microscope work, writing idea maps and storyboards for your presentations, getting graphics and animations from the Internet, and actually writing your presentation on the computer. We will have to plan our activities carefully so that everyone will have enough time at the computer and the microscopes to get the work done. To help you understand how you will be graded on your project, I will hand out a scoring rubric after you understand a little more about the project."

Jeff, astounded and interested, listens carefully to the specifics of the computer assignment. His teacher says, "I want you to include these topics in your computer project: parts of the cell, cell functions for both animals and plants, and a step-by-step explanation of meiosis and mitosis."

"I want you to include a picture that shows an example of each major idea, like the parts of a cell. And I want you to show mitosis and meiosis graphically, either with an animation, video, or a series of graphics. I will give you some ideas about where you can find this information on the Internet. I also want you to write and record a short audio piece—about one minute—to include in your presentation, on how cells differentiate to perform different tasks.

Defining a product

"Your finished presentation should have between fifteen and twenty-five screens and should start with a title page followed by a menu page. Your program should allow a user to get to any piece of information with three clicks of the mouse. Every word in your report that is not common knowledge should have some kind of hyperlink to an explanation that could be text, a graphic, an audio, or a video clip. Only half of your hyperlinks can point to text. The rest should point to audio, graphic, video, or animation. You will also want to document all of your sources by providing a page called "References" at the end of your presentation. We will talk about copyright rules and how to set that page up tomorrow because you will want to document information as you get it.

Working with information

"Spend the next fifteen minutes just browsing through the chapter in your book on cells and think about how you might organize the information you need for the hypermedia presentation you are going to write. Then, I will give you some ideas about how to start." Jeff looks at his textbook and begins thumbing through the chapter and starts thinking about how he will organize his hypermedia guide to plant and animal cells.

Now that you have read a little about what happens in a classroom before students start a hypermedia project, we will look at some of the reasons why Jeff's teacher thinks that this assignment using presentation software will replace learning activities she has used in the past.

■ PRESENTATION SOFTWARE

Presentation software is a unique blend of formats for displaying information. It has three names: presentation, multimedia, and hypermedia software, but software with any of those names usually will do about the same thing. In this book we generally use the term presentation software. Its power lies in its ability to display information in many different formats arranged in a variety of helpful combinations. Presentation software enables people to do the following:

Methods of displaying information

■ Display information in *five* different formats: text, video, audio, graphic, and animation
■ Present information in a hypertext (non-linear) format, allowing the user to jump from one related idea to another

Names of software

Beyond these two fundamental functions found in all presentation software, the user must supply everything else, including organization and content, thereby setting up an excellent opportunity for learning. Names of different presentation software include PowerPoint, HyperStudio, Digital Chisel, SuperLink, and, oddly enough, Internet browser software. For younger children, teachers use KidPix and KidWorks. Prices range from free (for Internet browser software if you already have it) to around $100 per copy for the other kinds of software.

Characteristics of presentation software

This genre of software is menu-driven and allows authors to easily import graphics, animations, audio, and video to pages, cards, or screens. It allows authors to draw geometric figures such as squares, rectangles, lines, and circles using color, as well as to display text in many fonts, sizes, colors, and styles. Finally, it allows authors to link information any way that they deem appropriate. Presentation software is simple to learn, and is quite intuitive after some instruction and a little practice.

Some presentation software allows advanced authors to write "script" (computer programs) that actually get input from the end user. This capability allows authors to create exercises and tests within their finished product, and generally provides for more forms of interactivity. Scripting is beyond the scope of this book.

Presentation software and learning

How can students learn better when they create presentations? Presentation software helps them see relationships among facts, which is helpful for two reasons: When students organize isolated facts into a presentation, they remember the facts better (Plotnick, 1997; Pohl, 1998); When students see relationships among facts, they often generalize and come to understand some problem or process more deeply.

Now, do you remember the assignments Jeff has to complete for his hypermedia project? He has to do an outline and an idea map. He also has to do a storyboard, which may be new to you. A storyboard helps people translate the ideas in their outlines and idea maps into a blueprint that guides them as they work on their presentation at the computer. Looking at Table 5.1, you can see that a hypermedia assignment,

Presentation software and Bloom's Taxonomy

TABLE 5.1 ■ Bloom's Taxonomy and Hypermedia Lessons

Level of Thought	Description	Hypermedia Activity
Knowledge	Name, locate, tell, list, repeat, point to	Gathering facts Outlining
Comprehension	Define, summarize, infer, describe	Idea mapping Outlining Flowcharting
Application	Used, solve, adapt, relate, perform	Idea mapping Flow charting
Analysis	Compare, classify, screen, test for	Idea mapping Flowcharting Storyboarding
Synthesis	Create, develop, generate, build, compile, design	Storyboarding Flowcharting Writing the hypermedia presentation
Evaluation	Judge, reject, criticize, rate, rank	Critiquing other students' work

if designed properly, challenges students at all levels of the taxonomy. Consider how important it is to teach students to think critically and how difficult it is to design lessons that encourage this. You can see from the table that hypermedia-supported lessons provide many opportunities for students to think at the highest levels of the taxonomy. Any successful work that they do above the "knowledge" level of Bloom's Taxonomy involves critical thinking.

Before we continue with Jeff, Mrs. Hansen, and the assignment, you need to understand a few more basics about how and why hypermedia is so powerful. Knowing how and why will help you decide which kinds of content you teach are best suited for hypermedia-supported lessons. Presentation software does not help teach all content most efficiently.

Displaying Information: Key to Creating Understanding

Researchers tell us that some people learn better when they read information, others when they hear it, others when they see it presented graphically, and still others when they interact with it in some physical way (Gay, 2000). Computers accommodate all of these learning styles because the machines can present information in five different formats:

> Building context with varied formats

- Graphics
- Text
- Audio
- Audio and video
- Animations

Also, computers encourage complex interactions with content. The act of organizing information helps people learn. The richer the information they organize, the richer their learning will be. Student or teacher presentations with presentation software are *not* the reason for using computers to teach. The value of presentation software does not lie so much in the finished product as in the process of creating it.

> Process is as important as product

The Role of Interactivity

For many years, the primary way people learned to organize their writing was the outline. Organizing ideas with presentation software is like outlining in three dimensions. To prepare a hypermedia assignment, a student does a traditional outline, an idea map (an outline of relationships), and a storyboard. The storyboard translates the facts and relationships derived from the idea map and outline into a blueprint for the computer. For a student author this task is complex enough that it can supplant many traditional activities such as doing worksheets, answering questions at the end of the chapter, and writing definitions.

> Supplants many traditional activities

Conveying information with hypermedia is different than conveying it in print. Hypermedia adds a third dimension to the formatting of information. Print media runs front to back, beginning to end. It operates in a single dimension. With print-based information delivery, students are taught how to think about a beginning, middle, and an end for the story, report, or paragraph. Then they chunk the information they want to convey into paragraphs, decide on an order for the paragraphs (or at least they are told to think about an order), and finally write their piece.

Allows students to think nonlinearly

Knowledge itself does not naturally fall into paragraphs that start at one place and end at another. If you were writing a report on geographic regions of the United States, you might divide the country into six regions: Northwest, Southwest, Northeast, Southeast, Midwest, and the Plains. In your written report, you would have to talk about each of these areas in some order. Although there is no reason that Northwest should be first and Southwest should be second, given the limitations of print you will have to talk about some region first, another next, and another last.

From another perspective, if people do not understand a word in your report, they might need to go to the glossary or a dictionary to look it up. Most likely, they will try to guess from the context and move forward. Hypermedia allows us to transcend these limitations of print if it is designed properly. It is in the act of designing the product that students learn from the information that they are trying to organize.

Author must always think about relationships

Think about Jeff and the hypermedia report he was just assigned to do. Knowledge about cells does not start at one place and end at another. A cell performs both mitosis and meiosis. But what about cell function and structure? You have to know something about cell function and structure to understand mitosis and meiosis. You also have to know something about structure to understand function, and vice versa. Furthermore, you have to think about cells in order to make the decision to describe cells based on their function and structure.

If you think about the possibilities for creating hypermedia reports, you can see that the nonlinear environment provided by presentation software nudges its users into thinking clearly and logically. The writer must spend time working out relationships in ways that transcend the traditional paper outline to make a coherent, understandable, and informative hypermedia presentation.

The life cycle of a hypermedia-supported assignment is straightforward. Let's look in on Jeff's classroom to see how he and his classmates are doing with their new project, *A Hypermedia Guide to Cells.*

FIELD TRIP 5.2

Cells Project Continues

Jeff and his classmates began their work in earnest. After they spent a few minutes getting an overview of the information from their textbooks, Jeff's teacher explained their assignment. She gave them a partially completed idea map about cell function and structure to start their thinking. She also gave them a list of graphics to find on the Internet. Mrs. Hansen gave the class the names of some pictures she wanted them to find. She said, "I know you will need at least these graphics (vacuole, mitochondria, and nucleus), so you can get started. As you work on your presentation you will learn which others you will need to find or prepare for your project." Finally, she gave them a template to help them build their storyboards. Jeff's head was spinning. This was all so new!

Organizing information

Because this was the first time Jeff and his classmates had studied a unit using hypermedia, they had to learn a few things. They had all done regular outlines half-heartedly in their English classes, but they had never tried *idea mapping.* Therefore, their teacher had to show them how to do it. At first Jeff thought idea maps were going to be easy. All he would have to do was draw some boxes with lines between them, stick some relevant-sounding words in the boxes, and that part of the assignment would be done.

Jeff discovered that idea mapping is quite a challenge. When the teacher asked, "OK, now what are some of the things that all plant and animal cells, have in common?" Jeff could not figure out why she thought "structure" was a better answer than "nuclei." Then, after a lot of practice with the teacher and the rest of the students, Jeff learned how to look for relationships among things and ideas.

By the time Jeff was done with the outline and the idea map, he had come into contact with quite a few facts. To fully understand how knowledge about cells is organized, a person has to know and understand some detail.

As Jeff's idea mapping efforts progressed, his teacher helped him understand that most of the key ideas in his concept map could be shown in ways other than with words. He spent his computer time consulting his idea map as he hunted for information from the Internet, scanned pictures, and made audio recordings to put in his presentation.

As the pieces of information about cells began making sense, Jeff started his storyboard. To make a storyboard, he drew each screen of the presentation on a piece of paper. He wrote down information about fonts and colors, as well as "hot words" (words users can click on for information or navigation). He recorded the instructions for linking each page to the others in his flowchart. He made notations of the names of graphics files and their locations. He wrote headings and paragraphs about cells, what they do, and their composition. In addition, he created definitions and added pictures along with some audio clips to further explain the ideas he was working with.

> Preparing to display information

As his storyboard began taking shape, Jeff used his computer time to create the actual product with PowerPoint (other software would have served as well). Because of his preparation, Jeff was able to use his limited time at the computer efficiently. He had done all of the organization. He could finally pay attention to the mechanics of creating a hypermedia presentation—thinking about which key to press, experimenting with special effects and just making it look good.

> Creating the project

At the end of three weeks, the unit was finished. Mrs. Hanson narrowly averted three classroom management disasters. She underestimated the amount of computer time the students would need. Fortunately, she was able to send some students to the computer lab on certain days and others to the library computers. In a classroom with five computers and 30 students who were only in the room 50 minutes a day, the maximum amount of time a student could get was two hours over three weeks. Next time she would provide the students with a small library of graphics (the best of this year's efforts) rather than ask the students to do the Internet search themselves. This time she quickly provided some modest graphics when she realized they would not have enough time to find them individually. She also overestimated what the students would remember about running presentation software from last year's computer applications class. Next year she vowed she would spend a day re-acquainting students with the skills they would need to use it. And then there was that one day when almost everyone was confused about the idea map—more on that later.

> Error #1: Underestimating time and resources needed

> Error #2: Overestimating students' recall of skills

> Error #3: Failing to teach idea maps before assigning them

She asked the students to hand in their idea map, outline, and storyboard. Students gave a short, five-minute demonstration of their presentation for the whole class. Then she divided the class into four groups. Group members individually gave in-depth displays of their presentations to the other members of their group. The group then chose one of the presentations to display on the Internet and save as an example for next year's class. She gave the class a 30-question multiple-choice test followed by an essay question to evaluate what they had learned about cells. As she corrected the tests, it was clear that the test was easy for Jeff and most of the others—quite a change from last year.

> Presenting the product

As she looked over the students' products, she realized that she had more information than she needed for grading the unit. Rather than grade each piece of work, she quickly scanned each storyboard and idea map and placed a check by the student's name if the work was acceptable. She then wrote a short, one-sentence, "What You Did Right" comment on each paper. She could see that the students

> Evaluating the product

would need more practice with idea mapping and storyboarding, but this was a good first step. She graded the students' tests, listened, and watched as they gave their presentations. Their next hypermedia presentation, *Organ Systems in Mammals,* would be a little easier.

■ EXECUTING A HYPERMEDIA-SUPPORTED LESSON PLAN

Browse Table 5.2 for a list of the activities in a typical hypermedia-supported unit. The elements are the same whether the learner is in kindergarten or twelfth grade. The difference lies in how much help the teacher provides and how much information the student is required to process. Bear in mind that students will do other things, too, such as read their text, take tests, and participate in class discussion. They will do fewer worksheets, answer fewer questions, and memorize fewer lists and definitions.

It is important to match the computer portion of the assignment with the students' abilities. Table 5.3 will help you understand what this means. It is divided into three different segments: beginning, intermediate, and advanced. As a teacher, you know that these divisions do not necessarily refer to grade levels. I would, and have, given the assignment for beginners described in Table 5.3 to adults. I have seen students in upper elementary grades and middle school who are easily capable of doing the advanced assignment. The goal is to move everyone forward as much as possible toward the advanced level. Why? Because the advanced level gives students practice doing high-level analytical thinking tasks and provides opportunities that create context for the information that they are learning. This context will help them remember the information better for a longer period of time (Woolfolk, 2000).

You probably recognize that the advanced lesson plan does require some creative thinking. However, you might ask, "Why are the beginning and intermediate plans any better than a worksheet?" The answer is that the plans provide opportunities to learn from text, graphics, audio, animation, and video while the student is physically inter-

> The information students process varies by grade

TABLE 5.2 ■ Activity, Materials, and Products

Activity	Materials	Product for Evaluation
Outline	Pencil/paper or computer	Written outline
Idea Maps	Pencil/paper or computer	Hand-drawn or written idea map
Storyboard	Pencil/paper or computer	The completed storyboard
Flowchart	Pencil/paper or computer	The completed storyboard
The Software	Computer	CD or Internet display is graded on: • Following directions • Completeness • Design of the information (presented logically) • Screen design

TABLE 5.3 ■ Assignments Using Presentation Software

Level of Learner	Kinds of Assignment
Beginner • The learner does not have presentation software skills. • The learner is young (grades K–4). • The content is very difficult or foreign to the learner. • The learner has never created a concept map before. • The learner has had difficulty reading and mastering idea mapping and storyboarding.	Create the outline and idea map together as a class. Provide the storyboard. Provide all of the graphics on the network or disk so students do not have to look for them. The number of links between pages depends on the age and cognitive abilities of the child. A kindergartner might be required to make two or three pages while a 12th grader might have to manage 10–15 pages on his/her first attempt.
Intermediate • The learner is aquainted with presentation software. • The learner has the cognitive ability of an average middle school student. • The learner knows how to create concept maps. • The learner has access to the Internet and knows how to look for graphics and text information.	Give the list of concepts you want them to know and ask them to write them in outline form. Give them a half-finished idea map. Give them a template for a storyboard and work through the title screen, main menu, and two or three screens with them.
Advanced • Learners are familiar with presentation software, file formats, and downloading information from the Internet. • They have had practice creating concept maps. • The learners know and understand how concepts can share properties or characteristics.	Give students a list of topics they should cover. The topics Jeff's teacher gave the class are plant and animal cells, what they are made of, what they do, and how they reproduce. Students should use this list as the basis for the outline, idea map, and storyboard.

acting with the machine that delivers the information. Those five information delivery modes play to a variety of learning styles. Again, you are providing opportunities for students to put the content that they are learning into a context so that they can understand and remember it better.

■ SUMMARY

Planning a lesson that uses the full capabilities of presentation software involves more than having students go to the computer and construct a series of slides inhabited by some text and graphics. Using presentation software to maximize learning involves planning the lesson in such a way that students are required to organize and connect the information that they are learning. There is a process for developing a presentation that provides opportunities for students to interact with the same information in several different contexts: the outline, concept map, and storyboard.

Furthermore, students should consciously search for different representations of the information they are organizing so that they have two or three different opportunities for making links in their memories to what they are learning. If they are learning the definition of the word "urban" they will want to write about urban (text), show pictures representing an urban setting (graphics), and find or create either a video or animation that also represents some element of "urban." Furthermore, they will probably want to think about consequences or implications of "urban" and represent these topics in multiple formats as well.

■ REFERENCES ■

Gay, G. (2000). *Thinking and learning skills.* Center For Adaptive Technology, University of Toronto. http://snow.utoronto.ca/Learn2/mod3/mistyles.html.

Plotnick, E. (1997). Concept mapping: A graphical system for understanding the relationships between concepts. ERIC (ED 407938).

Pohl, M. (1998). Hypermedia as a cognitive tool. ED-MEDIA/ED-TELECOM 98 World Conference on Educational Multimedia and Hypermedia & World Conference on Educational Telecommunications. Proceedings (Tenth Freiburg, Germany).

Woolfolk, A. (2000). *Educational psychology.* Boston: Allyn and Bacon, p. 283.

■ ANNOTATED RESOURCES ■

Ray, L. Multimedia authoring tools: Challenges to effective use. *Computers in Schools,* 1999, Vol. 15(1).

Using multimedia authoring tools is not always easy. This article examines the challenges of the appropriate use of multimedia authoring for students. Ray especially focuses on literacy development.

Reed, W., & Wells, J. Merging the Internet and hypermedia in the English language arts. *Computers in Schools,* 1997, Vol. 13 (3/4).

This article provides some detail on merging the Internet and Hypercard for students studying *Hamlet.* Whether your class is studying *Hamlet* and using Hypercard does not matter. You will read about some interesting strategies and methods for using the Internet and hypermedia in language arts.

Graphic and Interface Design Principles

OBJECTIVES

- Appreciate the value of planning and designing effective screens.
- Design screens that present information effectively.

As students prepare their presentations, they must also think about how to make the presentation convey information well. We have established that clarity of thought is an important element in the preparation of a presentation. It is not comforting to know, however, that bad graphic design can destroy all of the hard work involved. The task of building a good presentation is not over when all of the outlining, idea mapping, and storyboarding are finished. Unless your students use some basic principles of graphic design as they build their screens, their work may not communicate well and may reflect poorly on both them and you.

Simplicity and consistency are *the* principles of graphic design for computers. Understanding graphic design is a matter of your own practice and your observations of screens that other people make. Expecting good graphic design techniques of yourself as well as your students is as important as expecting students to use good spoken and written grammar. The reason people use grammar at all is to make their communication more clear and precise. Graphic and **interface** design are the grammar of the eye.

As you teach interface design, consider the age and ability of your students. Work on a few rules at a time. There are some rules that very young students cannot understand—see a rule about type justification, for example. Not much is gained by teaching kindergartners about type justification unless a student accidentally stumbles upon the control in the software and wants to know what it is for.

> Simplicity and consistency are the basis of graphic design

interface
The consistent color, font style, and placement of informational and navigational elements of a program or an operating system. A good interface is essential.

Graphic design is
a large field—teach
students the basics.

Whole books have been written on the topic of good graphic design for computers. I have listed two of the best in the references at the end of this chapter. The guidelines I provide below do not cover technical details such as kerning and anti-aliasing, among others. The guidelines I have chosen are fundamental ones that novice designers often violate, making a presentation difficult to view and understand. Using presentation software to convey information is a strange, new world for many people. They must understand the basics first. We will approach the topic as a series of rules with examples.

Rule 1: Orient Users

Provide information on each screen that tells users where they are in the presentation. Use headings and captions as organizers. Headings and captions should reflect the way students organize content in the outline and idea map. Level-one items often serve as screen headings. Menus are level-two items, and level-three items serve as individual facts that students display in text boxes, audio and video clips, animations, and sound files. At this point it is easy to see why so much planning is important. Without it, the students' products are just a collection of disorganized facts and pictures.

Though the colors cannot be seen in Figure 6.1, the layout that Jeff developed uses both color and screen location to help users assimilate and understand content as well

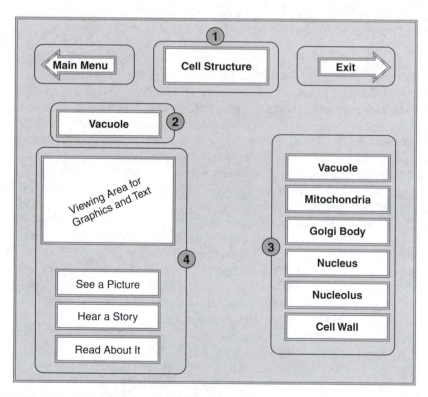

FIGURE 6.1 ■ Helping Users Know Where They Are in a Title

as navigate the program. The list below describes the parts of the screen that are indicated on the figure.

1. Area 1 is the title of this topic—one of three main topics in Jeff's presentation. The other main topics are Cell Function and Cell Reproduction. Jeff decided to use gray as the background color for this section. This topic title is in a dark blue-green box, similar to the other colors on this screen but different enough to stand out. For the Cell Function topic, Jeff used a green background, and for Cell Reproduction he used purple. In other words, the background color of the screen, along with a title at the top, cues Jeff's user to a change in topic.
2. This box contains the title of the subtopic that the user has chosen from the bank of buttons at the right (in area 3). The subtopic title box is blue and matches the color of the subtopic buttons in area 3. Jeff wanted his users to mentally connect the subtopic title box with the related buttons.
3. These six buttons represent the subtopics a viewer can choose. When a user clicks on one of these, the new subtopic title appears in area 2.
4. This is the display area with three selection buttons below it. This is where information on a subtopic is presented. In this example with Vacuole chosen as the subtopic, when the user clicks on See a Picture, a picture of a vacuole appears in the display area. When the user clicks on Read About It, text about vacuoles appears. When Hear a Story is selected, there is no change to the display but the user hears an audio segment about vacuoles that Jeff has recorded. These three buttons are a different color from the six subtopic buttons, because they perform a different set of functions.

Not numbered in this figure are the two primary navigational buttons. The Main Menu button takes a user back to the menu that lists this and the two other main topics in Jeff's presentation. The Exit button takes a user out of the presentation. These buttons occupy the same positions on all the screens in Jeff's presentation.

To see how a presentation author can achieve consistency from screen to screen, now look at Jeff's screen for Cell Reproduction (Figure 6.2) The background color has changed, but the topic title is still at the top of the screen. All navigational buttons are in the same place, along with the viewing area for content. This is the kind of consistency that good planning yields.

Rule 2: Justify Text Appropriately

Everything should be left-justified except for numbers in a table, which should be right-justified. Numbers should be right-justified so that they line up correctly as the number of digits to the left increases. However, if the numbers include decimals, then they should be aligned on the decimal point, if the software being used has that capability (and most software does). Table 6.1 shows left-, decimal-, and right-justified text. Figure 6.3 shows a different type of justification, where both left and right margins are straight because extra spaces have been inserted (by the software) between words. Although traditional books use justified margins, on the screen justified text can be hard to read.

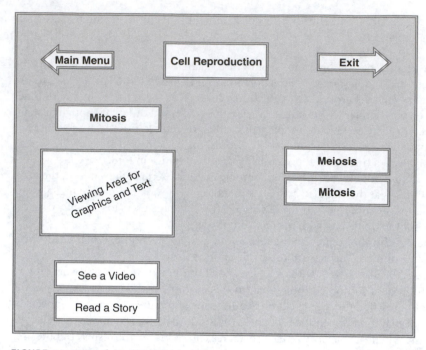

FIGURE 6.2 ■ Mock-Up of Cell Reproduction

TABLE 6.1 ■ Numbers and Justification

Left-justified	Decimal-justified	Right-justified
1	1.0	1
12	12.0	12
123	1.23	123

Rule 3: Limit Type Styles

Do not use more than three type styles per screen.   You may use one style for headings, one for text, and one for navigation buttons and controls, although even this much diversity is not necessary. These text styles should remain consistent throughout a short hypermedia product and at least within sections of longer products. Navigation text (button and menu text), especially, should remain consistent through a presentation. Different font styles beyond this minimum should have a real reason. For example, you may import a graphic or graphics with different text styles than the ones you are using. Don't worry about it. Do not follow the rule if there is a good reason not to. On the other hand, if you adhere to the rule you are less at risk of producing "busy" screens.

> **Difficult to Read**
>
> Although it seems like a good idea, justified text is hard to read. The variable spacing and the monotony of the margins make it difficult to read quickly. Just like everything else on a computer screen, spacing means something.
>
> **Easier to read**
>
> Although it seems like a good idea, justified text is hard to read. The variable spacing and the monotony of the margins make it difficult to read quickly. Just like everything else on a computer screen, spacing means something.

FIGURE 6.3 ■ Justification Examples

Rule 4: Limit Colors

Do not use more than three or four colors per screen. Colors should stay consistent for the entire product if it is short, or could change somewhat to accommodate different topics (consisting of several screens) within a presentation. Colors in imported graphics do not count toward the three- or-four-color specification. Have a good reason for using color. Reasons for using color include:

- To attract, hold, or direct attention; in that sense, color could be a navigational tool
- To show relationships
- To provide data (example: a blue line changing to red implies cold to hot)

Rule 5: Standardize Use of Colors

Set up a color scheme and use it consistently. Some colors work very well for certain tasks. Blue, for example, is a great color to use for a background rather than a foreground because the human retina has fewer blue-sensitive cells than sensors for any other color. Additional colors for backgrounds are black, white, and yellow, but consider two things—contrast and expense in printing. Too much contrast between type and background is hard to read for some people. And be considerate if you think your audience might appreciate your presentation enough to want to print a personal copy; solid black or dark-colored backgrounds consume a lot of expensive printer ink. Consider using red and green in locations where you intend the viewer to focus. Otherwise, the viewer is likely to miss them. When choosing colors for text and its accompanying background, do not use low-contrast colors (for example, orange on yellow, green on blue, or white on beige). Also, avoid the following color combinations: red on green; green on blue, and red on blue. They are hard to read and create after-images (Marcus, 1991).

Rule 6: Enhance Text with Graphics and Interactivity

Do not allow students to hand in screens that are only text.   Text-heavy documents are perceived as difficult to read (or worse—boring), whether on screen or on paper. Text-heavy presentations also do not take advantage of the computer's power to organize information. Text should be accompanied by charts, illustrations, diagrams, boxes, and—above all—*interactivity* (menus, hotwords) because these elements make documents visually appealing, which is important if you want people to read what you've researched, written, and produced.

Rule 7: Eliminate Superfluous Items

Every object on the screen should have meaning.   Decoration for the sake of decoration is superfluous. Examples of superfluous designs are elaborate borders that do not contribute information to the presentation and clip art that has only a vague relationship with the objective of the screen.

Rule 8: Use Upper- and Lower-Case

Don't use all-caps.   Instead of using all capital letters, use both upper- and-lower-case type (Figure 6.4) because it is easier to read.

Rule 9: Keep Text Lines Short

Keep line lengths between eight and ten words.   Short sentences and paragraphs are more visually appealing and are more likely to be read.

ALL-UPPER-CASE TEXT IS REALLY DIFFICULT TO READ BECAUSE OF THE LACK OF CONTRAST. USERS MISS WORDS AND PUNCTUATION, AND READING SLOWS DOWN SIGNIFICANTLY. PEOPLE GENERALLY SCAN COMPUTER SCREENS RATHER THAN READ THEM CAREFULLY, SO CLARITY IS ESPECIALLY IMPORTANT.

All-upper-case text is really difficult to read because of the lack of contrast. Users miss words and punctuation, and reading slows down significantly. People generally scan computer screens rather than read them carefully, so clarity is especially important.

FIGURE 6.4 ■ Upper- and Lower-Case Text

Rule 10: Use Single Spacing

Double-space between paragraphs rather than indent.

Rule 11: Simplify the Structure

Make it is as easy as possible for a user to find information in the program.   People using hypermedia products prefer consistency in the structure of screens. It is difficult to know how to get around when the structure changes frequently. Remind students that a hypermedia product should not be a hide-and-seek game (the author hides the information and the user looks for it). The student's goal should be to structure information so it is easy for someone to access and understand.

Rule 12: Limit the Focus

Feature one idea per screen.   A good rule of thumb is to have only one main topic per screen, but this main topic may have several subtopics. The best guideline for grouping subtopics on a screen is "Miller's 7 ± 2" rule (Gagne, Yekovich, & Yekovich, 1993). This means that the reader of the screen can most easily handle between five and nine ideas at one time. Fewer than five ideas do not give the user enough information upon which to generalize, and more than nine ideas are confusing. This is especially true of concepts. Notice in Figure 6.1 that there were six different topics from which to choose. Jeff could have added three more without making the screen too confusing.

Rule 13: Provide Emphasis

Use bold, italics, or underlining to emphasize ideas.

Rule 14: Know Your Audience

Decide ahead of time on the purpose and audience for the product.   If the student will present the product to the whole class, certain elements, particularly the type size, will be much different than if the product is meant for the use of one person at a time. In *Illustrating Computer Documentation* (1991), William Horton cites a study by Kantowitz and Sorken on recommended sizes of type for different distances from the monitor (Figure 6.5). Although font size may seem like a minor consideration, it is another way of getting students to reflect upon the purpose for their work and to think about the audience for whom they are writing. Also, because computer screens have lower resolution than the printed page, **sans serif** fonts are recommended, especially for small type, as in **body text.** (In traditional printed media, serif fonts were considered to be more legible.) Arial and Helvetica are two common sans serif fonts.

Rule 15: Do Not Flash

Do not use flashing text to get the attention of the users.   It irritates rather than interests them. Flashing text makes it hard for the user to focus on anything else. Use color and location to call attention to information.

sans serif
Lettering styles with lines and curves of uniform thickness (usually), and no decorative "feet," "tails," or other flourishes—all of which were descended from hand lettering.

body text
Text that comprises the main part ("body") of written communication. Contrast this with *titles,* which are "display" text.

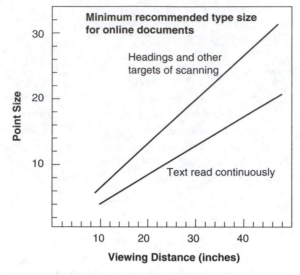

FIGURE 6.5　■　Using the Right Font Size

Rule 16: Use Lists

Lists are especially helpful on computer screens.　They help people find information quickly. There are several ways to delineate lists: numbers, bullets, and check boxes are the most common.

Rule 17: Navigate Consistently

Keep navigation buttons in the same position from one screen to the next.　Jeff did this, as you saw already (Figure 6.1).

Rule 18: Do Not Stack Text

Stacked (vertical) text is hard to read.　See Figure 6.6. The label for the figure on the left is hard to notice and read.

Rule 19: Include Multiple Graphic Types

Remember that pictures are only one kind of graphic element.　Other kinds of graphics include charts, maps, tables, lists, diagrams, photographs, and clip-art.

Rule 20: Organize the Screen

Group objects for meaning and better visual clarity.　Use borders, lines, white space, or color backgrounds to group objects with similar functions and make them stand out.

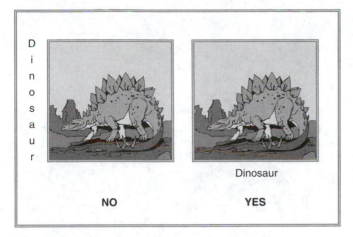

FIGURE 6.6 ■ Stacked and Unstacked Text

The images used herein were obtained from IMSI's MasterClips® and MasterPhotos™ Premium Image Collection, 1985 Francisco Blvd. East, San Rafael, CA 94901-5506, USA

Rule 21: Size Matters

Realize that the relative size of an object on a screen determines its importance to the reader.   Examples of this principle are illustrated in Figures 6.7 and 6.8. A menu for the life cycle of a monarch butterfly that is arranged like the one in Figure 6.7 emphasizes the adult stage in the cycle. The user of this software will most likely see, remember, and click on the adult. However, if the viewers of this presentation must know about each stage of the monarch's life cycle, they are at a disadvantage—and a very quiet, sneaky disadvantage, at that. In fact, this is a very good point to make to your students, who must not only make presentations but also view the presentations of others. Someone may be trying to manipulate their perception of reality by the way graphics are displayed on a screen. Figure 6.7 implies that the adult monarch is most important without using a single element of text to do it, whereas Figure 6.8 implies that all stages in the life cycle of a monarch are important, again using no text.

Rule 22: Placement Matters

The location of items on the screen determines their importance.   Items at the top of the screen appear to the viewer to be more important than items at the bottom of the screen. If, for example, you were displaying a picture of your class on the computer screen with individual portraits of the class officers, the pictures of the class officers would be placed above the portrait of the class. If you were graphically representing the wars in which the United States has participated, the most important (whatever your criteria for importance is) should be at the top of the screen and the least important at the bottom. If a student were doing a presentation on major and minor romantic poets of the early 1800s, pictures of the major poets would belong at the top

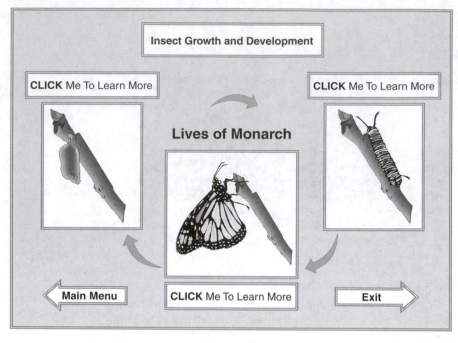

FIGURE 6.7 ■ Size Matters—Undue Emphasis on the Adult

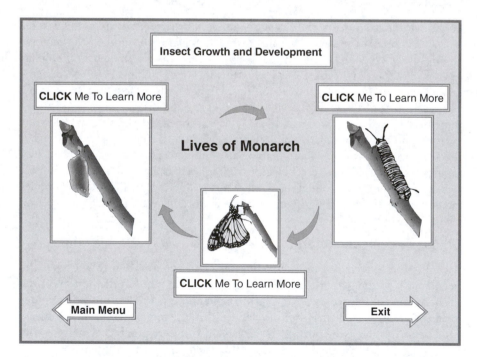

FIGURE 6.8 ■ Size Matters—Correct Proportions

The images used herein were obtained from IMSI's MasterClips® and MasterPhotos™ Premium Image Collection, 1985 Francisco Blvd. East, San Rafael, CA 94901-5506, USA

of the screen with minor poets below them. This is a simple principle, but again, a principle that the informational literate student should understand. Newspaper design is a good example of hierarchy in design. The more important the story, the bigger and higher the headline is placed on the page.

■ SUMMARY

Teaching fundamental graphic design principles to students is neither time consuming nor superfluous. Graphic design is an emerging literacy that many students will use often in their academic and professional lives. In addition, thinking about design often involves thinking about the content that has generated the design problem, which provides students with another way to interact with what they are learning.

Design problems for computers involve both page layout and interface design. While solving page layout problems, students grapple with who their audience will be, the relative importance and relationships among chunks of information, and how their audience can easily read and understand the information being displayed. Interface considerations require students to think about how information is linked. In the process of thinking about links among chunks of information, students must come to understand the structure of the knowledge itself. If they do not, the presentation that they build will appear disorganized and hard to move through. Graphic design, then, is not just one more topic for teachers to present, but rather one more tool to help them build a deep understanding of the information their students learn.

■ REFERENCES ■

Gagne, E. D., Yekovich, C. W., & Yekovich, F. R. (1993). *The cognitive psychology of school learning.* Boston: Little Brown.

Marcus, A. (1991). *Graphic design for electronic documents and user interfaces.* New York, New York: ACM Press.

Horton, W. (1991). *Illustrating computer documentation.* New York: John Wiley & Sons.

Outlines, Idea Maps, and Storyboards

OBJECTIVES

- Apply your knowledge of outlining to the design of a presentation.
- Convert an outline into an idea map.
- Design and develop idea maps for concepts and processes.
- Convert an idea map to a storyboard.
- Provide several examples of how students benefit from making idea maps.
- Know how to convert a storyboard to a finished presentation.

After looking in on Jeff's class, we learned that a hypermedia-supported lesson plan must be thought through carefully before it is executed. Almost any hypermedia assignment can be broken down into the components listed below:

Steps in a presentation assignment, each results in a product

Step 1:	Outline
Step 2:	Idea map(s)
Step 3:	Storyboard
Step 4:	Flowchart
Step 5:	Development of software product
Step 6:	Presentation of the final product (explaining it to a group, burning it to a CD, putting it on the Internet)

Ideally, the student must complete each step in the planning process to make a product. Each product may be graded, although they all do not have to be. The organization and sophistication of the final product is a reflection of the planning that goes into it. Consequently, if a student does not do an adequate outline and idea map, the resulting storyboard and software product probably will be poor, as well. Let's look a little deeper into how each of these steps fits together.

■ OUTLINES

If we were to look at Jeff's outline on plant cells, we would see something like the outline in Figure 7.1. Jeff has done nothing more than a traditional outline. But doing it has caused him to start thinking about the topic. It is an easy, comfortable skill that he already knows, and his teacher is taking advantage of that by using it as the springboard for the assignment.

Notice that the three-level outline is not complicated. One way to relate an outline to a finished hypermedia presentation is to think of moving between levels of the outline by way of mouse clicks. For example, a user of the finished presentation who wants to learn about chromatin will need three clicks: one click to choose one of the main topics, *Structure of Cells;* a second click to go to the submenu *Nucleus;* and a third click to go to *Chromatin.*

The idea mapping and storyboarding phases will flesh out these topics so that the students study them from many different perspectives. Planning is not entirely a step-by-step process. A student may start a storyboard after finishing an idea map and realize that the idea map is wrong and needs to be re-done. Or a student may do an idea map and find out that the outline is wrong. A student may be working on a computer product and find out that the storyboard could have been done better a different way. When this happens, students go back to the part of the process where they went wrong and correct their mistakes.

> Planning a presentation is iterative

> Levels of information in electronic documents

    I. Function of Cells
        A. Plant Cells
        B. Animal Cells
    II. Structure of Cells
        A. Vacuole
        B. Nucleus
            1. Nucleolus
            2. Chromatin
        C. Mitochondria
    III. Cell Reproduction
        A. Meiosis
            1. Interphase
            2. Prophase
            3. Metaphase
            4. Anaphase
            5. Telophase
        B. Mitosis
        1. Interphase
        2. Prophase
        3. Metaphase
        4. Anaphase
        5. Telophase

FIGURE 7.1 ■ Jeff's Outline

Outlines need three layers—at most

Generally speaking, for most information displays, a person should be able to get anywhere in the content in three clicks (Lopuck, 1998). Consequently, the outline may be simple. This rule helps students use the outline as a tool. The outline will seem less like busywork to students when they see its relationship to the software that they will build. Younger students may build two-level outlines, and advanced students studying complex topics may add another level or two to the outline. Idea mapping and storyboarding will tease out the details, revealing additional relationships that simple outlines miss.

In the old days, the organizational part of writing a paper or report required an outline. In one sense, computer technology has not changed the need for outlining, but it has certainly changed the purpose of an outline and the amount of outlining that must be done. My favorite metaphor for organizing hypermedia products is "outlining in 3-D." Writing a traditional outline as a guide produces only a traditional report displayed on a screen instead of a piece of paper. Though writing an outline is part of the process, an outline alone does not take advantage of the power of the computer, the software, or most importantly, a student's mind. There are other organizational techniques such as idea mapping that teachers can use to provide context and interaction with content for students.

■ IDEA MAPS

Presentation software makes copying more difficult

When I ask students to interact with content, I try to eliminate any opportunity for them to copy information and hand it in "untransformed." Many times the student paraphrases an encyclopedia article or other nonfiction, or even worse, chooses a few words to change and leaves the rest intact. Current practices encourage this kind of laziness. The wide availability of information on the web and the ease of cutting and pasting facilitates the act of copying information without thought. It is difficult to copy others' writing and put it into a hypermedia report, however. The delivery mechanisms are so different that information transferred directly from long text passages looks silly and is virtually useless when a student pastes it directly into a presentation.

Presentation software encourages students to think about relationships

Using presentation software to organize and explain information requires thinking through ideas and breaking them into smaller chunks of information that can be displayed on a monitor and linked together logically. It is the difference between approaching every topic with the mindset of "What comes first, second, and last?" compared to "How are these ideas related to each other?" This is the point at which idea mapping becomes a valuable tool. Pohl's (1998) observations indicate, "The efficacy of concept mapping as a methodology of learning is to a certain extent supported by empirical evidence."

Although idea mapping may be done by hand, computer tools make the process faster and easier for students. Two important tools are Inspiration and Visio. A version of Inspiration for younger students is Kidspiration.

We will leave Jeff to his own devices for a while and look in on a fifth-grade class studying world history and culture. As a part of this study, the students are working on a yearlong project to develop a multimedia presentation on the exploration of this planet and beyond. Their teacher, Mr. Hess, hopes that this presentation will provide some context for the dates and names that his students must inevitably memorize during the course of the year.

Explorations

Mr. Hess shows the class a presentation on the Internet made by a student from last year's class, the *History of Inventions* (the theme that year). He told his class that they would put their presentations on the Internet as well, so that anyone who has a computer and a connection to the Internet would be able to see their work. Jamie, a student, is excited that she will get to use a computer to draw pictures other people will see, though she is not particularly interested in exploration, this year's theme.

Motivating and preparing the class

The teacher divides the class into groups and asks them to begin working on the presentation by outlining what they think a presentation on exploration might look like. After the students have spent about twenty minutes in their groups, he asks each group to write its outline on the blackboard for the other students to see. Their assignment for tomorrow is to think about what they have seen and talked about and be ready to make suggestions on the construction of a perfect outline for the topic.

Outlining

Tomorrow comes, and the teacher hands out copies of all of the groups' outlines from yesterday. The class again discusses how a topic such as exploration should be organized. Some think it should be organized by the name of the explorer, others by the name of the country explored. To solve the dilemma, Mr. Hess tells the students to use a tree map to describe how the presentation should be organized. He gives the students fifteen minutes to draw their maps.

Idea mapping

Jamie is confused. She thinks the easiest way would be just to list the explorer and what he or she explored, but she cannot make her tree map work. There is no way to put branches on it. As she tries to visualize the piece of software that she will create, all she can see is one page after another listing explorers and their biographies. That isn't how the *Inventions* project created by last year's students looks. It is cool: you can see categories of inventions depending on your interest. So, Jamie thought, "How would this map look if I did it by areas of the world? Let's see. I know America was discovered and explored. So were the North and South poles."

Jamie makes a tree map representing her current knowledge of exploration. "America" is one branch of the tree, "Poles" the other branch of the tree, and "North" and "South" were branches from Poles. Her fifteen minutes were up and she found that others in the class had come to similar conclusions. Among all of them, they came up with six areas of the world where exploration had occurred: the Americas, Asia, the Pacific, the Poles, Africa, and Space. Mr. Hess again had the students work in groups to flesh out this general tree map into a more specific map. He asked them to use their textbooks and other reference materials to define more clearly the areas where exploration had occurred. Their ideas were starting to take shape.

Using an idea map

The next day Mr. Hess asked the students to put their tree maps on their desks in front of them and "put on their thinking caps." Mr. Hess said, "We have decided where exploration happened, but we want to put more in our presentation than just a place. Is there something more to exploration than just the place? We all know about Columbus exploring the Americas. And we just read the story in our reading books about Marco Polo in China. Using Columbus and Marco Polo as examples, let's think of some other things that are important for exploration. For the next five minutes talk with the person next to you about possible topics related to exploration. Use a web map to help you plan."

Finding the properties of exploration

Martin, Jamie's partner, immediately said, "Well, you always hear that the Queen of Spain was the person who gave Columbus the money to go on his trip. Maybe the country the explorer came from or worked for is important." So Jamie began a web. In the first circle she wrote, Exploration. In another circle she wrote Home Country, and connected it with a line to the first circle. The planning went on for several minutes until Mr. Hess called the class to order again. He began methodically combining the children's suggestions on the blackboard by making a web of five different ideas, all connected to the central circle, Exploration. The lesson was over for the day.

The next day, as the project resumed, one of the more vocal students commented, "I hope you aren't going to make us PLAN any more. When do we get to use the computers?" Mr. Hess laughed and said, "This is a good news/bad news situation. Making a presentation takes a lot of computer time, so each of us has to plan very carefully. You must make every minute that you spend at the computer count. But the good news is that you have done the hardest part of the planning and now you get to dream about what your presentation is going to look like. Today I am going to show you how you can use your tree map and your web map to design the first four screens of your presentation. After that you can begin your storyboard. Once you have the first page of your storyboard, you can begin working on your presentations at the computer. You will rotate. While some people work at the computer, others will begin their next set of storyboards. Some of you can go to the library to use the computers to get materials, such as pictures and videos from the Internet for your presentation. Tomorrow I am going to teach you a little bit about how to do good Internet searches and give you the addresses of some sites to get you started."

Jamie was elated. She was finally going to get to draw and collect pictures and organize them all into something that other people would see.

The fundamental rule for using computers to display information is to use the organization of the content to guide the organization of the hypermedia presentation (Pohl, 1998). If you look in Appendix D, you can see some examples of templates for idea maps. Notice that they all have names. This is because knowledge has some basic "shapes." All knowledge can be classified in one of three categories: conceptual, procedural, and conditional knowledge. Concepts have properties and examples, procedures have steps, while conditional knowledge is the meta-knowledge of when and why to apply conceptual and procedural knowledge (Woolfolk, 2000). Once your students understand the significance of these categories and begin to see information as belonging to one of them, they will have a better idea of how that information is organized and, consequently, will organize it correctly for their presentations. A good analogy for this understanding of concepts and procedures is knowing how to solve word problems in arithmetic or algebra. Once you learn a pattern, you can solve a variety of problems—whether it is two boats meeting mid stream, two trains meeting between points A and B, or two cars meeting on a drive between Leadville and Coppertown. Understanding concepts and events gives students a formula to apply to the organizing process for their presentations.

Concepts: Examples and Properties

Concepts are facts or ideas. They usually belong to a family of related facts or ideas. They appear in the curriculum as themes that children study: exploration, English literary periods, inventions, the westward migration, biomes, and the short story. Concepts have two characteristics that are helpful for learners. They have examples and they have properties (Gagne, Yekovich, & Yekovich, 1993).

Examples   First, let us discuss examples. Tundra is an example of a biome; the Renaissance is an example of a period in English history; the jet engine is an example of an in-

---

Sidebar labels:

Making a storyboard

Using the Internet for research

Information is conceptual, procedural, or conditional

vention; and Cortez in Mexico is an example of exploration. Many times examples can be classified into categories and subcategories. Consider Exploration, which could fall into categories including (from a European point of view) the exploration of Asia, the Americas, Africa, the Pacific, the North and South Poles, and Space. These categories could be further broken down into more categories with examples for each. To represent Exploration visually, students might use a tree map or a brace map because these maps graphically demonstrate the hierarchy of categories that they are studying. A student should be able to use either a brace or a tree map to divide a concept into categories. Figure 7.2 shows the categories of Exploration with a brace map, and Figure 7.3 shows the categories of Exploration with a tree map. Neither is superior to the other.

> Examples have categories and hierarchies

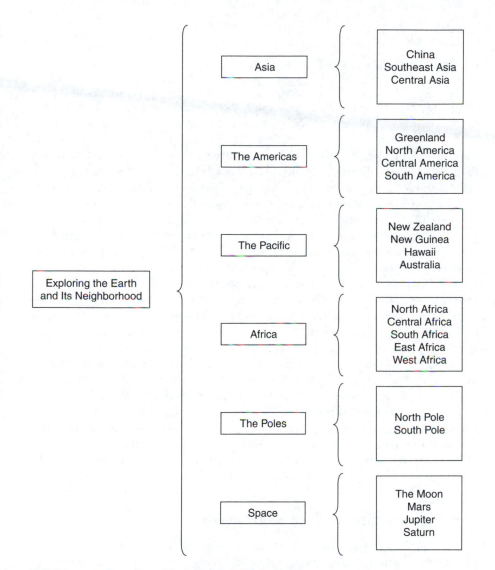

FIGURE 7.2 ■ Brace Map of the Categories of Exploration

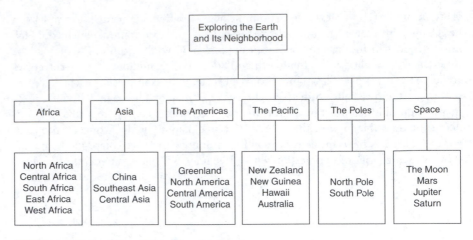

FIGURE 7.3 ■ Tree Map of Properties of Exploration

One represents ideas horizontally and the other vertically. (Their contents do not match exactly because they were generated by different student groups.)

Properties   However, really understanding a concept means more than just being able to categorize it and provide examples. Concepts also have properties. Think of properties as the defining characteristics of a concept. The properties of concepts are often those items related to a concept that you want the children to learn. Table 7.1 shows examples of some concepts accompanied by a few of their properties. One example from this table, Exploration, is further represented as an idea map (called a "web map" in the story about Mr. Hess's class) in Figure 7.4. Notice that a properties map is not hierarchical. It is descriptive, and all properties have the same weight.

> Properties are
> not hierarchical

When students structure a concept with tree and properties maps, they are taking their first step toward visualizing the navigational system and screen design of the presentation they will write. The center or hub of their properties map, or the main concept heading of their tree or brace map, will be the title screen. The brace or tree map will define one set of menus and the properties map will define another set of menus or hot words. The properties map provides the organization for information about the topics on the final level of the brace map. You may observe in Figures 7.5 through 7.8 mock-ups of the screens derived from the idea maps in Figures 7.2 through 7.4.

> Relating idea maps to the
> design of the presentation

As you can see, it is three clicks of the mouse (after the title screen) to the most detailed information in the presentation. All of the screens are consistent, and at worst, it would be hard for a user to get lost. At best, a user of such a software title would be learning from the structure of the software as well as from the information on the screens. How much more would the *designer* of the software (your student) learn?

Questions and Answers about Idea Mapping

We have spent many pages on a subject that does not appear to have much to do with presentation software. Although the connection should be clearer now, you may still have questions about using idea mapping to support your use of presentation soft-

TABLE 7.1 ■ Sample Concepts and Their Properties

Concept	Properties
Explorations	Name of explorer Country explored Native country of explorer Time period when exploration took place Was the exploration a success or failure
English Literary Periods	Major Discoveries Artistic styles Musical styles Literary styles Historical events
Inventions	Name of the invention Time of the invention Importance of the invention Country where the invention happened People involved with the invention Names Number Knowledge needed to make the invention Materials necessary for the invention
The Westward Migration	Reasons people moved west When they moved west How they moved west Changes they made to the west
Ecosystems	Name Kinds of animals Kinds of plants Climate Soil Topography
Short Story	Theme Plot Character Setting Mood

ware. Following is a question and answer session that should help clarify a few ideas that still might be a little fuzzy to you.

How extensive should an idea map be? Remember the three-click rule? Don't forget that an outline only needs to be three levels deep. The same is true for an idea map. The maps do not need to be extensive. Detailed explanations can be written later and assembled as resources for the presentation. The purpose of the idea map is to tease out the organization of the content for students, and to create a template with cubbyholes where students can tuck away the facts.

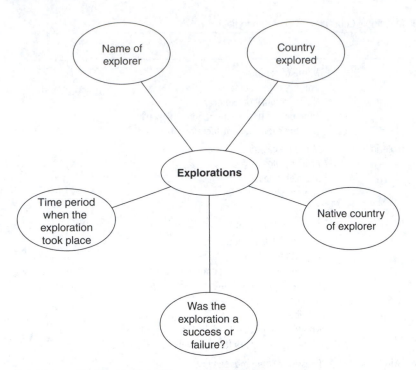

FIGURE 7.4 ■ Concept Map of Properties of Exploration

How should I grade idea maps?   The grade on the idea map should not be a large proportion for the grade on the multimedia project. If you use a rubric to grade presentations, you might consider having one row in the rubric for the outline and one row for the idea map. The work done with the idea map will influence the student's success on the project as a whole. Idea mapping can be treated like practice problems. The teacher challenges the students to create an accurate idea map and then immediately provides an example for them to see. Students can do this alone or in groups. Groups should review idea maps created by single students, or the class should review maps created by groups. Ultimately, the teacher, when he or she is sure that the students have a clear pic-

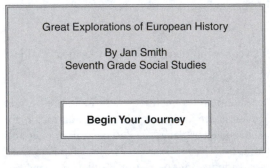

FIGURE 7.5 ■ Title Screen of Exploration Presentation

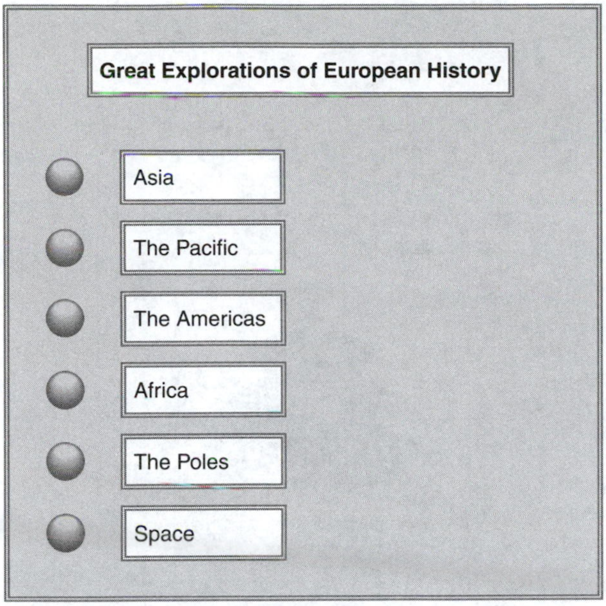

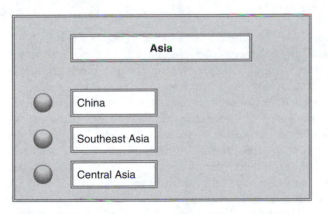

FIGURE 7.6 ■ First Menu Level of Exploration Presentation

ture of how the elements of their multimedia project are connected, may decide not to require each student to hand in a correct idea map as a part of the assignment.

How do I teach idea maps?   Most students do not learn how to do idea mapping without some trial and error. Since idea mapping is not consistently taught in our educational system, teachers should plan to spend some time training students in this process. In fact, it is better to teach students the skills for completing a multimedia assignment (outline, idea map, storyboard, presentation software) separately rather than overwhelming them with four new activities at the same time.

FIGURE 7.7 ■ Second Menu Level of Exploration Presentation

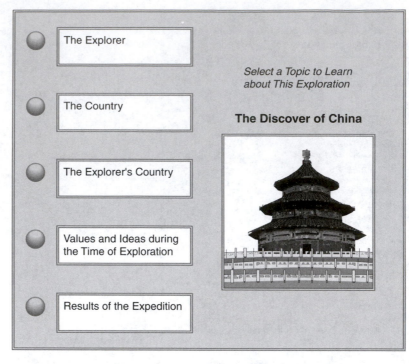

FIGURE 7.8 ■ Final Menu Level of Exploration Presentation

The images used herein were obtained from IMSI's MasterClips® and MasterPhotos™ Premium Image Collection, 1985 Francisco Blvd. East, San Rafael, CA 94901-5506, USA

You can begin teaching idea mapping by supplying your students with completed idea maps and discussing them. Next, ask students to fill in blank maps that you have created. Do it as an assignment in class and immediately show students the correct entries. Another way of teaching the skill is to give them an outline and ask them to turn it into an idea map. Finally, name the content that you want your students to map and then ask them to do it.

What did Jeff's idea map look like? Jeff's final map is shown in Figure 7.9. It is about "average" in regard to the detail and accuracy asked for by his teacher. (Some of the information in the map in this figure is truncated because of space, but you can get the idea.) Some students drew more detailed maps; some students drew maps where the information was incorrectly placed. Jeff's teacher encourages the students to turn in legible, readable idea maps. Usually students draw several maps during the course of the assignment. Jeff's first map was his best initial guess at what a map should look like. He made his second map with the rest of the class during an interactive discussion with the teacher. Jeff drew the map that he finally handed in using his first two attempts as a guide. He used a ruler and compass to make straight lines, square boxes, and round circles, and he printed information carefully and legibly. These maps can be done more quickly and neatly online if your students have access to Inspiration, Visio, or Kidspiration.

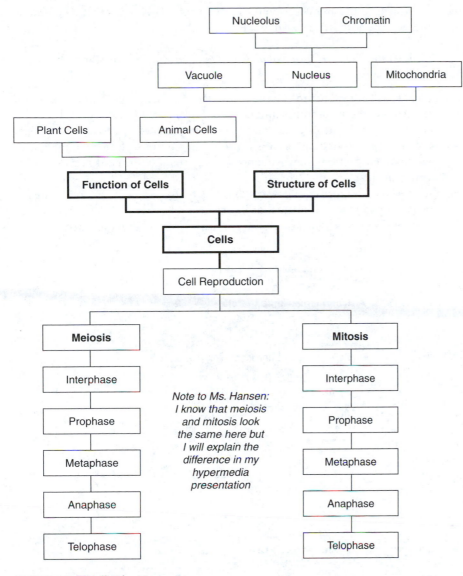

FIGURE 7.9 ■ Jeff's Idea Map

Looking at Jeff's map in Figure 7.9, you can see some of the patterns that we have just studied. The topics connected with the thick, black lines came from a concept map of properties. Cell Function and Cell Structure are tree maps arranged upward (truncated here because of space). Reproduction, the third characteristic or property of cells, is really two processes that look alike but unfold differently. They are represented as chain maps. Students often must tape several pages together to complete their idea maps.

What did Jeff's menu screens look like? This is the best question of all. To answer it you will have to look at another illustration. Figure 7.10 has two examples of Jeff's menus.

In the first menu, if the user clicks on the button next to Anatomy of a Cell the computer presents the next menu shown there.

How might I justify the use of idea mapping to my students? Here are some advantages of using idea maps:

■ Students will not waste time on the computer with many false starts. False starts are costly. Without careful planning, students may spend a great deal of time working before they realize their plan is awkward, uninformative, or unworkable.

■ Students will be searching for information with a purpose. Instead of memorizing lists and definitions, they will uncover patterns and form links that will help them remember.

■ Outlines and idea maps are "low overhead" activities. They require only a pencil and paper and may be as formal or informal as a teacher wishes to make them. They allow students to make best use of precious time at the computer.

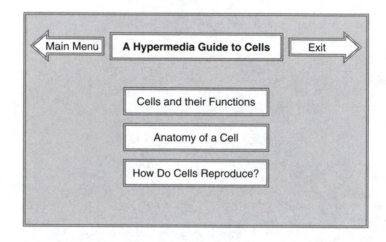

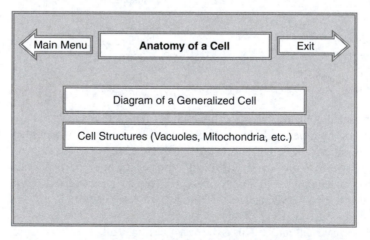

FIGURE 7.10 ■ Screens Jeff Built Based on His Outline and Idea Maps

Is there idea-mapping software and how useful is it? Yes, there are two affordable titles available for idea-mapping software. Inspiration Software, Inc., has two titles—one for very young students called Kidspiration and one for older students called Inspiration. Both are intuitive and easy to learn, and both run on Mac and PC platforms. One of the nicest features of the product is the ability to convert outlines to concept maps and concept maps to outlines. This makes the planning process much faster by providing students instant visual feedback. Microsoft also has a very usable product called Visio.

■ STORYBOARDS

The storyboard is started after the idea mapping process is well along. The students must have identified all of the concepts and processes in the content they are preparing. After the students know how a topic is structured, they can start building menu screens and designating screen areas for graphics, text, video, audio, and navigation. They can decide on color and font size and record all of their information on cards or paper, one card or sheet per screen. They can start gathering resources, the text, audio, video, graphic, and animation files they will use to build their presentations. And finally, they must decide how all of these screens will fit together. Idea mapping provides only the main branches of the software. As students begin to gather and format resources for their project, they will add more screens.

The storyboarding process

Young students, or students who are just beginning to learn how to write hypermedia presentations, will not be able to respond to every design principle that you reviewed in the previous chapter. For a kindergarten child who is new to the process, one to three connected screens with a background color, a few graphics, and few words or letters should be acceptable. On the other hand, an advanced student who knows the mechanics of creating hypermedia presentations very well could be responsible for every specification in the storyboard template and every design principle that you learned in Chapter 6.

Because you are the first generation of teachers to use this medium, you will work harder preparing both materials and your students for the first few hypermedia-supported projects that they do. Some of your students may have created idea maps before, but at this point there will be very few who know how to storyboard. You will have to lead most of them, step-by-step, through the creation of their storyboards. You may also have to teach many of your students how to use presentation software.

Teach your students how to storyboard

In fact, you should consider discussing storyboard format with other teachers who teach in the grades above and below you. If your school were to develop a scope and sequence for storyboarding, ultimately you would only spend a small amount of time teaching storyboarding instead of the content that you must teach. Storyboarding, once students know how to do it, will enhance the amount of information that they retain because storyboards are another type of organizational device, like idea maps and outlines.

Looking at an idea map is like looking at a molecule represented as a flat object, such as the one in box A of Figure 7.11. An idea map gives us a general understanding of how ideas are connected. A storyboard is much like the 3D molecule in box B of that figure. It defines the actual method of displaying the information, the links between hot words and their explanations, the links between menus and pages, and choices of fonts and colors that all add meaning to the ideas the student is organizing.

A

B

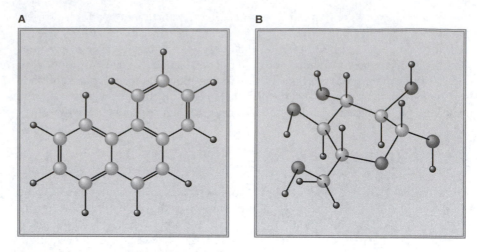

FIGURE 7.11 ■ Flat and 3D Representations

The images used herein were obtained from IMSI's MasterClips® and MasterPhotos™ Premium Image Collection, 1985 Francisco Blvd. East, San Rafael, CA 94901-5506, USA

FIELD TRIP 7.2

Return to the Biology Class Example

Now we'll look in on Jeff again.

Jeff, almost finished with his idea map (he has the rough draft done), began his storyboard. He was waiting to do his final draft of the idea map until he had mostly finished the storyboard. Mrs. Hansen previously told the class that storyboards sometimes bring out ideas that are overlooked in the idea-mapping process.

He had a rough idea of the kinds of pictures she had found for the class and placed in a library on the server. Mrs. Hansen decided that there was not enough time for every student to search for every picture. She downloaded the graphics from the Internet, gave each file a descriptive name, and printed the directory listing for the class. Now students will only need to look for enough additional graphics, audio, or video to customize their work.

Mrs. Hansen said that she wanted the class to make the storyboards with a pencil, ruler, and compass, and to use the template (Figure 7.12) as a guide for the information to put into the storyboards. She told the class that the first page of the storyboard had to be a title page. Items on that page would include the following:

- Title of the hypermedia report
- Name of the author
- Date
- Two navigation buttons (next, exit)
- A relevant graphic

To help her students, she filled in some of the blanks in the first column of the table. Since this was their first storyboard, she gave the class many clues. In later assignments, she would coach them by talking to them about what should go in the blanks. Mrs Hansen had a stack of blank template forms for the students to use—one template form for each screen of their presentations. So Jeff filled in the blanks and wrote a description of what could happen on each screen.

Blank screen

Rough draft of screen design goes here. Student draws it with a pencil.

Object	Color/Font	Branch/Link
Page or Screen Number		
Background		
Foreground		
Controls		
Button: Next		
Button: Back		
Button: Home		
Button: _____		
Button: _____		
Button: _____		
Selection Area		
Background		
Foreground		
Item 1: Caption		
Item 2: Caption		
Item 3: Caption		
Item 4: Caption		
Item 5: Caption		
Item 6: Caption		
Item 7: Caption		
Item 8: Caption		
Item 9: Caption		
Text Display Area		
Background		
Foreground		
Video Display Area		
Background		
Foreground		

FIGURE 7.12 ■ A Storyboard Template

While working on his main menu screen, Jeff raised his hand, suddenly unsure of himself. It had occurred to him that if he started out wrong and did very much he would waste a lot of time. Putting together a computer screen is a lot of work. And then there are the links. Undoing and re-doing links between pages is confusing and really easy to do wrong. Worse yet, because each student's computer time was so limited, he didn't have time to make a mistake.

"How should this work?" he asked himself. "I have one concept (cells) and two processes (mitosis and meiosis). So should my main menu (Figure 7.13) look like box A? Or like box B, or C, or D?"

His teacher arrived and looked at his four attempts. She complimented Jeff for trying several ideas and said, "Look back at your idea map (Figure 7.9). Usually the name of the idea map is the title of the menu page. Notice the names of the boxes at the ends of the spokes (structure, function, and reproduction). Those names will be the labels for buttons on your main menu page. If you click on structure, then where will you go, Jeff?" she asked.

With his eyes, Jeff followed the line from "structure" to the next level of detail on the idea map. He guessed that he would set up a page to show the names of the cell parts as well as the text, pictures, video, or sound resources that he has made or collected from the Internet.

Jeff answered Mrs. Hansen and could now see which experimental screen in Figure 7.13 is the best menu screen: screen B. As he used his idea map to guide him, he realized that following a line and going from one box to the next represents one click of the mouse. Each box usually represents a screen. Jeff easily visualized the next set of screens. Figure 7.14 is one of Jeff's finished storyboard pages.

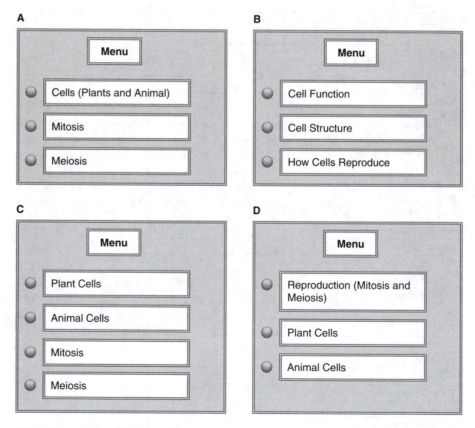

FIGURE 7.13 ■ Possible Menu Pages

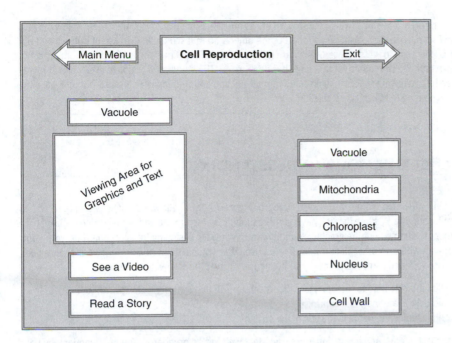

Object	Color/Font	Link
Page		
Background	Blue	None
Text	Yellow; Times 12/Button	None
Controls		
Button: See a Video	Grey/Times 12/Button	None
Button: Read a Story	Grey/Times 12/Button	Link to audio file selected in "Click on a…"
Button: Main Menu	Grey/Times 12/Button	Link to Main Menu
Button: Exit	Grey/Times 12/Button	End Presentation
Selection Area	Beige/inset	None
Click a Topic	Gray/Times 12/Inset box/	Each hot word links to an identical page with the information about that hot word on it.
Vacuole/hot word	Black/Times/12	To Storyboard 12
Mitochondria/hot word	Black/Times/12	To Storyboard 13
Chloroplast/hot word	Black/Times/12	To Storyboard 14
Nucleus/hot word	Black/Times/12	To Storyboard 15
Cell Wall/hot word	Black/Times/12	To Storyboard 16
Text Display Area	Beige background/black text/box	None
Video Display Area	Light Blue background/box	None

FIGURE 7.14 ■ One of Jeff's Storyboards

The area at the top is where the student draws and labels the features of the screen. Below the proposed screen are the specifications for all of the objects on that screen. In the case of buttons and hot words, the page to which those objects are linked is listed. Sometimes the actual page number is not known until the storyboard for that page has been made. The storyboard template even gives students a little help, allowing spaces for links to no more than nine different topics (e.g., mitochondria, vacuole, etc.) according to Miller's 7 ± 2 rule.

✔ CHECKING YOUR UNDERSTANDING

7.1

Use Jeff's idea map (Figure 7.9) and storyboard (Figure 7.14) to help you draw the storyboard screen for mitochondria. Assume that Jeff has a graphic showing mitochondria and has recorded a short audio segment to supplement the graphic. You might even consider designing this storyboard on your computer with whatever presentation software you use. After you have finished drawing your picture, look at Figure 7.15 and compare your work to the figure. Answer the following questions.

1. Did I indicate bold for the hot word that is selected so that the user will know where he/she is?
2. Did I eliminate the video controls?
3. Did I change the name in the title of the screen?

Are the text, media, and navigation areas consistent with Jeff's storyboard? (You may wonder why your text, media, and navigation areas must be consistent with Jeff's, because you have some good ideas of your own. The answer is because within a presentation they must be the same. Consistency is the rule.)

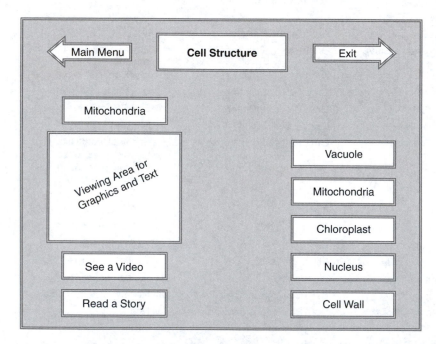

FIGURE 7.15 ■ The First Page of Your Storyboard

■ SUMMARY

It is clear that presentation software is more than a motivational device. Used well, presentation software adds significantly to the number and quality of interactions students have with the content that they are studying. We know that repetition is one way to learn facts. When students use the complete process for preparing a presentation, they work with the facts that they are learning at least four times—in the outline, concept map, storyboard, and the presentation itself. Within each step (for example, the concept map) they may work with a fact or idea several more times—arranging it and rearranging it within the structure of the topic they are studying.

Another way students learn is by developing an understanding of the organization of a topic when they work to put the facts into their hypertext context. Students must understand the organization of a topic to do a presentation "in 3-D." To design a menu screen and use links that take viewers three mouse clicks into a topic requires an active organization effort on the part of the student.

Finally, students see content represented in many different formats: audio, video, text, graphics, and animation. These different representations of information provide avenues for students with different styles of learning. They also increase the richness of the context of the information, thus increasing the likelihood that the students will retain the knowledge with which they are working.

■ REFERENCES ■

Gagne, E. D., Yekovich, C. W., & Yekovich, F. R. (1993). *The cognitive psychology of school learning.* Boston: Little Brown.

Hyerle, D. (1996). *Visual tools for constructing knowledge.* Alexandria, VA: ASCD.

Jonassen, D. (2000). Computers as mindtools for schools. Upper Saddle River: Merrill.

Pohl, M. (1998). Hypermedia as a cognitive tool. ED-MEDIA/ED-TELECOM 98 World Conference on Educational Multimedia and Hypermedia & World Conference on Educational Telecommunications. Proceedings (Tenth Freiburg, Germany).

Woolfolk, A. (2000) *Educational psychology.* Boston: Allyn and Bacon.

■ ANNOTATED RESOURCES ■

Harrington, M., Holik, M., & Hurt, P. Improving writing through the use of varied strategies. (1998).

This article describes an action research project that investigates the use of graphic organizers (concept maps) and other strategies to improve student writing. The project is focused on upper elementary children. A summary may be found in ERIC (ED-420874). The project itself is 67 pages long and includes examples of graphic organizers.

Using graphic organizers (concept maps)

Integrating the computer into language arts in a fifth-grade classroom: A developing instructional model. ERIC (ED417381).

This paper was presented at the 1997 annual meeting of the National Reading Conference in Scottsdale, Arizona. It discusses a study focused on using Hyperstudio, a tool to help children learn process writing. The results of this study indicate that writing quality and quantity improved along with student motivation. This paper provides a good example of how to develop an assignment to help children learn process writing.

Dimitriadi, Y. (2001). Evaluating the use of multimedia authoring with dyslexic learners: A case study. *British Journal of Educational Technology*, Vol 32(3).

Practical wisdom indicates that children with learning disabilities and attention deficit disorders find learning with multimedia motivational. This is a case study involving two children with learning difficulties. These children, with the author of the study, developed a multimedia presentation and in the process learned authoring, composition, revision, proofreading, and presentation skills. The author believes that this experience was both positive and motivating for the children.

If you would like more examples and information about concept maps, see Appendix D.

CHAPTER 8

Evaluating Student Presentations

OBJECTIVES

- Describe the criteria relevant to your content area that you could use to evaluate student presentations.
- Adapt or build a scoring rubric based on criteria for evaluating student presentations.

■ RUBRICS

Evaluation of multimedia projects, though time consuming, can be fair and consistent. In order for presentations to be evaluated fairly, students should be given evaluation criteria before they start the project. Rubrics are a great strategy for grading presentations. Creating a clear, well-organized rubric for students and explaining it carefully at the beginning of the project will save both students and teacher some grief when evaluation time comes. Construction of your rubric depends on the age and sophistication of your students, their experience using presentation software, and the content for which you are holding them responsible. In the outline below are some suggestions for elements that you might include in a rubric.

> Rubrics are good for evaluating presentations

I. Writing
    A. Structure
        1. Grammar
        2. Sentence Mechanics
        3. Vocabulary and writing level
    B. Content
        1. Coverage of Topic
        2. Organization of Information

II. Navigation
    A. Branches and Links
        1. Branches and links work
        2. Branches and links are logical
    B. Necessary branches always present (e.g., Menu, Exit)
III. Screen Design
    A. Rules for color
    B. Rules for fonts
    C. Rules for displaying text
    D. Rules for consistency
    E. Rules for displaying information
IV. Development of Presentation
    A. Outline
    B. Idea Map
    C. Storyboard
    D. Completed presentation

The preceding outline listed suggestions for topics that you might include in a rubric. But what would a real rubric look like?

Creating Standards for Your Students

If you look on the Web or in educational journals for assessment ideas, you will see many sample rubrics (Barnett, 2000). You can gain much insight into how to design a rubric by reading those created by others. It is rare, however, that you can simply lift a rubric from some source and use it unmodified. In my own practice, I have never used the same rubric for the same content two years in a row because classes and areas of focus are different. Tables 8.1 through 8.4 are examples of rubrics that cover elementary through high school multimedia projects. Although these sample rubrics are based on specific assignments ("The Four Seasons" for the elementary rubrics and "Poetic Devices" for middle/high school) they are worded in such a way that they could be modified to suit any topic. The three elementary examples on the four seasons illustrate three approaches to designing a rubric:

Grading rubrics should be based on the assignment

- Students who are just learning how to use presentation software or are very young (Table 8.1).
- Students who have completed one or two assignments with presentation software and are acquainted with the process as well as the basic mechanics of using presentation software (Table 8.2).
- Students who understand the development process well, the mechanics of using the software, and for whom the creation of graphics, audio, and video is easy (Table 8.3).

Consider your students' skills as you construct a rubric

An average kindergartner may never get beyond the Acceptable level in Table 8.1, while a precocious fifth grader may be able to score often in the Excellent column in Table 8.4 which we haven't yet mentioned. Consequently, if you were constructing a

TABLE 8.1 ■ Rubric for Elementary Beginning Users of Presentation Software

Topic: The Four Seasons

	Excellent (3)	Acceptable (2)	Needs Improvement (1)
Development of presentation	The student has developed an idea map that represents both main ideas for the menu screen and detail for information screens.	The student has developed an idea map that reflects the menu screen.	The student's idea map is not developed or it is wrong.
Writing	The student is writing to the standard of the grade level. This will vary by grade level and teacher.	The student is generally writing at grade level but the writing has some spelling or grammar errors.	The student is not writing at grade level or the errors interfere with the reader's understanding or appreciation of the presentation.
Navigation	The student has a main menu from which the user chooses the season to display. The seasons on the main menu are in order.	The user navigates through the program linearly, i.e., first a title page, next the first season, then the second season, etc.	There is only one page in the presentation with all seasons on the page or the links between pages don't work.
Content	All content is covered and is illustrated with two or more of the following ways of representing information: text, graphics, video, audio, or animation.	All content is covered.	Not all content is covered.
Screen design	The student has followed the rules of screen design that the teacher has chosen for emphasis in this presentation. At this level the teacher might emphasize 3 or 4.	The student has followed half of the rules of screen design that the teacher has chosen for emphasis in this presentation.	The presentation exhibits serious screen design problems.

rubric for your kindergarten class you might use something like the "Acceptable" standards in Table 8.1 as your standard for "Excellent." On the other hand, if you are constructing a rubric for experienced, second-semester first graders, the "Acceptable" column in Table 8.2 could be the "Excellent" column in your rubric. It is so relative that the example rubrics are meant only to help you in a general way. Your curriculum and your class will determine the specifics.

Table 8.4 provides a rubric for an assignment based on the assumption that students are older, more cognitively developed, and more experienced users of presentation software. I did not develop rubrics for beginning and intermediate users at this age level. If you read Tables 8.1 through 8.3, you can see how you might make the rubric easier for beginners and intermediates. The same principles that worked in these tables will also work for Table 8.4. For inexperienced users, decrease the number of organizational tasks (omit an outline or idea map), decrease the difficulty of building the navigational structure (let them do a linear presentation the first time), and do not add any extra writing tasks, such as requiring specific sentence constructions or vocabulary. For the second presentation assignment, add a few more requirements, for the third assignment add a few more, and finally require something on the scale of the rubric in Table 8.4.

TABLE 8.2 ■ Rubric for Elementary Intermediate Users of Presentation Software

Topic: The Four Seasons

	Excellent (3)	Acceptable (2)	Needs Improvement (1)
Writing	All spelling is correct.	Spelling is mostly correct.	Spelling errors interfere with the user's ability to use or appreciate the presentation.
Content	Each season is described by three sentences. Each sentence is accompanied by one descriptive graphic.	Each season is described by two sentences. Each sentence is accompanied by one descriptive graphic.	One or more seasons aren't described by a sentence. There are no descriptive graphics or the graphics do not reflect the meaning of the sentences.
Navigation	A menu follows the title page. The seasons are listed on the main menu in order. From the menu a user can choose any of the seasons.	The presentation starts with a title screen. From there the presentation goes from one season to the next in order. Each season is described on one page of the presentation. The pages are linked and go from one season to the next.	One or more links don't work. Seasons aren't listed in order either in a menu or in a linear presentation.
Screen design	The student has followed the screen design guidelines that teacher has requested. At this level, 4 to 6 guidelines are appropriate.	The student has followed most of the screen design guidelines that teacher has requested.	The student has not followed the guidelines. The screens are hard to read and disorganized.
Development of the presentation	The student has developed an idea map and the main ideas on the idea map match the main navigational options. The student has written a storyboard that is consistent with the idea map and also consistent with the finished presentation. The student did both the idea map and storyboard before keying in the presentation.	The student has developed an idea map and there are major similarities between the idea map and the navigational structure of the presentation. The student has developed a storyboard that resembles the finished presentation. Both the idea map and storyboard were developed before the presentation was keyed in.	The idea map is missing or does not resemble the presentation or The storyboard is missing or does not resemble the presentation or The idea map and storyboard were developed after the presentation.

Some Notes on the Components of the Rubrics

As you develop the rubric, remember that you may add required components in the "Writing" section that are completely unrelated to doing presentations but rather support good writing skills. As teachers in the content areas are pressed to teach "Writing Across the Curriculum," these presentations act as a display opportunity for the writing skills students study. Be careful when you add these extra requirements. Make sure that your students are not struggling with the mechanics of using presentation soft-

Make sure students aren't trying to learn too much at once

TABLE 8.3 ■ Rubric for Elementary Advanced Users of Presentation Software

Topic: The Four Seasons

	Excellent (3)	Acceptable (2)	Needs Improvement (1)
Writing	All spelling and grammar are correct. Student uses construction (such as compound sentences) on which the teacher has asked him/her to focus.	Grammar and spelling are mostly correct. Student attempts to use constructions on which the teacher has asked him/her to focus and are mostly correct.	Spelling errors interfere with the user's ability to use or appreciate the presentation.
Content	Each season is described by a paragraph. Each paragraph is accompanied by another way of presenting information than text (graphic, video, audio, animation). Alternate forms of presenting information may not all be graphics.	Each season is described by a paragraph. Each paragraph is accompanied by a graphic.	One or more seasons aren't described by a sentence. There are no descriptive graphics or the graphics do not reflect the meaning of the sentences.
Navigation	A menu follows the title page. The seasons are listed on the main menu in order. Each season is described on two screens. From the menu a user can choose any of the seasons. The user can get back to the main menu from any screen.	A menu follows the title page. The seasons are listed on the main menu in order. Each season is described on one screen. From the menu a user can choose any of the seasons. The user can get back to the main menu from any screen.	One or more links don't work. Seasons aren't listed in order either in a menu or in a linear presentation.
Screen design	The student has followed the screen design guidelines that teacher has requested. At this level, 7 to 10 guidelines are appropriate.	The student has followed most of the screen design guidelines that the teacher has requested.	The student has not followed the guidelines. The screens are hard to read and disorganized.
Development of the presentation	The student has developed an outline. The student has developed an idea map and the main ideas on the idea map match the main navigational options. The student has written a storyboard that is consistent with the idea map and also consistent with the finished presentation. The student did both the idea map and storyboard before keying in the presentation.	The student has developed an idea map and there are major similarities between the idea map and the navigational structure of the presentation. The student has developed a storyboard that resembles the finished presentation. Both the idea map and storyboard were developed before the presentation was keyed in.	The idea map is missing or does not resemble the presentation or The storyboard is missing or does not resemble the presentation or The idea map and storyboard were developed after the presentation.

ware. They will be frustrated because they are trying to learn too many things at once. Once you are sure that they are confident users of the software, understand the development process, and possess some basic screen design knowledge, then you can begin adding challenges that will improve their writing.

TABLE 8.4 ■ Rubric for Middle School/High School Users of Presentation Software

Topic: Poetic Device

	Excellent (3)	Acceptable (2)	Needs Improvement (1)
Writing	All spelling and grammar are correct. Student uses constructions (such as compound sentences) on which the teacher has asked him/her to focus.	Grammar and spelling are mostly correct. Student attempts to use constructions on which the teacher has asked him/her to focus and are mostly correct.	Spelling errors interfere with the user's ability to use or appreciate the presentation.
Content	Each kind of imagery is accompanied by an example from a poem the class has studied. Three different forms of explanation (text, graphic, video, audio, animation) accompany each example. Explanations are clear, accurate, and complete.	Each kind of imagery is accompanied by an example from a poem the class has studied. Two different forms of explanation (text, graphic, video, audio, animation) accompany each example. The student does not always use a graphic and text to provide the explanations. Explanations are clear, accurate, and complete.	One or more poetic devices are missing. Examples are incorrect. The student explains a device(s) with only text or a graphic.
Navigation	A menu follows the title page. The major sections of the presentation appear on the menu page. Those devices with sub-categories (alliteration: consonance, assonance) allow navigation to a separate page for each. The user can get back to the main menu from any screen.	A menu with the names of all of the poetic devices for the lesson follows the title page. Each device and its subcategories is described on one screen. The user can get back to the main menu from any screen.	One or more links don't work.
Screen design	The student has followed all screen design guidelines listed by the teacher on a style guide.	The student has followed most of the screen design guidelines listed on a style sheet.	The student has not followed the guidelines. The screens are hard to read and disorganized.
Development of the presentation	The student has developed an outline. The outline and idea map are similar. The student has developed an idea map and the main ideas on the idea map match the main navigational options. The student has written a storyboard that is consistent with the idea map and also consistent with the finished presentation. The student did both the idea map and storyboard before keying in the presentation.	The student has developed an outline. The outline and idea map are similar. The student has developed an idea map and there are major similarities between the idea map and the navigational structure of the presentation. The student has developed a storyboard that resembles the finished presentation. Both the idea map and storyboard were developed before the presentation was keyed in.	The outline is missing or does not resemble the idea map. The idea map is missing or does not resemble the presentation or The storyboard is missing or does not resemble the presentation or The idea map and storyboard were developed after the presentation.

When you see sample rubrics you will often see "number of screens" or "number of cards" specified. I am reluctant to make this specification because it makes the development process more difficult for students. If they do their idea maps and flowcharts correctly, they will plan and produce the correct number of screens. It is not a bad idea to give them a range, like between five and eight screens or between twenty and twenty-five screens just to help them understand the scope of the assignment. However, in specifying the number of screen/storyboards for them to do, you are trying to make sure that they cover the content. You can really judge this outcome more effectively by telling them whether they did or did not provide the correct coverage in the "Content" section of the rubric. Furthermore, it is better to look at their idea maps and storyboards and say, "Don't you think you should include something about this?" Alternatively, "You know, maybe you should narrow this down and leave this section or screen out." Your students will learn more if their goal is to deal with the content they need to know rather than produce a specific number of screens or storyboards.

Table 8.5 is a list of fundamental screen design guidelines that we spoke about earlier which have been summarized in a format that students could use to check their own

Help students understand the level of detail you expect

Give students specific screen design guidelines

TABLE 8.5 ■ Sample Screen Design Style Evaluation Sheet

Guideline	Yes	No
1. Windows provide regions for different kinds of content.		
2. Window for each kind of content appears in the same place on every page.		
3. Text is left-justified. Numbers in tables are right- or decimal-justified.		
4. Navigational buttons for the same function appear in the same place consistently.		
5. Larger items are more significant, smaller items less significant.		
6. Items at the top of the screen are more important than the items below them.		
7. The background does not interfere with the delivery of information—it is an integral part of the presentation.		
8. Buttons reveal their purpose immediately.		
9. The size and location of the control buttons are proportional to the purpose they serve.		
10. If the presentation uses transition effects, the effects are consistent.		
11. Audio is clear and easily understood.		
12. Video is short and to the point.		
13. Text is easy to read against its background.		
14. Different kinds of graphics are used (scanned images, clip art, screen dumps, charts, diagrams, lists, maps, tables, and student-drawn graphics).		
15. Each screen has at least one relevant graphic.		
16. Users always know where they are in the presentation.		
17. There are three or fewer text styles per screen.		
18. Each screen has four or fewer colors (excluding imported graphics).		
19. Every object on the screen is meaningful.		
20. All text is in caps and lower case.		
21. The font is readable for its intended purpose.		
22. Each screen should have one idea or purpose.		
23. No flashing text is used.		
24. Vertically stacked text is not used.		
25. Lists are used where appropriate.		

presentation or a peer's presentation. As noted in the rubrics, however, the first time, second time, or even third time that students build a presentation is not the time to ask for compliance with every standard. Pick a few standards and teach them; review them at the beginning of the next assignment, and then add some more. If a student violates one of the guidelines to good effect, be flexible and figure out why the violation works and show it to the rest of the class. That is one way to foster creativity without grading it.

Students peer edit
using a rubric

One suggestion that helps students apply these guidelines and saves you time is to have students check each other's work against the guidelines and perhaps even the grading rubric before the work is handed in. This may not work for very young children since they cannot read well enough to interpret the rubric and apply it. But for children who can, it is the analog to peer editing in a writing class. Not only will peer editors learn more about the presentation design process, but they will also cover the content one more time in a different context.

Creativity is difficult to
grade and to justify

One difficult issue that arises is that some rubrics include a row for creativity. Most descriptions are too vague to be helpful in scoring the presentation. For example:

> Good original artwork is included. Clip art, photos, and so on are used in creative ways. Color carries the theme and sets the tone for the stack. Animation is used very effectively to illustrate a concept. (Barnett, p. 31)

First, requiring students who have no native drawing ability but who are toiling toward some kind of grade in science (social studies, language arts) to produce good original artwork isn't fair. That they can't draw good pictures doesn't mean they aren't creative; it means they can't draw. Secondly, could the originator really define to an angry parent or a hurt child the standards for the sentence, "Clip art . . . (is) used in creative ways." The sentence is so broad as to be meaningless. The author of this rubric probably means that the students should follow the rules of good screen design for displaying graphics. This holds true for the last two sentences of this rubric as well. Because the student used color and animation doesn't mean that the student is especially creative. It means that the student followed screen design rules for color, thought carefully about the concept, and decided that animation would represent the concept well.

David Jonassen (2000) suggests a different way of approaching creativity. He lists the different parts of developing a presentation and then defines specific creative thinking skills associated with those parts of the presentation. Table 8.6 summarizes Jonassen's approach. If you were to attach a row of cells labeled "creativity" to one of the rubrics mentioned previously, Table 8.7 would give you an example of what this row might look like. Remember that this is aimed neither at the highest nor the lowest grades, nor at any particular content area. If you were to use this creativity block as part of your rubric, you would have to modify it to suit your needs. Notice that the row "Synthesizing" in Jonassen's table is not included in Table 8.7. That is because we have covered that topic quite thoroughly in the previous evaluation rubric.

Creativity is difficult to teach

I am inclined not to attempt to judge other forms of creativity or the lack of it, because it is difficult to score and even more difficult to defend. You and others will recognize special creativity when you see it, but you cannot teach it in such a way that you can grade it. Some students follow every rule of screen design, every writing and

TABLE 8.6 ■ Creative Thinking Skills Described by Jonassen

	Researching Information	Organizing and designing presentation	Managing project
Elaborating			
Expanding	X	X	
Modifying	X	X	
Extending		X	
Shifting	X	X	
Categories			
Concretizing		X	
Synthesizing			
Analogical thinking			
Summarizing	X	X	
Hypothesizing			
Planning			X
Imagining			
Fluency		X	
Predicting		X	X
Speculating		X	
Visualizing		X	
Intuition		X	

Jonassen, D. (2000). *Computers as mindtools for schools.* Upper Saddle River, NJ: Merrill Prentice Hall, p. 224.

TABLE 8.7 ■ Rubric for Judging Creativity in a Presentation

Excellent	Acceptable	Needs Improvement
Research for the project included expanding upon what was found. The student modified what he or she found to fit the context of the project. Some categories of information were used to explain and amplify the meaning of other categories of information.	There is no evidence of cutting and pasting re-searched information from sources into the project. All information the student obtained was paraphrased and re-ordered.	Evidence of cutting and pasting exists. Information appears to have been obtained from only one or two sources and slightly modified.
The student used the information that he or she found to provide original conclusions. The form that these conclusions can take include: predictions not made by the authors of the research the student has gathered but based on that information, speculations and hunches that could be wrong but show that the student has done much "What If" thinking, and/or visualizations, i.e., original visual interpretations (graphics, diagrams, tables, charts) of textual material	The student does provide predictions, speculations, or visualizing, but relies on other authors to provide those insights. The student has not engaged in original "What If" thinking.	The student simply reports information.

content specification, and use appropriate grammar and spelling—producing a good presentation but not a creative one. Other students will do the same and produce a spectacular presentation. Those students who produce the creative presentations will receive the intrinsic rewards of creativity—appreciation from you and their classmates. This is probably enough. The primary goal, remember, is for the student who produces the presentation, either spectacular or average, to learn the content in a way that is motivating and which adds rich connections to the knowledge the student already has.

✔ CHECKING YOUR UNDERSTANDING

8.1

Many school sites on the Internet provide examples of student-created presentations. It is likely that the schools in your town have such a site. Choose a site that has examples of student presentations at the grade level that you teach or intend to teach. Choose a set of student presentations. With a group of students in your class, decide what the assignment must have been for that group of presentations. Then, as a group, develop a rubric to judge the presentations. Grade each presentation yourself and then compare your grades and your justification for them with your colleagues. You might even take this exercise one step further. Have one of your peers choose a presentation that did not receive an "A." Role play the situation between the parent of the student and the teacher, or role play the teacher explaining to that student why he/she did not receive an "A."

■ QUESTIONS AND ANSWERS ABOUT USING MULTIMEDIA PRESENTATIONS

Do students always do their projects alone?   Not at all—students often work in teams to complete projects. In another year or two when Jeff's teacher gets more confident with presentations, she will have the entire class cooperate on a presentation called "The Physiology of Mammals." Then the class would divide into groups and take sections of the topic to outline, to map, storyboard, and write presentation software. Groups could organize themselves in several ways. They could assign themselves roles such as editor, researcher, story boarder, software writer, etc. and do the project jointly. Or, each could take a topic, develop it alone, and then figure out how to merge everyone's individual project into a unified presentation. The way the teacher actually manages the assignment depends on the personality and skills of the class.

When is it appropriate to make hypermedia-based assignments?   Not every kind of content should be the basis for a hypermedia assignment. Sometimes it is more efficient to use a spreadsheet, database, or word processor or even to say, "Memorize this." For example, there are more efficient ways to teach students how to bisect an angle or factor an equation than to have them make a hypermedia presentation on the topic. A spreadsheet might be a better way to learn about the lever, and using a database might be a better way to study presidents of the United States.

Presentations are good for summaries, for taking the large view, and for helping students tie together ideas whose relationships get lost over weeks and months. You may spend six weeks on a literature or reading unit. Rather than having students do several small hypermedia assignments, it would be better to have them do one project for the unit that ties together themes, character types, or whatever you must emphasize.

Is it ever appropriate for a teacher to be the author and presenter of a hypermedia title? Yes, there are times when it is appropriate for you to be the author of a presentation. Most teachers do not have extra time to really do a presentation correctly very often, i.e., do an idea map, storyboard, and finally the presentation with appropriate graphics, audio, and video. If your goal is to put an outline in front of your class as you speak, and you have to check out an LCD projector and set up a computer with all of the attendant hassles, your time is better spent in other ways. Over time, you may develop a set of very nice presentations that introduce units or help you teach particularly difficult topics. These are the kinds of presentations that you want to spend your time on. You should put your best efforts on CD for your class and allow them to check the disks out for review. They will be good models for students.

Should students add videos to their presentations? Student videos should be very short. A one-minute video on most topics would be sufficient. Realistically speaking, if every student in the class does several one-minute videos, your class will use considerable space on the school's server or on your local classroom machines. Use this space limitation to your advantage. Require your students to make every word count and to structure and practice their oral presentation carefully. Your students can record these videos as .avi files using one of the ubiquitous "quickcams" which are made by many different companies and which come with many different features. These cameras are easy to install and many cost less than $100. One or two cameras for the entire class would be enough.

■ SUMMARY

Teachers should approach the assessment of hypermedia presentations thoughtfully. Giving the student one grade for the whole presentation with a comment is not adequate feedback. As teachers plan a presentation assignment, they should include an assessment rubric that students are aware of at the beginning of the assignment. The rubric should cover both the process of developing the presentation as well as the finished product. The rubric should assess the quality of the presentation, the quality of the writing, and the quality of the coverage of the content. The teacher should weight each according to its importance.

For students who are new to developing presentations, scoring rubrics and expectations should be simple. It is important to avoid teaching students too many skills at the same time. For beginning users you may want to use it as a tool for reviewing information that you have already covered. If, on the other hand, your students are skilled users of presentation software and understand how to capture and process digital audio and video you can use presentation software to explore a new topic.

■ REFERENCES ■

Barnett, H. (2000). Assessing the effects of technology in a standards-driven world. *Leading and learning with Technology,* 27(7), p. 31.

Jonassen, D. H. (2000). *MindTools: Computers in the classroom.* Englewood Cliffs, NJ: Merrill.

Educational Applications of Word Processing

CHAPTER 9

OBJECTIVES

- Understand classroom management issues related to word processors.
- Know which lower level learning activities the word processor supports.
- Know which higher level learning activities the word processor supports.
- Use tables and the word processor.
- Use the word processor to organize Internet links for your class.
- Direct your students in the effective use of a spell checker.
- Use readability statistics to sharpen your students' writing skills.
- Know how to use text-reading software to help poor readers acquire information.

To successfully complete this chapter, you should be able to perform the following tasks:

- Cut and paste
- Make a table
- Create or remove borders
- Create an outline using the outline function
- Scan text and use OCR to transform it
- Import graphics into a word processor
- Use the graphics program associated with your word processor
- Create bulleted and numbered lists
- Import information from spreadsheets
- Set up and use a spell checker, thesaurus, and grammar checker

This chapter is really a follow-up to Chapter 5, "Presentation Software." In that chapter, you learned much about the organizational process, the precursor to actually keying in

Same principles as in creating presentations

the screens for the presentation itself. All of the information you learned about outlining and idea mapping applies to word processing as well. As with creating a presentation, writing with a word processor is a solitary activity. Yes, you can have steps in the process that are not solitary, such as group brainstorming and peer editing. However, the final act of writing becomes the interaction between the writer and the machine— one person to one computer. You will learn later that almost the opposite is true of spreadsheets and databases: A group of children, even an entire class, may profitably use a database or spreadsheet simultaneously. That is not the case with word processing.

Help people think about larger ideas, much as calculators do in math

Since people learned to write, they have sought ways to make the physical process more efficient. The word processor is a great improvement over typewriters, which represented the same scale of improvement over pens and pencils. Word processing has made composition possible for people who could not write before, such as young children and people with learning and coordination disorders (Yuehua, 2000). For those who become somewhat adept with a keyboard, good writing is attainable and with work, improvement is steady. The challenge for educators is to structure the limited access that students have to word processors in a way that is most beneficial.

■ MANAGEMENT ISSUES: HOW MANY COMPUTERS DO YOU HAVE?

One-Computer Classroom

One computer mostly a teacher's tool

Word processing in a one-computer classroom helps teachers with administrative chores. However, it is difficult to rely heavily on a word processor in a one-computer classroom and still give students a meaningful learning experience. In a typical class, during the school year the maximum time a student would have to do word processing assignments might be seven hours if the computer were used for other center activities involving the rest of the tools on an equal basis. In this case, you cannot count on the word processor to significantly improve the writing of your students. In a one-computer classroom, the computer is largely a tool for the teacher.

Five-Computer Classroom: "Jigsaw Model"

"Jigsaw" model for word processing skills

The five-computer classroom provides students with a more realistic amount of time to complete assignments on a regular basis. In a well-managed five-computer classroom, a student can expect to have access to a computer for writing at least an hour a week. An ideal situation for using these five computers is to train students to use a word processor in two or three one-hour sessions in a laboratory first. However, if a laboratory is not available, students can still learn word processing skills using a "Jigsaw" model. Students start with a home group. Then each person in the home group goes to a different expert group to learn a skill or a set of skills. Forming the expert groups is as easy as having each student in the home group count off. Then all "ones" go to Group One, "twos" to Group Two and so forth. Once in their expert groups, students investigate a set of word processing skills defined for them by the teacher. They

	See		22
	How		44
	The		56
	Colors		22
	Change	Sum of Column 5 =	144

FIGURE 9.1 ■ Table Exercise

learn these skills by using the help menu and by completing, as a group, an exercise designed by the teacher. Group One may learn page-formatting skills, such as fonts, spacing, portrait/landscape orientations, and justification. Group Two may learn about importing and formatting graphics; Group Three importing spreadsheets, charts, and graphs; Group Four creating and formatting tables and columns (see an example of a "Table Exercise" in Figure 9.1); and, Group Five, headers, footers, footnotes, selecting, cutting, and pasting. The students return to their home groups to teach what they have learned and to learn what the others in the group have to teach. After this initial activity in which students learn or refresh their word processing skills, they can rotate through the computers to complete selected writing assignments.

Laboratory

Laboratories helpful for teaching skills

A laboratory is the best place to teach students how to use processors. Several long or many closely spaced shorter blocks of time help students learn how to use a word processor quickly. It is important that students get to use their new skills early in the learning process in several closely spaced assignments. Students should learn the same topics that are suggested in the section on the five-computer classroom. The best way to do this is to provide an activity for each skill. Then assign a project that involves content where they use most or all of the skills they have learned.

Another effective way to use a laboratory for writing is in conjunction with a five-computer classroom. If students have to write a report or do a research project, they can do the first draft with a pen and paper. Entering this first draft on the computer takes some time, and if possible, the school laboratory should be reserved for this assignment. Once the first draft has been entered and printed out, then students edit their own papers as well as submit them to others for peer editing and review. In a five-computer classroom, there is time for students to do revisions.

■ THE MODELS: USING THE WORD PROCESSOR TO TEACH CONTENT AND SKILLS

Now that you have looked at some general management and skill issues, it is time to turn to content, the real reason you have the computers with word processors in your classroom. Review the models for word processing in Table 9.1. Most of these uses are

TABLE 9.1 ■ Models for Word Processing

Targeted Learning Problems	High-Level Analysis

1. Ordering/Classification
  a. Sorting
  b. Outlines
	1. Rewrite (style, content)
	  a. Revision
	  b. Editing

2. Substitution Exercises
  a. Supply the missing
    (words, sentences, paragraphs, pictures)
  b. Remove the extra
    (words, sentences, paragraphs, pictures)
	2. Information analysis
	  a. Research report
	  b. Journaling
	  c. Lab reports
	  d. Note taking

3. Grammar
  a. Thesaurus
  b. Spell checker
	3. Newspaper
	4. Brochure

4. Logical sequencing
  a. Follow directions
  b. Writing directions
	5. Group investigations/brainstorming
	6. Composition
	  a. Creative writing
	  b. Letters
	  c. Writing roulette

[margin note: Word processors speed student work]

self-explanatory, and most of these activities may be done with pencil and paper. The benefit of using a word processor is the speed with which children can manipulate information. Take outlines, for example. Children have been outlining with pencil and paper for a very long time. However, think about the outlining process. People outline when they are just beginning to think about a topic—when their thoughts may not be entirely clear. Sometimes the entire outline must be rewritten because the writer has more or different ideas. Changing an outline with a word processor is only a matter of cutting and pasting or pressing the Enter key to make a new line.

It is important to notice that a student product is implicit in each model in Table 9.1. Furthermore, the process that is used to create the product for the "High-Level Analysis and Skills" model may require the use of additional tool software. On the other hand, the "Targeted Learning Problems" models require students to manipulate smaller chunks of information often represented as text, a function that is facilitated by a word processor.

High-Level Analysis and Skills

[margin note: Students experiment with different formatting]

"The Newspaper," the "Research Report," creative writing, and writing roulette are activities that you no doubt have models for already. Using a word processor doesn't change the activity much. It does provide for a better-looking product from the students and it allows them to add graphics that they might not ordinarily use.

Journaling, lab reports, and note taking activities may be improved with computers if students know how to keyboard. However, using computers for these activities is questionable considering the other functions computers do that students cannot do with pencil and paper (databases and spreadsheets). In a science class, precious computer time might be better spent with probes and spreadsheets than with entering lab reports or note taking.

Let us look an example of how a teacher might execute a high level activity using a word processor. Producing a newspaper requires a different set of skills than producing a research report. Students use a different writing style as well as more and different formatting techniques. To get the flavor of how a newspaper assignment can be used as a tool for learning, let us visit Mr. Harrison's fifth grade social studies class. They are studying medieval Europe.

FIELD TRIP 9.1

Creating a Newspaper

Adam, an avid fan of both Mr. Harrison and sixth grade social studies, was excited to begin the new unit on medieval Europe. In preparation for the unit he had spent the previous evening slaying dragons in the back yard with his wooden sword. Today was the day they would actually start reading and learning about knights, castles, and the misty world of the middle ages.

Mr. Harrison began the unit by asking students what they knew about the world a thousand years ago. He had a computer and projector and was using a word processor to list the students' contributions. Before class he had made a table with headings to help students remember what they knew about the period. Headings at the top of his table included: government, military, daily life, religion, language, common people, aristocracy, pastimes, important events, medicine, and law. As students begin trying to fill in cells in the table, they discuss their contributions and decide that there are some things that they do not know. In fact, there are quite a few things they do not know. Mr. Harrison said, "Adam, if you were to wake up tomorrow morning and the date were March 1, 1066, what would your day be like? What would the headlines in the newspaper that day be?" Adam was smart enough to know that there would be no newspaper and said so, which made everyone laugh. But he had to admit that he didn't know much more than that.

Mr. Johnson used the laughter and Adam's answer to propose to the class the method they would use to learn about medieval Europe. He said, "Newspapers reflect the daily life of the people that write them." Quickly he double clicked an icon at the bottom of the computer screen that opened to some excerpts titled "100 Years Ago Today" he had scanned from his local paper. He read them to the class. After the class listened to and reflected on the newspaper examples, Mr. Harrison suggested to the class that they write a newspaper that would reflect daily life in England on October 15, 1066. The class was delighted, and full of energy they began collecting information from their textbooks, the library, and a selected list of Internet sites that Mr. Harrison had prepared for them. Each student could pick six topics from the table that Mr. Harrison and the class had brainstormed. In fact, Mr. Harrison printed the table and duplicated it so that each student would have a copy. On the days students were doing their research, Mr. Harrison also lead class discussions on newspapers and how they are written and formatted. Mr. Harrison gave the class some guidelines for their articles.

After each student had researched and written on six topics, the class then used a word processor to format and publish individual newspapers. When all of the newspapers were finished, each student printed a copy and the students read and critiqued each other's work. In cases where students disagreed about the facts, Mr. Harrison arbitrated the discussions and helped students make accurate conclusions. After students made corrections, Mr. Harrison then put all of the newspapers on the class website for students' parents, relatives, and friends to see.

Setting up a problem

Providing tools to help students solve the problem

Analyzing and judging information

Adam was excited about his project and handed in this newspaper as a first draft:

King Harold Defeated!

King Harold was defeated yesterday at Hastings. Surviving soldier stated that they creamed us. It was a sad ending For King Harold who so boldly defeated King Harold of Norway. Duke Williams army was an army looking for plunder and conquest. They were not fighting for any humane reason. Men of education suspect that this invasion will have an effect on the English language. Orevua!!

An Explanation

Duke Williams raided England because he wanted every body to be Roman catholics. Normandy had been getting stronger and stronger Because of all the strong lords they had been having. Harold promised the Throne to William but Harold refused to give up the throne. So that is Why Wiliam invaded, out of greed.

An Effect

An effect will be the change in our language. There will be a lot of French words introduced To our language.Dumb, huh!

We the media suspect that Normandy England will be more powerful than before.

Dear Lord Abby, I am a poor bloke Who can barely survive. I don't have any money because I spent it on the paper to write this letter. How can I get some money? Sighned poor Man.

Dear Poor man, get a life!

Second letter.

Dear lord Abby, I own a business and it isn't going to well my business is farming. What can I do? Dear Farmer, Your business Is not my business.

Sports

Yesterday's Joust was very exciting, the lists were filled the fans were chearing, Blake had just finished with Nare and was chooseing an opponent. He chose Drake The only one who hadn't he hadn't won. (Blake was getting a lot of armor and horses). They both mounted Their horses, and charged. Strangely they both Knocked each other off their horses, but Drake fell harder. Blake Quickly got up and hammerd him With his mace. Blake had almost torn of Sir Drake's helmut when Drake swung his sword up and hit Blakes hand broad side. Blakes hand was paralyzed for the moment. Drake saw his chance and quickly tore off Blakes helmet, there by Having to challenge and fight all the other men Blake had beaten.

Obituary

This morning Cathy Robin died this morning of unknown cause.
Blake III Died of pox, at age 40.
Trank Blabber died of Apoplexy at age 19.
Araph Linger died of a club at age 15.
Fander Fish died of Apoplexy, age 10.
Lady Crane died of a curse, kitchen maid suspected.

Editorial

Topic: chamber pots

I think that people should find a better way to empty their chamber pots. There are problems with just dumping it out a window. For instance, people could get waste on them if they happened to walk by when somebody was emptying their chamber pot. Here is another reason why people should find another way, if someone dumped the contence of a chamber pot into a stream The fish might die from the foulness of the waste, and that wouldn't be good for the fishermen. Here is my solution, you build a system of gutters (something you'll hafto invent) that all lead to a pit just outside of the village. You dump the waste into these gutters and the waste will flow into the pit.

Advertisements and Announcements

Cany Flounder is sick and will probably die on Tuesday. Flan's Fats is having a sale on fat. Remember Flan's Fats don't taste like rats. Lord Lutany has Bought a fresh shipment of fish from Ireland, you can to at a very low price (price will be yelled at town auction). Dave Thatcher will thatch your roof for only two hundred poinds. The fishing fleet will be back the fourth. Most of the men will be back from the trip, I don't think anyone has drown. Sowrenson's Swords is having a sale on German and French Imports. Lady Becket is turning to a rip old age of forty.

Lorsa Cling died of Child birth.

Table Tips

Remember to have a blessing, don't belch, don't touch your ears or your nose, be sure to have a toothpick, and don't forget to keep your elbows on the table, clean your nails and hands.

The draft shown here is an actual rough draft submitted by Adam, a sixth grade student. You can see that the process of writing the newspaper has connected the student with many facts about daily life in the middle ages. Furthermore, the student has not simply memorized these facts but put them into a larger context. He tried to think about them as though he were there when they happened. The word processor helped him express his thoughts in a way that other people could read them because Adam had never been able to print or write legibly. You can also see that Adam has some editorial work to do. Mr. Harrison has teamed with the language arts teacher so that the editing will take place in her class.

✔ CHECKING YOUR UNDERSTANDING

9.1

1. Since this is the first draft of this student's work, explain how you would manage your classroom as you helped this student and the rest of the class work on spelling and sentence mechanics. Since your will post these on the web, you will want students to hand in final copies that are very clean. Assume that you have a five-computer classroom.

2. Since you will ultimately want to assess your students' knowledge of the middle ages with a test of some kind, use this student's paper to develop one essay question and five multiple-choice questions that you could use on an assessment. Remember one activity in this unit is for all of the students to read each others' newspapers. An example of one multiple-choice question would be:

    1. Probably the most common reason that women often died young during the middle ages was:

        a. Childbirth problems
        b. Household accidents
        c. Jousting injuries
        d. Travel dangers

Targeted Learning Problems

Like the models for "High Level Analysis and Skills" and "Targeted Learning Problems," models may be used with either group or individual learning activities. In most content area topics, students need a basic level of knowledge or skill in order to progress further. A word processor can provide a different context and medium for student interaction with these problem areas.

"Removing or supplying text" requires students to work with the language of a discipline and hone their vocabulary skills. Ordering steps in procedures is another way of practicing a skill in the early stages of learning it. Teachers can build sorting exercises for word processors quite easily. Figure 9.2 is an example of a sorting exercise

Build traditional worksheets

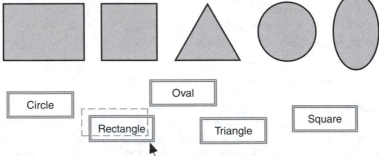

FIGURE 9.2 ■ Classification Exercise Using the Mouse and a Word Processor

for geometric shapes. Using a computer, children either cut and paste or drag the labels to the appropriate graphics. They do similar exercises with pencil and paper by drawing lines, or cutting and pasting–for "real," this time. If you have computer resources, you can create these kinds of activities for your children. If your resources are marginal, have your students use the computers for something they can't do as well or as fast with pencil and paper.

■ WORD PROCESSING TIPS

Bullets and Numbered Lists

A numbered list indicates steps in an event or a prioritized list. Bullets indicate that there is no special sequence of events or order of importance. Students should learn to do each type of list using automatic numbering and bulleting features of the word processing software. Encourage more adept students to explore the different styles of numbers and bullets that can be used.

Using Tables to Organize Information

Teach your students to use tables to help you organize word-processed documents. When students include graphics in their documents, sometimes they appear cluttered and disorganized. Using a table as an organizational tool helps students keep their thinking straight and their presentation of information clear. Looking at the table in Figure 9.3, do you recognize some organizational tips that you learned in Chapter 7?

> Tables help students organize and format information

The page is organized around the concept "regions of the western hemisphere." The properties of the regions are native food and animal supplies. Examples of the properties are listed in the left-hand column. Note how the student has arranged the graphics with the northernmost landmasses first and the southernmost last. Furthermore, notice how easy it is for the reader to scan up and down the column of example foods and animals and observe how few foods and no animals moved north or south. The arrangement of the items in the table reflects what the words in the first cell of the table say. The student started with a table like the one in Figure 9.4.

Making Links to the Internet

Although students cannot use word processing software to present information nonlinearly as with presentation software, they can link to articles or other information on the Internet. Here is one scenario in which that capability is useful. Remember when we talked about "Information Literacy" in Chapter 3? We learned that students must learn to be able to judge the quality of information that they get from the Internet because so many different kinds of authors post their work there. Imagine that your students are working on a research project on the pros and cons of genetic engineering. Also, imagine that as a part of this research assignment you are trying to

Prehistory of the Americas

The Americas consist of three different regions—North America, Central America, and South America. Because of their arrangement (north/south), crops and livestock that thrive in one part of the Americas do not necessarily thrive in other parts of the landmass. Furthermore, because of impenetrable jungle and hostile conditions, crops and livestock from South America (the Andes) that might have thrived in North America because of a similar climate, never moved north or south (Diamond, 1999).

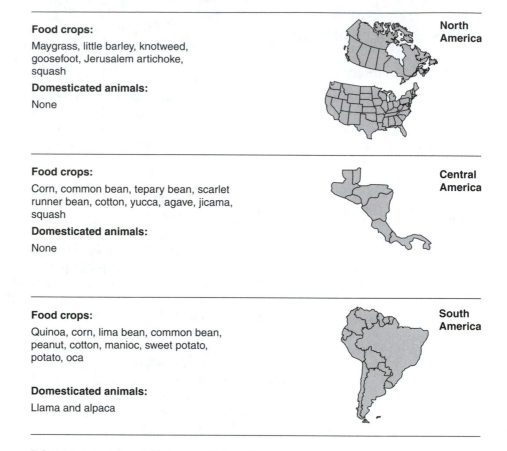

Food crops:

Maygrass, little barley, knotweed, goosefoot, Jerusalem artichoke, squash

Domesticated animals:

None

North America

Food crops:

Corn, common bean, tepary bean, scarlet runner bean, cotton, yucca, agave, jicama, squash

Domesticated animals:

None

Central America

Food crops:

Quinoa, corn, lima bean, common bean, peanut, cotton, manioc, sweet potato, potato, oca

Domesticated animals:

Llama and alpaca

South America

FIGURE 9.3 ■ Using a Table to Format Information

FIGURE 9.4 ■ Students' Starting Point for Figure 9.3

teach them the difference between reliable and unreliable information. Your assignment to them is this:

- Find three good Internet sources of information in favor of genetic engineering for food crops.
- Find three good Internet sources of information against genetic engineering for food crops.
- Find three good Internet sources of information in favor of genetic engineering for humans.
- Find three good Internet sources of information against genetic engineering for humans.

In this assignment, you are teaching them two things about information literacy: triangulation and judging the quality of sources. Now comes the hard part. How will you look at and grade or give them feedback on their sources? You have three alternatives:

1. Have them write down the address of the Internet site when they find it so that you can type it in and check it out.
2. Have them print out the Internet site.
3. Have them cut and paste the Internet site into a word-processed document and give you an electronic copy. When you are ready to look at their searches you will load their document into a word processor on a computer connected to the Internet, and click on the addresses they have cut and pasted. You will then review the documents they have chosen and type feedback or grades directly into the document they gave you, save it, and give it back to them.

You can tell right now that choice 1 will be quite ineffective. Students will write down some addresses incorrectly, and you will type some incorrectly. After you get the addresses right (if you ever do), you will have to create a new document and save it under their name. Choice 2 is wasteful but possible. You could underline portions of the printed pages and underline words or phrases that reveal biased opinions. Choice 3 is a winner: It is quick and easy. If you wanted to do something similar to underlining words and phrases that reveal biases, you could simply cut and paste them into your student's document.

Importing Information from Other Applications

Although we have not yet discussed spreadsheets, you should encourage students to import supporting work that they have done with spreadsheets into documents they make with a word processor. Reports no longer have to be all words. Students can include tables, charts, and graphs that they make with other electronic tools. When you read Chapters 10 through 12 you will learn that working with a database or a spreadsheet is usually never an end in itself. There is usually a requirement for some kind of product—a presentation, speech, or written report. Figure 9.5 includes an example of an imported spreadsheet and its accompanying chart.

Display information from other applications

	Clay	Humus	Sand
	5	5	5
	4	6	4
	6	7	7
	4	6	6
	4	8	7
	3	7	6
	4	8	5
Sum	30	47	40
Mean	7.5	11.75	10

Bean Height

FIGURE 9.5 ■ Spreadsheet and Chart Inserted into a Word Processed Document

When the students use a word processor, they can include many different kinds of information. Besides graphs, charts, and tables from a spreadsheet, they can import graphics. Students have some choices about how to display graphics. They can learn to wrap text around a graphic, or lay the graphic over the text or under the text. Figure 9.6 is an example of using word wrap around a graphic. Although the instructional utility of having this skill is marginal, learning how to format graphics and text on the same page is a minor part of basic computer skills for the information age.

Jupiter is the largest planet in the solar system. It has more mass than any

object in the solar system other than the sun. It is the sixth planet from the sun, and it is a very cold place at the top of its clouds and a very hot place below their surface. Its atmosphere is unbreathable for human beings. Composed of hydrogen, helium, ammonia, and methane, Jupiter is called a "gas giant" because it is mostly gas and liquid with a small rock core. Jupiter has 16 moons. Galileo saw them first.

Just what would it be like to be a human on Jupiter? You would need a special space. . . .

FIGURE 9.6 ■ Importing a Graphic and Placing Text Around It

Spelling and Spell Checkers

There has been a lively debate among English teachers about whether or not children should use spell checkers. A study done recently by Cope (2000) adds some perspective to this debate. He used two groups of high school English students in grades 9–12 and administered the California Test of Basic Skills (CTBS) for spelling as a pre-test. He disabled the spell checker on the computers used by the experimental group (n = 42). The control group of students (n = 64) continued to use their spell checkers with the auto correct feature. This feature changes errors it recognizes as the writer types without notifying the writer, who may never know about the errors. This treatment continued for a semester. At the end of the semester, Cope tested the students again using a different form of the CTBS test. Students in the control group (students using automatic spelling correction) scored significantly lower (p .05) than students in the experimental group who did not have access to spell checkers. Conclusions that Cope drew from this experiment are that spell checking with auto correct does not help students. You may want to make sure that this feature is turned off in your classroom.

> Be careful about spell checker settings

Readability Statistics and Grammar Checkers

Most word processors provide a simple utility that displays readability statistics for a selection or for a whole file. This allows students to measure themselves on a variety of different items (Figure 9.7). The "Flesch Reading Ease" is a scale from 1 to 100. The higher the number, the easier a selection is to read. Microsoft documentation (1997) indicates that for general readability at the adult level, writers should achieve scores in the 60s or 70s. "Flesch-Kincaid grade level" is tied to the United States school system

> Readability statistics give students one baseline

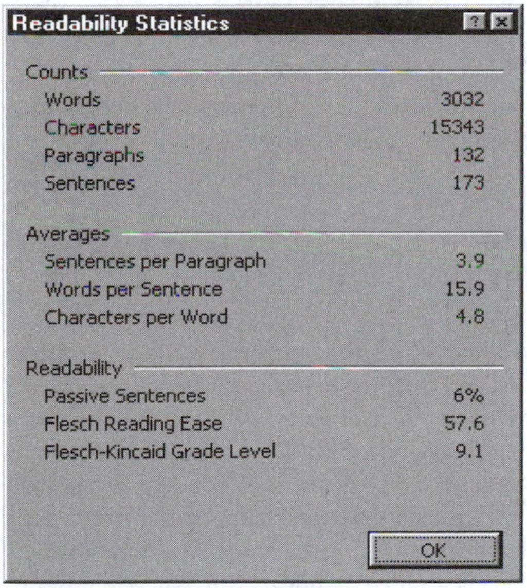

Readability Statistics

Counts	
Words	3032
Characters	15343
Paragraphs	132
Sentences	173

Averages	
Sentences per Paragraph	3.9
Words per Sentence	15.9
Characters per Word	4.8

Readability	
Passive Sentences	6%
Flesch Reading Ease	57.6
Flesch-Kincaid Grade Level	9.1

OK

FIGURE 9.7 ■ Readability Statistics

indications of grade level. On this scale, a level between 7.0 and 8.0 indicates general readability. Younger children, of course, would use different standards. Teachers at different grade levels can create standards for their students by scanning in items of work that they have judged to be outstanding at the grade level or performance level that they teach and recording the readability indicators and other statistics. These, then, could be given to students as one standard by which to judge their writing. Although mechanics can never substitute for content, it rarely hurts to give a student at least one concrete goal for which to aim.

Another way to use readability statistics is to have students accumulate them in a spreadsheet during the year. Once they do this they can graph or chart each statistic and look at their progress over the year. You may, for example, be teaching them to write complex sentences. This goal would translate into more words per sentence. Although the readability statistics don't tell you if the sentence is well constructed or meaningful, it can still be one piece of the puzzle that helps students measure their progress. You will be the one that gives them a grade on how meaningful their work is, and that grade can be entered into the spreadsheet along with the readability statistics. If grades are going up on how meaningful sentences are and numbers of words per sentence is going up as well, then the student is probably writing more good, complex sentences.

Grammar checkers can find some mistakes but . . .

The grammar checker on word processors is a valuable tool for students who are trying to learn the mechanics of writing. It is important to recognize that a grammar checker cannot check grammar as well as a teacher can. A grammar checker cannot help students with the logical connection they must make between paragraphs, for example. A grammar checker cannot check to see that every paragraph has a topic sentence and a summary sentence. A grammar checker can, however, alert students to purely mechanical problems with their writing, and there is a long list of those. See Figure 9.8 for a complete listing of mechanics checked by Microsoft Word.

Furthermore, you may use grammar checks in various combinations. Word provides for four basic styles: casual, standard, formal, and technical. This option allows writing teachers to help students understand the differences among writing styles. This option box is displayed in Figure 9.9. In addition, the software provides a "custom" setting which allows you to put checks in the boxes that you choose, enabling you to closely define the problems that you want your students to focus on.

Text reading software helps students who can learn but not read

■ TEXT-READING SOFTWARE

Text reading software, although not really a word processor in the traditional sense, can be used in conjunction with word processors to help with not only the reading process but also the writing process. When people with reading and writing disabilities are mainstreamed, they sit alongside those who can be told, "Read in your social studies book pages 52 through 57." If students cannot read but can learn social studies, understand and enjoy stories and literature, learn science and learn mathematics, there is an alternative to failure based on their inability to read. Using text reader software, a computer will read a story or a textbook to a student while the student follows along. Students may change the font, size, or color of the text to accommodate individual dif-

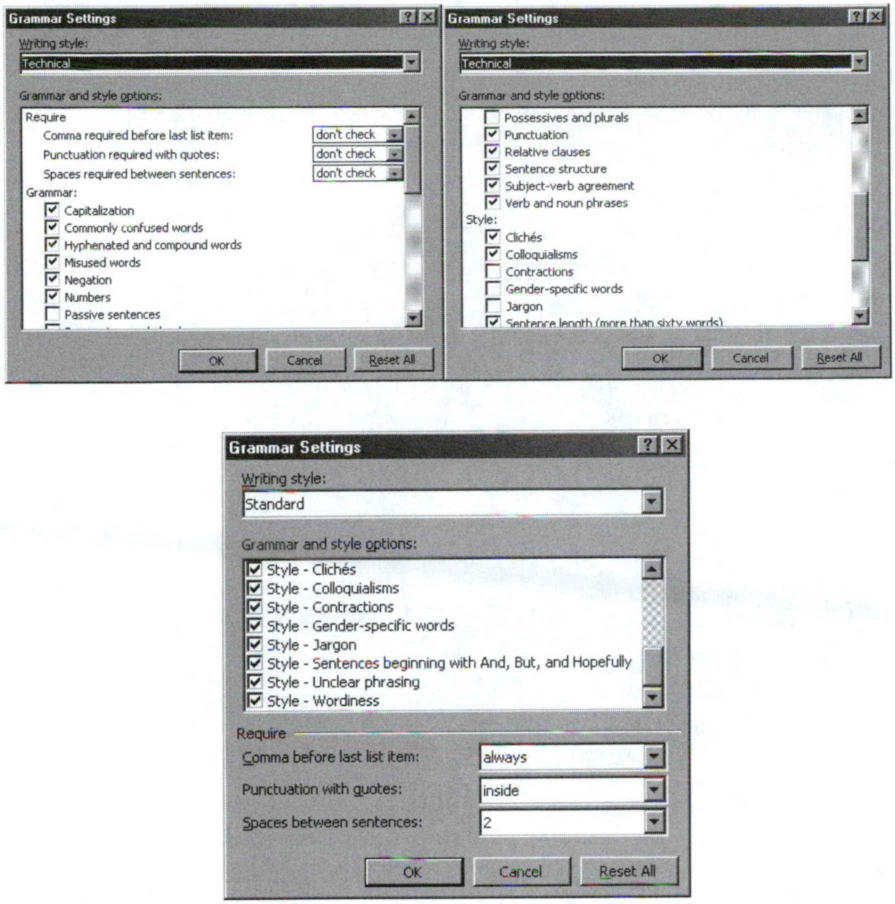

Grammar Settings (left dialog)

Writing style: Technical

Grammar and style options:

Require
- Comma required before last list item: don't check
- Punctuation required with quotes: don't check
- Spaces required between sentences: don't check

Grammar:
- ☑ Capitalization
- ☑ Commonly confused words
- ☑ Hyphenated and compound words
- ☑ Misused words
- ☑ Negation
- ☑ Numbers
- ☐ Passive sentences

OK   Cancel   Reset All

Grammar Settings (right dialog)

Writing style: Technical

Grammar and style options:
- ☐ Possessives and plurals
- ☑ Punctuation
- ☑ Relative clauses
- ☑ Sentence structure
- ☑ Subject-verb agreement
- ☑ Verb and noun phrases

Style:
- ☑ Clichés
- ☑ Colloquialisms
- ☐ Contractions
- ☐ Gender-specific words
- ☐ Jargon
- ☑ Sentence length (more than sixty words)

OK   Cancel   Reset All

Grammar Settings (bottom dialog)

Writing style: Standard

Grammar and style options:
- ☑ Style - Clichés
- ☑ Style - Colloquialisms
- ☑ Style - Contractions
- ☑ Style - Gender-specific words
- ☑ Style - Jargon
- ☑ Style - Sentences beginning with And, But, and Hopefully
- ☑ Style - Unclear phrasing
- ☑ Style - Wordiness

Require
- Comma before last list item: always
- Punctuation with quotes: inside
- Spaces between sentences: 2

OK   Cancel   Reset All

FIGURE 9.8 ■ Settings for Checking Grammar (Examples of Features)

ferences. The computer will also read students' stories or reports back to them as well. Such a text reader will read information continually or read it one word at a time, at the student's request. Students can select the volume, pitch, and speed of the computer's voice, as well. While the computer is reading, the student may also take notes in a special notes pane. Upon request, the computer will read the notes back to the student. "Ultimate Reader," which has been stable for several years, may be found at: http://www.tagrp.com/products/page47.html. CAST eReader is a similar product, with information at http://www.cast.org/udl/index.cfm?i=197.

How do students put text into a text reader? Some is available on the Internet at "etext" sites. Houghton Mifflin provides a disc with the text of its social studies books, for example. If both of those options fail, students scan in text with scanners equipped for OCR (optical character recognition).

Text readers are not especially new, but are underutilized in classrooms. The software itself costs around $200 per copy. A classroom would need a scanner, though not

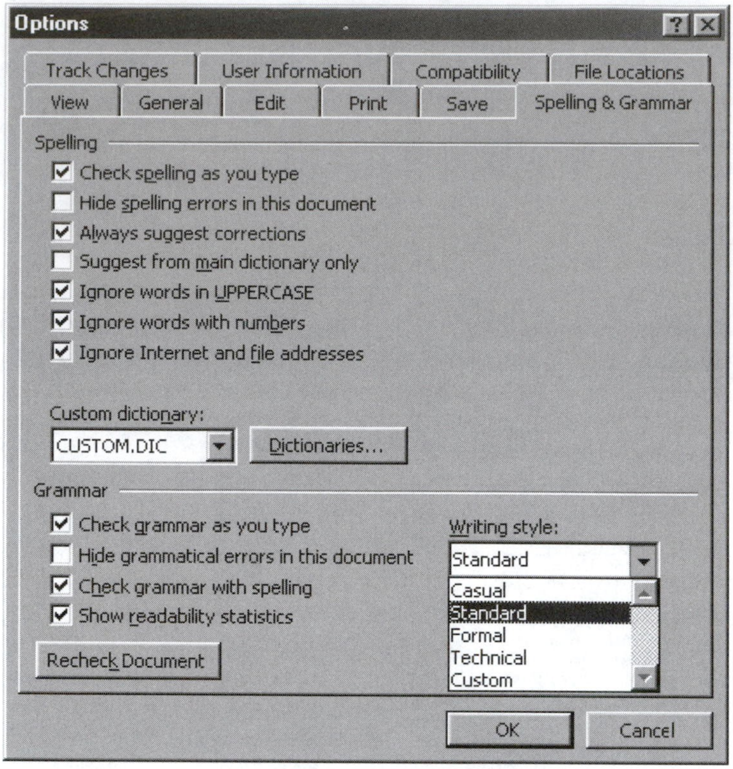

FIGURE 9.9 ■ Choose Your Writing Style

an expensive one. West (1998) lists six different activities for which she uses text read-ing software in her elementary school classroom, including:

- On-screen note taking
- Modified reading activities
- On-screen talking worksheets
- Creative writing activity
- Sight/articulation word practice
- A talking word processor

West has successfully used text-reading software to work with mainstreamed chil-dren with learning disabilities. She reports that "of the thirty-one students in my fifth grade classroom, nine tested at a second or third grade reading level and qualified for special education help. Three of these students had poor motor skills which made writing a long, difficult task. Attention Deficit Disorder and a lack of motivation were also challenges." Though her students were not measured against a control group, they were pre- and post-tested. She reports that for the nine students, "year-end test results showed increased fluency, decoding, and vocabulary skills."

There is also some evidence that this use of computers helps at least some children to *learn* to read. Richard Sirase (1997) completed a small study with thirteen children and concluded that scanned text read by a computer does benefit elementary children with "global" reading delay. He could find no evidence that scanned text is helpful for children with specific reading problems. This is only a preliminary study, and much work needs to be done in this area. Enough evidence exists to suggest that if you have children in your class who have reading problems for whom proven methods fail and you have the resources, a scanner and text-reading software might help.

■ SUMMARY

This is a short chapter, but not because word processing is unimportant. It is short because, of all the computer-based instruction tools, many teachers are already most familiar with using the word processor to teach writing and have methods for teaching with it. Word processors make writing faster, easier to edit, and easier to read. For students who do not write well with pencils, word processing software removes the barrier that prevents people from reading and understanding their work. For students who do not *read* well, a word processor is an integral tool in the text reading process. Word processors also perform many of the same functions as presentation software. Given an assignment that requires students to summarize and organize information (writing a brochure, outline, or newspaper) the word processor provides a medium that allows students to focus on constructing products that convey information effectively. Table 9.2 summarizes the instructional applications for the spreadsheet. The challenge is having sufficient computer resources to use these methods effectively.

TABLE 9.2 ■ Bloom's Taxonomy and the Word Processor

Level of Thought	Description	Word Processing Ability
Knowledge	Name, locate, tell, list, repeat, point to	Spell checking
Comprehension	Define, summarize, infer, project, describe	Sorting; supply the missing (words, paragraphs, pictures); remove the extra (words, sentences, paragraphs, pictures); thesaurus
Application	Use	Grammar checker; thesaurus; editing and revision
Analysis	Compare, classify, screen, test for, examine	Following directions; research report; journaling; lab notes
Synthesis	Create, develop, build, design, compile, generate	Writing directions; newspaper; brochure; creative writing
Evaluation	Judge, critique, rank	

✔ CHECKING YOUR UNDERSTANDING

9.2

1. Write a 500-word paper on using the word processor to improve student vocabulary and writing skills, in a content area of your choice. Your paper should be written with the "casual" style chosen in the grammar-checker dialogue box. Grade level should be 5–6.

   ■ Check your paper with the "standard" style chosen in the grammar-checker dialogue box. Rewrite to accommodate the two following restrictions: grade level should be 8–9; passive sentences should be below 10 percent.

   ■ Check your paper with the "technical" style chosen in the grammar-checker dialogue box. Rewrite so the grade level is 7–8.

   ■ Check your paper with the "formal" style chosen in the grammar-checker dialogue box. Rewrite so the grade level is 7–8.

2. Write a brochure describing the features of word processors and Internet communications activities that help students write better. Design your layout with a bi-fold (three panel) landscape orientation, using a table to help you place your text and graphics. The audience for your brochure is your students' parents.

■ REFERENCES ■

Cope, D. (2000). *The effect of a spell checker on the spelling ability of high school students.* Unpublished Master's Thesis, Boise State University, Boise, Idaho.

Diamond, J. (1999). *Guns, germs, and steel.* New York: W. W. Norton and Co.

Microsoft (1997). "Word documentation for grammar checker." Accessed online.

Sirase, R. (1997). "Using scanners linked to talking computers as tools for teaching children to read." *British Journal of Educational Technology.* Vol. 28, No. 4, pp. 308–310, October 1997.

West, P. (1998). *Integration of text reading software in an elementary school setting.* Unpublished Master's Thesis, Boise State University, Boise, Idaho.

■ ANNOTATED RESOURCES ■

Dowling, C. (1999), *Writing and learning with computers.* Acer Press, available from Stylus Publishing at http://www.styluspub.com.

Writing and word processors

Although the book is not only about word processors, three of the eight chapters are devoted to writing and word processors, including discussions of the writing process and classroom activities using the word processor. The remaining chapters focus on writing and the Internet, and writing and multimedia.

Pedler, J. (2001). "Computer spell checkers and dyslexics." *British Journal of Educational Technology.* January 2001, vol. 32, no. 1.

Computers and dyslexics

Although the focus of this study is on improving spell checkers for use by dyslexics, the article could be read to obtain a methodology for analyzing the kinds of errors that dyslexics make. As a result, teachers could help students analyze their errors with the use of the spell checker.

CHAPTER 10

Databases: What They Are and How They Work

OBJECTIVES

- Describe the functional difference between a list (table) view and a form view in a database.
- Predict how an ascending or descending sort on a given database will look.
- Describe the pattern of information that a query will yield.
- Know when to use a sort and when to use a query.
- Explain the difference in the kind of information in rows and columns of a table.
- Explain why an electronic database with a database engine is more than a collection of facts.

The following are skills you should know and practice before your read chapters 9, 10, 11, and 12.

- Set up a table
- Do simple and complex queries
- Build a report
- Distinguish between design view and data sheet view
- Explain and identify fields and records in list or table view
- Do ascending and descending sorts
- Build a form
- Format fields (text, date, numeric, etc.)
- Understand how to use Boolean terms to write queries

Many people understand that databases are collections of facts, and they are. However, electronic databases are *more* than just collections of facts. They provide tools for a skilled user to detect patterns among the facts from which they are built. The next question is, "What kind of patterns would people want to detect?" To begin to answer this question and to help you make the connection between databases and their practical

More than a collection of facts

applications, we will begin with three brief narratives describing how people use databases outside of schools.

■ SOLVING PROBLEMS OUTSIDE THE CLASSROOM: THREE STORIES

A Business Problem

Projecting trends and making predictions

Cornell Andrews is a buyer for a department store chain. He has worked hard, made good choices, and received promotions. He graduated from college twenty years ago—before electronic databases were such a key to being successful in his job. In the old days he would buy "by the seat of his pants." He had a sixth sense about what would be popular and when. After fifteen years he was handling accounts worth millions of dollars a year.

Then his lead began to erode. Younger buyers' sales volume moved closer and closer to his. Soon he was just an average buyer, and finally he began to fall behind. What was the problem? He went to Ann, one of the most successful buyers in his area, and asked her how she could be so right so often. Ann showed Cornell her database. By keeping a record of all the items she buys and how soon the items are sold, with the electronic database she was able to construct seasonal profiles of the best sellers as well as predict color and fabric combinations that would be successful.

A Scientific Problem

Describing unknowns

Susan Pacheco is an astronomer. She works for NASA and is the lead scientist analyzing information that is being returned to her computer from a deep space probe. The probe was launched ten years ago to study the furthermost reaches of the solar system. Information on Uranus has been coming in for more than a year now. She gets information on temperature, amounts of certain gasses at specific locations in space, and readings that indicate the location of solid bodies in space.

She puts all of this information into a database and then goes to work on her hunches. She relentlessly asks questions of the database, reformulating and refining her ideas. At last, with all the data gathered and all the questions asked, Susan realizes that she and her team have discovered a new moon circling Uranus.

An Ethical and Sociological Problem

Analyzing problems

Gary Johnson is an insurance company employee. He is working feverishly on a key project for the company. The state legislature is debating changing the speed limit from 65 miles an hour to 75 miles per hour. Opponents say that more people will be killed and insurance rates will go up if the speed limit is raised. Those in favor of the bill say that people will just get places faster. Gary's insurance company doesn't know and needs to know how his company should approach this issue.

One way Gary decides he can find out is to build a database of defining characteristics of past accidents. Then, by asking questions of the database, Gary hopes to find some patterns, like the conditions under which crashing at 75 miles per hour are most and least deadly, and how they compare to fatal accidents where the speed is less. Millions of dollars are at stake for both his company and consumers.

Databases Help People Think about Difficult Problems

People use databases widely in business, the professions, and science to enable them to sort through and analyze immense amounts of information. When people hear the term "database," they most commonly think of a place to find a specific fact or answer to a question. An almanac, for example, is a database. When people use an almanac in its print form they look up facts like the population of a country, its major products, or statistics about crime or education.

But what happens when a print database, like an almanac, is placed inside of a database engine (like Microsoft Works, or Claris Works, or Microsoft Access) on a computer? Then people can use databases to sift through the raw material to help them analyze complex problems. Why? Because a computer can reconfigure large amounts of information into many different patterns far more quickly than humans can with their minds, a pencil, and a piece of paper.

If all of the information in a print almanac were placed in an electronic database, then the almanac would become a much more potent tool. The difference to the user would be something like using a table saw rather than a handsaw. A table saw makes faster, more precise cuts just as an electronic database finds information faster and more precisely than people do when they use a print-based database. Used skillfully, databases provide the bridge between individual, seemingly unrelated facts and the synthesis that allows a user to describe unknowns, make predictions, and render judgments.

> Databases supply relationships

■ DATABASES IN THE CLASSROOM

An eleventh-grade American History class is studying Native American culture and history. Students have learned about Native Americans in different regions of the country and are nearly finished studying the major tribes of each region. Over the course of the unit they have built a database of Native American tribes, their main foods, clothing, and environmental challenges. The students are now ready for their major synthesis activity for Native American cultures.

FIELD TRIP 10.1

Databases and Native Americans

The teacher poses this problem for the class:

"As we have learned, Native American cultures weren't all the same. Cultures varied across the country, depending on the local resources and on the history of each tribes. If you were a Native American back then, depending upon the culture and the region in which you lived your answer to each of the following questions would be different: What would you eat? Where would you sleep? How would you stay warm? How would you get clothing? What would you do for fun? How long would you live? What would happen to you when you became ill?

The teacher poses a problem

Pretend, for this exercise, that you have come to America on a boat with the Pilgrims, and have decided that Pilgrim life is not for you. You strike out into the forest on your own, looking for a culture and lifestyle that suits you better. Which Native American tribe would you fit into best?"

After the teacher posed the problem, the students went to the computers in groups of five to do preliminary planning. Together they agreed upon a lifestyle for the sake of exploring the problem together. Later each student used a similar process to do the exercise alone.

Students see the solution more realistically

Students in one group decided that they would be most interested in being the member of a tribe that travels extensively, uses horses, lives in a warm climate, has plenty to eat, and has a long life expectancy. Together the students formulated the questions that would yield the name of the perfect tribe from the database. As they worked they discovered that they had to make some compromises because they found that no tribe was able to live in such continual prosperity. Then they began debating what to give up: Perhaps it should be the horses (if you are full and warm it might be better than having a horse and being cold or hungry).

Working with a database is iterative

After some practice together, students distributed themselves through the four centers in the classroom and began their individual database assignments. Students began by formulating questions. Then as computers become available they tested their questions, recorded the answers, and returned to their seats to rewrite and summarize the information they received from the database as well as write more questions. When the computers were not available, students did assigned reading, worksheets, and worked on maps of sixteenth century America. The teacher moved through the classroom, tutoring and asking questions. Occasionally she noticed that several students were having trouble with the same question and gave short mini-lectures to the whole class, giving them information about content or how to formulate better questions for the database.

Using database info to construct a presentation

After students had asked the questions of the database that enabled them to analyze the information and draw conclusions, they created a hypermedia presentation describing the Native American tribe they wanted to join and why they wanted to join it. Because there are only five computers in the classroom, they began this report with a hand-written storyboard. Then, over the course of two weeks, they rotated through the computer centers to get computer time to finish their work. They presented their work to the class and compared what they learned and inferred from the database to information they gleaned in encyclopedia articles and other reference works.

How Do Databases Support Student Learning?

Students, like their counterparts in the work world, process large amounts of information. When people use electronic databases, they not only access large amounts of information but also use that information to reason and draw conclusions if they know how to ask the right questions of the database. When students cover information, they usually memorize definitions, do worksheets, read books, listen to the teacher talk about the subject, and participate in discussions with their classmates. The database builds the bridges among rote memory work, reading, classroom discussions, and reports. In between learning facts and making judgments about what the facts mean, the students derive opportunities from the database to make some sense of the facts—to analyze them.

There has not been much empirical research done on the effects of database use in classrooms. Some studies show positive effects of database use relating to student skills in question asking (Ennals, 1995), classification (Underwood, 1985), and learning in science (Hecht, 1993). Both Jonassen (2000) and Grabe & Grabe (1996) build a case for the use of databases despite the lack of much research at this point. Their reasoning is based on students' use of higher-order thinking skills to complete database assignments. Based on that, we can reasonably assume that databases improve student learning. The challenge for the future is to further investigate this hypothesis and to define exactly how, what, and why students learn with databases.

> The value of databases lies in the higher-order thinking skills they promote

Also, databases are not equally effective across all content areas and grade levels. There are some uses for databases in a mathematics class. There are relatively more uses for databases in social science classes (such as history, government, economics, and psychology), in language arts and literature, and in the sciences—especially the sciences in which classification is key such as biology and geology. Students' ability to use a database differs by grade level and cognitive ability, as well.

> Databases are useful in most content areas

Field experience has proven that third-graders can understand the concept of a database when the teacher guides the class through an exploration of a topic. Some time during the fourth or fifth grade, students can begin to use small, pre-made or teacher-made databases effectively. By the time children reach junior high, their cognitive abilities are such that they can both create databases themselves and use large pre-made databases.

> Less useful in the primary grades

Databases have been used effectively with at-risk students as well. In a year-long study in a government class at an alternative school in Idaho, at-risk students used databases to predict the next president of the United States. They also completed a project that included choosing the worst war in which the United States has been involved (Fisher, 1996). Students and the teacher were trained to use the database software, but the project started slowly because the students could not see the point in what they were doing.

> At-risk students use databases successfully

Once the students began the actual assignments their skills improved, and they used the database to guide them as they completed their projects. By the end of the project, the students worked with the database and stayed on task as they began to understand how to ask meaningful questions of the database. When they understood that the skills they were learning would transfer to the work world, they expressed even more interest in learning how to use databases effectively.

What Do Students and Teachers Need to Know?

Everyone needs three different types of skills to use databases successfully. First, students *and* teachers need the nuts-and-bolts skills to build a database and navigate an existing one. Second, they need conceptual understanding that will enable them to perform sorts and queries (use filters). Third, they need analytical skills to interpret the resulting information and make inferences. Before we look at how a teacher builds a database lesson like the one on Native Americans, consider some basic terminology and concepts.

> Fundamental skills

■ GETTING STARTED: TEACHING THE TOOL

No matter what kind of computer or database software you use, you will find that databases from different software manufacturers have many common features. After all, they perform the same functions. They help us manipulate words and numbers to make predictions, describe unknown places, people, ideas, objects, or animals, and make decisions or analyze information. A person needs to understand the following concepts (listed in the order which they are explained):

- Form View
- Field
- Record
- Table View (List View)
- Sort
- Query (Find, Filter)

Students need to know these terms well enough so that a teacher can give instructions such as:

- "Do a descending sort on the *weight* field."
- "Find the *record* for 'black bears.'"
- "Do a query to find all of the records of presidents who went to college and were married."

As your students get better at using databases, they should be able to generate these kinds of tasks for themselves. For example, a student might write a position paper defending the 75-mile-an-hour speed limit on freeways. As the student searches for facts to support the argument, she or he might say, "I want to find out how many people were killed last year in traffic accidents in the states that have speed limits of 75 mph and in states that have speed limits of 65 mph. So, I will go to the database, and I will perform a query on 'speed limit equals 75 and deaths greater than some number per thousand.' Then I will do the same thing for states with speed limits of 65 miles per hour."

Most students will not reach this degree of sophistication quickly. It will take two or three database projects in several subjects, and there are some students who will never make such a sophisticated connection. Nevertheless, any student may someday become an anthropologist who uses databases to make inferences about ancient cultures, or a worker in the parts department of an auto supply store who uses a database to find the right part for your car. The tool can help students think about the information they must learn in school and provide them with skills they can use when they enter the work world.

Students must know how to use the tool before you give them a complex assignment

Form View

People who use databases usually work with them in two different formats. The format in Figure 10.1 is called "form view" because it represents a paper form that once would have been filled in with pencil or pen. The white rectangles on the form (which once were blank) are called *fields*. The information that is typed into each field is the field's *value* or *property*. For example, the field named Tribe has the property "Tlingt."

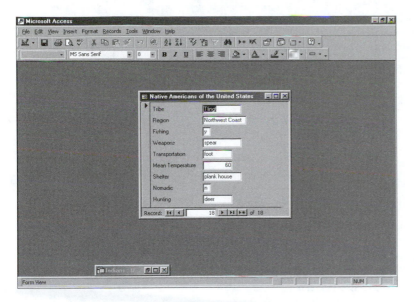

FIGURE 10.1 ■ Form View of Native American Database

When you design the record structure for a database, it is helpful to students if the first field in the record reflects the main idea of the database. In this example, the database is about tribes, so Tribe is the name of the first field on the record form.

The nine fields on this form comprise one *record*. As you can imagine, there are multiple records in this database—one record for each tribe. No two records have exactly the same field properties—unless there are duplicate records.

Someone who is putting new information into this database would start with a blank record and use the Tab key to move from field to field, typing information in each field.

Table View or List View

(Some database software calls the second viewing format "table view," and some software calls it "list view." In this book we will use both names together.) Information that has been put into the database using the form view that we just explored can also be viewed (or—for that matter—*entered*) in tabular format. Figure 10.2 shows eighteen records, each in a row of nine cells that represent the nine fields of the form view. Read across a single row to see all the properties of an individual tribe. Read down a single column to see the different values for each tribe in the field which that column represents.

Someone putting information in the database using this format would also use the Tab key to move from field to field (or with some software, the direction keys in the numeric key pad). Working in table or list view can be a faster way to enter data than the form view, but beginning users may find the form view more intuitive.

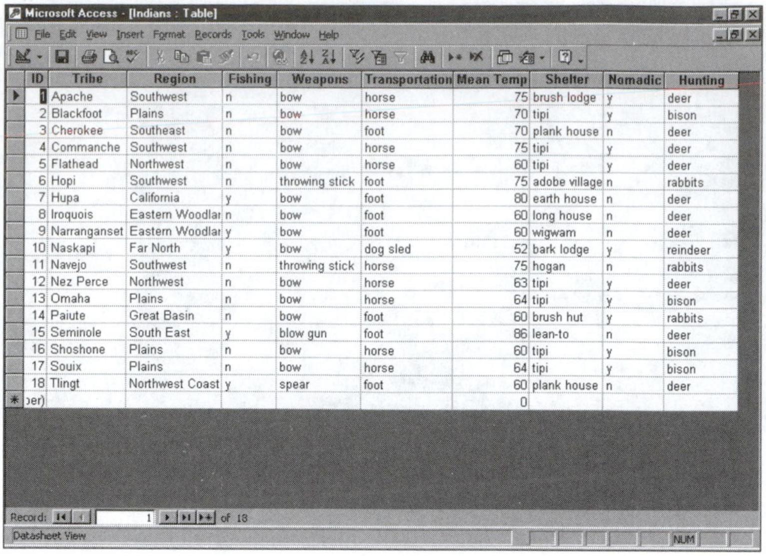

ID	Tribe	Region	Fishing	Weapons	Transportation	Mean Temp	Shelter	Nomadic	Hunting
1	Apache	Southwest	n	bow	horse	75	brush lodge	y	deer
2	Blackfoot	Plains	n	bow	horse	70	tipi	y	bison
3	Cherokee	Southeast	n	bow	foot	70	plank house	n	deer
4	Commanche	Southwest	n	bow	horse	75	tipi	y	deer
5	Flathead	Northwest	n	bow	horse	60	tipi	y	deer
6	Hopi	Southwest	n	throwing stick	foot	75	adobe village	n	rabbits
7	Hupa	California	y	bow	foot	80	earth house	n	deer
8	Iroquois	Eastern Woodlar	n	bow	foot	60	long house	n	deer
9	Narranganset	Eastern Woodlar	y	bow	foot	60	wigwam	n	deer
10	Naskapi	Far North	y	bow	dog sled	52	bark lodge	y	reindeer
11	Navejo	Southwest	n	throwing stick	horse	75	hogan	n	rabbits
12	Nez Perce	Northwest	n	bow	horse	63	tipi	y	deer
13	Omaha	Plains	n	bow	horse	64	tipi	y	bison
14	Paiute	Great Basin	n	bow	foot	60	brush hut	y	rabbits
15	Seminole	South East	y	blow gun	foot	86	lean-to	n	deer
16	Shoshone	Plains	n	bow	horse	60	tipi	y	bison
17	Souix	Plains	n	bow	horse	64	tipi	y	bison
18	Tlingt	Northwest Coast	y	spear	foot	60	plank house	n	deer
ber)						0			

FIGURE 10.2 ■ Table or List View of Native American Database

✓ CHECKING YOUR UNDERSTANDING

10.1

You may be wondering about topics in your content area and how they might be used to generate a database. Some topics are good for databases and others are not. In order to learn which kinds of topics are most suitable for databases, try the exercise below. Get a piece of scratch paper or index card and cover the answers to the list of possible topics for a database listed below. As you look at each topic, write down whether you think it could be the foundation for a database-supported lesson. Write "yes" if it could be used for a database or "no" if it could not. If your answer is "yes," then write down five related ideas that could serve as fields in your database. Then uncover the answer and explanation written in italics below the question.

Question 1: Short Stories

Yes, a database could support a lesson on short stories. Such a database would include the following kinds of information if a class were studying theme, character, and setting. If you are an English teacher, you might be able to think of other fields that could be included in the database. The kinds of information include:

- The socioeconomic status of the female and male characters
- Time period in which the story was written
- Occupations of the characters
- Time of year when the story takes place
- Theme (man against man/man against nature/man against himself/man against God)
- Philosophy (romantic, existential, etc.)

Question 2: Socialist Governments

"Socialist governments" would be another good candidate for a database. Some of the fields that could be included in the database are listed below:

- Name of countries with socialist government
- Time periods when the socialist government ruled the country
- Attitudes toward women
- Attitudes toward private property
- Productivity
- An environmental consciousness rating
- Gross national product
- Size of the military
- Length of time the government has been or was in existence

Question 3: Diagramming a Sentence

No, diagramming a sentence would not be a good topic for a database. Diagramming sentences is something that children **do.** An English teacher might use a database to teach parts of speech, but diagramming sentences is an event with steps.

Question 4: Biomes

"Biomes" is another example of a unit that could be enriched with a database. Examples of biomes are tundra, grasslands, northern coniferous forests, deciduous forests, deserts, and tropical rain forests. Some fields related to biomes are:

- Annual precipitation
- Plant life
- Animal life
- Temperature

Here is another question for you. Would the **examples of biomes** listed above (tundra, grasslands, etc.) be listed in a database as fields? Yes, they would. Examples of biomes are like the names of Native American tribes in the Native American database in Figures 1 and 2. They are what the database is about, but they are a field, like any other field.

Question 5: Writing a Paragraph

Writing a paragraph is another poor candidate for a database. Again, writing a paragraph is something people **do,** not a group of related facts.

Question 6: How the Heart Works

How the heart works is not a good candidate for a database. Organ systems of the human body, on the other hand, would be a good topic for a database-supported lesson.

Question 7: Governments of the World

Yes, governments of the world would make an excellent foundation for a database-supported lesson. Examples of fields that would make up the database include:

- Kind of government (socialist, capitalist, etc.)
- Size of country
- Number of violent revolutions in last 200 years
- Do women have the vote?
- Population of country

As you can see, one key to the successful use of databases to support student learning is choosing the right topic. As you think about databases and the information that you teach, remember that databases

TABLE 10.1 ■ A Simple Database on Native Americans

Name	Food	Travel	Housing	Tools
Nez Perce	Deer	Horse	Pole covered with hides	Bow
Example	Value	Value	Value	Value
Example	Value	Value	Value	Value

are mostly about facts and their relationships. A database, in the language of Chapters 6 through 8, is a concept. Its columns are properties of the concept, and the rows are examples of the concept. A database can help people see the relationships between many seemingly unrelated facts. See Table 10.1.

10.2

Now it is time to create a database on a computer. Choose one of the topics from "Checking Your Understanding 10.1" that is appropriate for a database.

1. Using your database software set up the database. Create five fields and complete five records.

2. Print out one record in form view, and label your paper "Form View."

3. Print out the whole database in table or list view and label your paper accordingly.

4. On the printout of the entire database, write the name of the main idea that you are describing.

■ SORTS AND QUERIES

Database engines

Now that you know how information in a database is arranged in records and fields, your next task is to learn how to make the database work for you. The key to tapping into the incredible, analytic power that lies dormant in a database is in the user's ability to formulate good questions.

One difference between a print database and electronic database is the "database engine." The "engine" for a print database is the user thumbing through the index, table of contents, and any other features that arrange information in the book for easy access. An electronic database offers more sophisticated techniques for extracting information. These techniques are called sorts and queries. Filter and find are synonymous for query in different brands of database software. A sort puts information in order, and a query extracts specific information or combinations of information from the database.

The Sort: Putting Information in Order

Sorts

Of the two major tools that a database provides, sort is the easier to understand and to work with. There are only four possibilities for a sort. They are displayed and defined in Table 10.2. Computers really only work with numbers, but programmers make it seem like the machine understands letters, too. Every letter and many symbols and sounds (like the beeps that you hear when your computer is booting up) have a num-

TABLE 10.2 ■ Kinds of Sorts

Direction of Sort	Description of Sort
A–Z	Ascending alpha sort
Z–A	Descending alpha sort
1–100	Ascending numeric sort
100–1	Descending numeric sort

ber associated with them called an ASCII code. When you tell the computer to do an "alpha" sort, it is really translating the letters on the screen to numbers and going from highest to lowest or lowest to highest. The result, however, is transparent to the user.

If you tell the computer to do a descending sort of the Tribe field in the Native American database, it will look at the first letter of every value in the Tribe column. Then it will rearrange the records in the database in reverse alphabetical order based on tribe names. Each row of the database, representing one record, is moved up or down in the table based on the alphabetical order of the value in the Tribe field. In the sort performed on the Native American database in Figure 10.3, all of the cells in the Tlingt record have moved to their new place in the database.

At first glance, the computer's ability to do a sort does not seem like much. Nevertheless, the utility of knowing how to do either a simple sort or a multiple-level sort can help people pluck information from large amounts of data. Put yourself in the place of the student in the American history class that is studying Native Americans and read the problem in Field Trip 10.2.

ID	Tribe	Region	Fishing	Weapons	Transportation	Mean Temp	Shelter	Nomadic	Hunting
18	Tlingt	Northwest Coast	y	spear	foot	60	plank house	n	deer
17	Souix	Plains	n	bow	horse	64	tipi	y	bison
16	Shoshone	Plains	n	bow	horse	60	tipi	y	bison
15	Seminole	South East	y	blow gun	foot	86	lean-to	n	deer
14	Paiute	Great Basin	n	bow	foot	60	brush hut	y	rabbits
13	Omaha	Plains	n	bow	horse	64	tipi	y	bison
12	Nez Perce	Northwest	n	bow	horse	63	tipi	y	deer
11	Navejo	Southwest	n	throwing stick	horse	75	hogan	n	rabbits
10	Naskapi	Far North	y	bow	dog sled	52	bark lodge	y	reindeer
9	Narranganset	Eastern Woodlar	y	bow	foot	60	wigwam	n	deer
8	Iroquois	Eastern Woodlar	n	bow	foot	60	long house	n	deer
7	Hupa	California	y	bow	foot	80	earth house	n	deer
6	Hopi	Southwest	n	throwing stick	foot	75	adobe village	n	rabbits
5	Flathead	Northwest	n	bow	horse	60	tipi	y	deer
4	Commanche	Southwest	n	bow	horse	75	tipi	y	deer
3	Cherokee	Southeast	n	bow	foot	70	plank house	n	deer
2	Blackfoot	Plains	n	bow	horse	70	tipi	y	bison
1	Apache	Southwest	n	bow	horse	75	brush lodge	y	deer

FIGURE 10.3 ■ Rows Sorted in Descending Order by Tribe

FIELD TRIP 10.2

A Student's Point of View

We rejoin the eleventh grade American History class working on their Native American database project. As one student works on the assignment to find the tribe that would be most suitable for her, she thought temperature would be a primary consideration. (She lives in the South and would like to go somewhere where it is a little cooler.) So she looked at her database and decided that even though "mean temperature" doesn't tell her everything, she can get a good idea of where the cool places are by doing an ascending sort on "Mean Temp."

Asking questions of the database

Figure 10.4 is the result of her sort. She got closer to her goal as she glanced at the names of the ten tribes that seem to live in cooler climates. Some of them seem a little too cool, but she isn't going to worry about that now. The next problem is to figure out which of them have horses, one of her other criteria.

Databases speed information analysis

In the case of the American Indian database, it would not be too difficult for the student to look for and write down names of tribes who live in lower temperatures along with the values of the rest of the fields in those records, requiring perhaps five or ten minutes. The database accomplished the same function in less than a second. The student can do many sorts on an electronic database in the same amount of time that it takes to do only one manual sort. Consider also the possibility of the student making clerical errors or dealing with a database consisting of fifty, a hundred, or even a thousand records. The power of the database to do a tedious job quickly and precisely is evident. Sorts combined with queries make an even more powerful tool. A query will help our student decide how to satisfy her next criterion. She wants to live with a tribe that has horses.

ID	Tribe	Region	Fishing	Weapons	Transportation	Mean Temp	Shelter	Nomadic	Hunting
10	Naskapi	Far North	y	bow	dog sled	52	bark lodge	y	reindeer
5	Flathead	Northwest	n	bow	horse	60	tipi	y	deer
9	Narranganset	Eastern Woodlan	y	bow	foot	60	wigwam	n	deer
18	Tlingt	Northwest Coast	y	spear	foot	60	plank house	n	deer
14	Paiute	Great Basin	n	bow	foot	60	brush hut	y	rabbits
16	Shoshone	Plains	n	bow	horse	60	tipi	y	bison
8	Iroquois	Eastern Woodlan	n	bow	foot	60	long house	n	deer
12	Nez Perce	Northwest	n	bow	horse	63	tipi	y	deer
13	Omaha	Plains	n	bow	horse	64	tipi	y	bison
17	Souix	Plains	n	bow	horse	64	tipi	y	bison
3	Cherokee	Southeast	n	bow	foot	70	plank house	n	deer
2	Blackfoot	Plains	n	bow	horse	70	tipi	y	bison
11	Navejo	Southwest	n	throwing stick	horse	75	hogan	n	rabbits
1	Apache	Southwest	n	bow	horse	75	brush lodge	y	deer
6	Hopi	Southwest	n	throwing stick	foot	75	adobe village	n	rabbits
4	Commanche	Southwest	n	bow	horse	75	tipi	y	deer
7	Hupa	California	y	bow	foot	80	earth house	n	deer
15	Seminole	South East	y	blow gun	foot	86	lean-to	n	deer

FIGURE 10.4 ■ Result of Ascending Sort on Temperature

✓ CHECKING YOUR UNDERSTANDING

Before you start on queries, make sure that you understand the mechanics of how a database works. Try the problem below. Cover up the answer in italics while you write your answer.

Problem: If you did a descending sort of the Mean Temp field, what information would be found in the first row of the database represented in table or list view? Write the values and check them against the answer below.

Seminole, South East, y, blow gun, foot, 86, lean-to, n, deer

The Query: Classifying Information

People classify information on a daily basis. Grocery stores, for example, are giant physical databases. When you walk into the store you look for cereal, then corn flakes, and finally a particular brand of corn flakes. Or, you go to the produce area of the store, look for apples, and then choose a Braeburn or Jonathan. The store is the database and you are the search engine. You know from experience that a good store is organized to help you find what you want quickly. The Yellow Pages of the telephone book is another example of a database. The difference between these two databases and an electronic database is the amount of time that it takes to find an item of information, especially if you don't know exactly what you are looking for.

Information in databases is even easier to find than products in stores if you know how. The tool that databases provide for finding information is called the *query* (synonyms are *filter* or *find*). To employ the query function, the user must have a small vocabulary of special words called comparison operators and logical operators. Comparison operators include the following symbols:

> Queries reveal patterns

- ■ is equal to (=)
- ■ is less than (<)
- ■ is greater than (>)
- ■ is less than or equal to (<=)
- ■ is greater than or equal to (>=)

Logical operators are the following words:

- ■ and
- ■ or
- ■ not

To form queries, combine comparison operators, logical operators, and the names of the ideas, places, or things. Thinking back to the student in the class who wants to find the Native American tribe to which s/he could adapt most easily, let's look at how the student might approach the problem with queries. Remember the student looking for a cooler climate whose sort resulted in Figure 10.4? Now she wants to find a tribe that used horses because they would be an advantage in both war and hunting.

In this situation, a sort is not really a possibility. Sorts order information, but they do not find specific pieces of information. Therefore, the student attacks the problem with a query. First she states the question in ordinary human language:

**Asking questions
of a database**

"Database, tell me the names of all the tribes that use horses for transportation."

Then she goes to the database and translates the question into language that it will understand by pressing the keys or using menus that are appropriate for whatever brand of database software is available in the classroom.

The procedure typically consists of several steps that are listed below.

1. Choose the field for comparison, in this case "Transportation."
2. Choose the criterion for comparison. In this case the student wants to find all entries in the field that are equal to (=) "horse."
3. Execute the search by choosing the appropriate function provided by the software.

The student's translation to the language of the database is made easy with the user interface shown in Figure 10.5. What you see there is the screen the student created just before pressing the "Apply Query" button. The database's response to the student's query is a list of every record in which horse is listed as transportation. Figure 10.6 shows the computer's response.

This database is small enough to allow the student to just look at the "Mean Temperature" column and the "Transportation" column and decide that she would like to live with either the Flathead or Shoshone or even the Nez Perce. However, a student who is dealing with a larger database with hundreds of records would need to do a

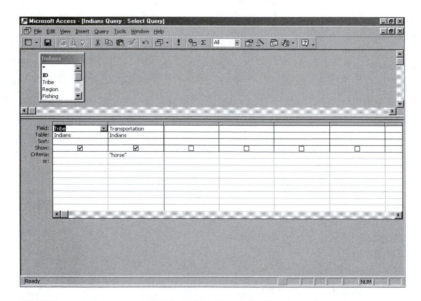

FIGURE 10.5 ■ Query for All Tribes Using Horses for Transportation

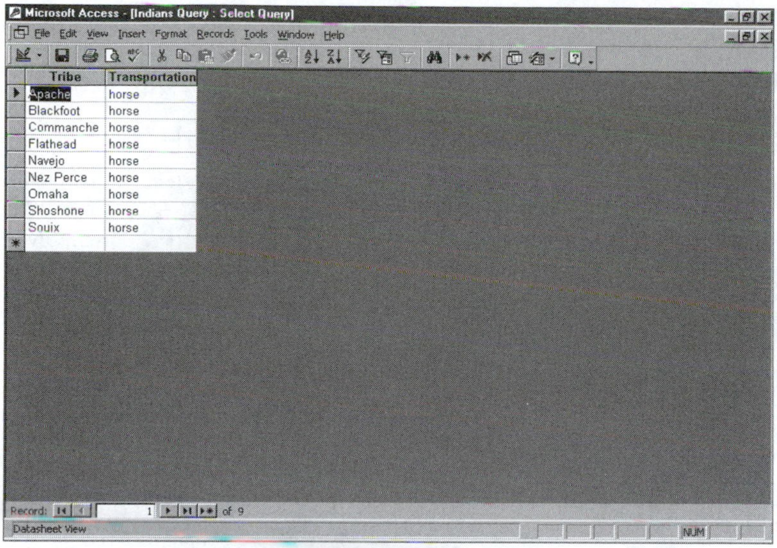

FIGURE 10.6 ■ Results of Query for All Tribes Using Horses for Transportation

query using conjunctions (the logical operators *and, or,* and *not*). If a student did such a query, the set-up would look something like Figure 10.7. The results of this query would give the student a look at just the records of interest. The results for the query in Figure 10.7 are shown in Figure 10.8.

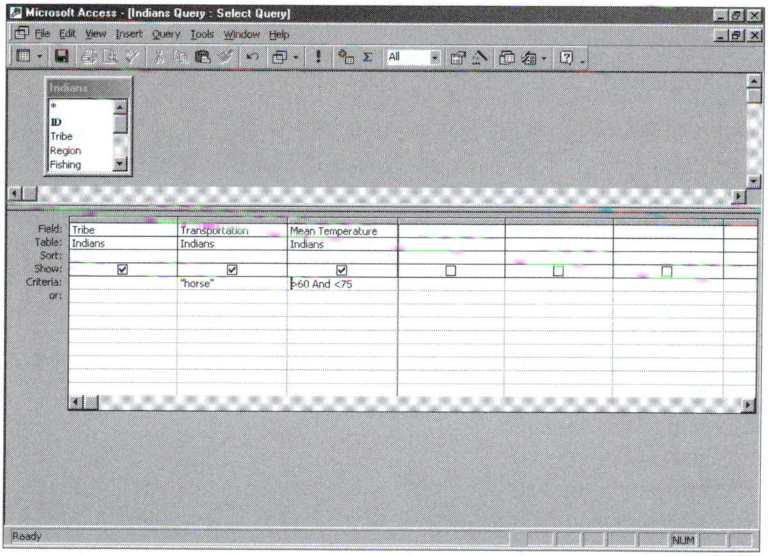

FIGURE 10.7 ■ A Query with More than One Criterion

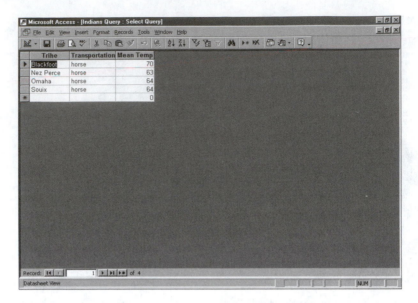

FIGURE 10.8 ■ Results of a Query Involving Temperature and Transportation

When teaching novice users, it is important to tell them that after they have performed a query, the other records have not disappeared. They are only hidden and can be seen again when the user tells the computer to show all of the records.

Grade Level Suggestions

The query in Figure 10.7 is quite complex. For a child to think independently of such a query and to enter it into a computer successfully requires cognitive abilities that not all children possess. An average fifth grader would not be able to do such an operation. Many seventh graders would also have difficulty, both with the skills for entering the query and the ability to think of such a complex query. If we were to analyze the task, we would find that the student would have to know or be able to do all of the following:

Adjusting database skills
to grade level

- Know why s/he is asking the question
- Understand how to phrase the question in ordinary language so that it is easy to translate into a language that a computer understands
- Understand that a query is needed and not a sort
- Understand which areas on the menu to click in order to get this query screen (Figure 10.7) to appear
- Understand inequalities
- Know how to use conjunctions
- Know how to interpret the results of the query and draw a conclusion (Figure 10.8)
- Know how to use the results of the question to generate more questions

This list of skills associated with queries shows that students are juggling eight different plates at the same time. Younger students or novice database users will have dif-

TABLE 10.3 ■ Task Analysis for Database Assignments and Recommendations for Teacher Assistance

Student task	Upper Elementary or Beginning Database User	Middle School (if student has used databases previously)	High School (if student has used databases previously)
Know why student is asking the question.	Needs assistance	Needs assistance	Student is independent
Understand how to phrase the question in ordinary language so that it is easy to translate to language a computer understands	Needs assistance	Student is independent	Student is independent
Understand that a query is needed and not a sort	Needs assistance	Student is independent	Student is independent
Understand which areas on the menu to click in order to get this menu screen to appear.	Student is independent	Student is independent	Student is independent
Know that a string (series of letters) needs quotes in order for the computer to interpret it correctly. This is not true of all software. Each database has its quirks, and this item is representative of the kinds of special action students need to do to make a database work.	Student is independent	Student is independent	Student is independent
Understand inequalities	Needs assistance	Student is independent	Student is independent
Know how to use conjunctions	Needs assistance or not applicable	Student is independent	Student is independent
Know how to interpret the results of a sort or query	Needs assistance	Needs an introduction and practice, then can work independently	Student is independent
Know how to use the results of the sort or query to generate more sorts and queries	Needs assistance	Needs an introduction and practice, then can work independently	Student is independent

ficulty with this procedure, while older or more experienced students should be expected to perform this routinely. There are ways of lightening the cognitive load on younger or less able students or those students who are just learning how to use databases no matter what their academic ability. In Table 10.3 are some suggestions for grade-level abilities and parts of the process with which teachers can assist students.

The assumption behind Table 10.3 is that students have had actual training in the use of database software. They would know which keys to press to go to form view or table view and how to do a simple sort or query. Table 10.4 (Thorsen, 1995) is a list of suggestions for the grade levels and database skill introduction.

How to Provide Student Assistance

Table 10.3 has many cells indicating that students need assistance. As you know, a teacher's time is at a premium. Considering everything that must be taught, we have little time to move around the classroom telling students which keys to press and in-

TABLE 10.4 ■ Database Skill Introduction in Grades K–12

Grade	Skill
3	Teacher demonstrates use of database in classroom projects
4	Use a teacher-made database to enhance learning in a lesson Enter data into a form and use sorts and queries to manipulate the data
5–6	Enter data into an existing database Recognize fields, records, files, and entries Compare paper and computer databases Move cursor around the database Use a database to make simple inferences
7	Use basic functions of a database (report generation and creation of address books) Enter data into a previously prepared template Make increasingly complex inferences by using the sort and query function of the database
8	Give examples of appropriate database use Plan and create a database Reinforce sort and query skills Use a database to explore content Generate reports Integrate database research into a word processed report
9	Have the following skills automated: sort, query Be fluent with the following terms: list view, form view, search criteria, conjunctions Use databases on a regular basis to solve problems and analyze information in science, social studies, and English
10–12	Create a form Add and delete fields in an existing database Add and delete records in an existing database Create reports from a database Arrange information using sorts and queries Query a database for specific information Edit, move, and change field properties and sizes Manipulate numeric fields—calculations Import and export database information to spreadsheets and documents Use software-specific help Use logical operators when querying a database Create macros to present database information Create links within a relation database Draw conclusions from a database query or report Use databases on a regular basis to solve problems and analyze information in science, social studies, and English

dividually guiding students from thought to thought as they attempt to use a database to get their thinking about a particular problem done. The solution to this problem lies in three different methods: teacher modeling, group work, and lesson templates.

Teacher modeling is important. The first time that you use a database to solve a problem with your class (whether they are third graders or twelfth graders new to databases), you will want to show the database on a computer projection device to the whole class. You will also want to choose a student who already knows how to use databases, or you should train one to operate the computer for you while you talk to the class.

Your best approach will be to downplay the mechanics (e.g., what keys to press to do a sort) and concentrate on the kinds of problems that the database can help your class solve. With a third-grade class you might have a database of dinosaurs and help them learn how to ask questions such as:

> **Teach the value of asking questions before the mechanics of sorts and queries**

- "Which dinosaurs ate plants?"
- "Which dinosaurs ate animals?"
- "Were dinosaurs that ate animals generally bigger or smaller than dinosaurs that ate plants?"

As you work with students, gradually move from being the only source of questions to guiding the class as they ask questions of the database. At the end of a class database activity, you will want to require some kind of product of the students such as a short paragraph or story that summarizes the information and inferences that they have made from both their questions and yours.

> **Be sure their questions lead to a conclusion**

Small-group work is also important. Once students understand what databases do and have a *general* idea of the meaning of the terms record, field, table view, form view, sort, and query, the next step is to teach them the specific meanings of those terms. This can be done in a five-computer classroom with small groups. A fun activity to help students learn the mechanics of how to use a database is a database of the class itself.

> **Groups database work uses high-level skills**

For this project the students decide what they want to know about the class members. Together with the teacher, the students brainstorm field headings such as favorite food, favorite book, age, height, gender, favorite subject, favorite musical group, and so on.

> **Students set up a database**

The teacher has to help students understand that information must be entered consistently in order for the database to be usable. For example, the class has to decide whether Gender will be entered as boy/girl or as m/f. Numbers also must be consistent. When students talk about the Height field, they need to decide whether the measurement will be metric or English. If they decide on the English system of measurement, for example, they need to decide which would be more useful, feet and inches or just inches. These kinds of questions all help students think more carefully and develop foresight and planning skills.

Once the teacher and students have selected and defined the fields, each student writes the name of each field and his or her own information on a three-by-five-inch card. Depending on the age of the students, either the students themselves enter the information or the teacher or an aide enters the information into a class database.

If students enter the information themselves, they get many good lessons in the importance of spelling and accuracy. One good strategy is to have the students enter information and not caution them ahead of time about the importance of accuracy. Then, as the class tries to do sorts and queries which are either inaccurate or do not work at all, the teacher can point out the reason why. For this strategy to be successful, the teacher needs to have entered all of the information accurately ahead of time and have disks ready to hand out or the correct database accessible on the network once students see how and why they have failed. Then the lesson can move forward. The process creates some confusion and consternation, but students are generally more careful about their spelling when they use databases after such an experience.

One variation on this exercise is to have the students not write their name, but rather give each student a secret letter or number as an identifier. One of the activities for the class can then be to guess the name of the person represented by each letter in the database. One fifth grade teacher uses this activity as an icebreaker at the beginning of the year. Over the summer she sends a survey to her new students requesting all of the information she needs and enters the information into the database herself so that it is ready for the first week of class.

The culmination of the lesson after students have an accurate class database in front of them is a series of sorts and queries. The teacher provides the questions and the students work in groups to provide the answers. Students rotate so that each one gets to press keys at the keyboard, but the student at the keyboard may only strike a key when told which key to strike by the rest of the group. This activity may be performed as a class under the direct supervision of the teacher, or it may be performed from a worksheet as a center with students writing their responses.

Not all students will be able to work on a database independently after this exercise. However, all will have a better grasp of the skills necessary to operate a database. Students working in groups will have enough skill to do a database assignment in a content area after this exercise if the assignment is well planned and written.

■ PLANNING YOUR DATABASE

Planning a database is a high-level thinking activity

Planning the database is a key element in making any database assignment work. If you are building the database yourself, then it should work flawlessly for your students. If it doesn't, they will be confused and the value of the lesson could be lost in the resulting chaos. Planning databases that students will create themselves is an excellent way for them to work with content. They have to think carefully about the content of the database and how they will use it. As students plan the fields of the database, they will discover two important pieces of information about the topic they are studying:

1. First, they will have to decide on field names for the topic.
2. Next, they will have to decide on a consistent method for expressing the contents of each field.

Data should be formated carefully

Numbers present a challenge for students. For example, students will have to determine how to represent temperature in the Native American database. Will they use sixty degrees, 60°, or 60° F, or just 60? Whatever they decide should make sorts and queries easy. When they understand how a sort works, they will learn to put measurement data in the column heading (insert it as part of the field name) and have numbers as the only entry in the field. They will also learn that there are special formats for date and time as well as currency and that being careful about these formats makes a great deal of difference in the usability of the database.

Text also presents a challenge for the novice database user. If some of the entries in the transportation field are spelled "horse" and some are spelled "horses," the database will not give an accurate response to student's queries about which tribes used horses for transportation.

Another pitfall students often overlook is putting a space before an entry, whether it is text or numeric. The computer sees the space as a character and will sort the contents of the field according to the ASCII code assigned to the space, not the first letter of the word or the first numeral in the number. These errors are particularly problematic because the space is invisible. When you are working on your own database or with students as they create their databases, this is a common error that is difficult to spot if it is not in a checklist of "debugging" strategies in your head.

✔ CHECKING YOUR UNDERSTANDING

10.4

Now that you have focused on what databases can do, it is time for you to try your skills. Below is a set of eight questions about a database of mammals. Fields in this database include: height, color, nocturnal/diurnal, herbivore/carnivore, life span, habitat, length of reproductive cycle, and number of young per birth. Put a card or piece of paper over the answer to each question. Then answer the following question: Would you **sort** the "Animals" database or **query** the "Animals" database to get the data that you need?

Question 1: What is the tallest animal?

(Sort)

Question 2: What are the names of all nocturnal carnivores?

(Query)

Question 3: Which animal has the most young per birth?

(Sort)

Question 4: Which animals have a reproductive cycle greater than 60 days and less than 100 days?

(Query)

Question 5: Which animals are herbivores and live more than 10 years?

(Query)

Question 6: Which animal has the longest reproductive cycle?

(Sort)

Question 7: Are there any animals that are nocturnal and white?

(Query)

Question 8: Which animal has the shortest reproductive cycle?

(Sort)

Question 9: Are there any animals that live on the tundra and are black?

(Query)

10.5

Here is another set of questions for you. Below is the name of each field in the "Animals" database. While you cover the answer, decide how each field should be formatted so that the database will yield accurate search results. Below, in italics, is a suggested answer.

Height

(Inches or centimeters)

Color

(A text string chosen from a list of colors—avoid using many different colors unless the distinction is important)

Time When Most Active

(Nocturnal/Diurnal)

Food Preference

(Herbivore/Carnivore)

Life Span

(Days)

Habitat

(Name of a biome [tundra, deciduous forest, etc.])

Length of Reproductive Cycle

(Days)

Number of Young Per Birth

(A number [3, 5, 8, etc.])

■ SUMMARY

Databases are powerful tools used by many different kinds of organizations to help them access information efficiently. A database is as useful to an automotive parts store sales associate as to a NASA scientist.

Basic skills for using databases include understanding how information is formatted and set up in tables and analyzed using sorts and queries. It is important that teachers ensure that their students understand these basic skills before they ask them to work independently with databases. Students are motivated to learn these skills when you demonstrate the power of the database by showing them how to ask questions and solve problems with the information they receive.

It is often better to encourage groups to manipulate databases together rather than assign students to work on projects alone. When students in groups brainstorm questions and how to format them so the computer can understand them together, they are often more successful than when they work alone.

■ REFERENCES ■

Ennals, R. (1987). "Micro-prolog and classroom historical research." Chapter in Ivan Reid and James Rushton (Eds.). *Teachers, computers, and the classroom.* Manchester, England: Manchester University Press.

Fisher, T. S. (1996). Integrating computer database applications into the social studies curriculum. Master's Thesis, Boise State University.

Grabe, M., & Grabe, C. (1996). *Integrating technology for meaningful learning.* Geneva, IL: Houghton Mifflin Company.

Hecht, J. B., Dwyer, D. J., Roberts, N. K., Schoon, P. L., Kelly, J., Parsons, J., Nietzke, T., & Virlee, M. (1993). *Project homeroom second year experiences: A final report on the project in the Maine East High School, New Trier High School, Amos Alonzo Stagg High School.* Illinois State University. ERIC (ED366638).

Jonassen, D. (2000). Computers as mindtools for schools. Upper Saddle River: Merrill.

Underwood, J. D. M. (1987). Chapter in Ivan Reid and James Rushton (Eds.). *Teachers, computers, and the classroom.* Manchester, England: Manchester University Press.

CHAPTER 11

Building a Database-Supported Lesson

OBJECTIVES

- Describe three kinds of problems to which databases apply.
- Know the steps and products in a database assignment.
- Write an appropriate problem.
- Develop database-supported lessons for three kinds of problems.

■ TEMPLATES FOR BUILDING DATABASE-SUPPORTED LESSONS

Teacher-made lesson templates provide students with a great deal of guidance and provide the bridge between directed and independent activity. Building a lesson template takes some time and thought, but the result is a product that will substitute for and improve upon a number of traditional activities. Some traditional activities that can be replaced when an appropriate database is available include answering end-of-chapter questions, writing and memorizing definitions, and doing worksheets.

Database lessons can be divided into three categories: describing an unknown, making a prediction, or making a decision. The process a teacher uses to create a template for each category is very similar. Once a teacher knows how to define a problem or set up a case, creating the rest of the lesson falls into place. Table 11.1 lists some examples of databases that we have talked about already as well as some new examples of topics for databases. These topics are classified according to one of the categories of problems (describe an unknown, etc.) listed above.

This chapter will be devoted to teaching you how to create templates for students to explore these different kinds of problems. The activities in these templates promote

TABLE 11.1 ■ Topics for Databases

Describe an Unknown	Make a Decision or Analyze a Problem	Make a Prediction
Find a city, country, culture, county, or state different from yours in specific ways & describe it.	Trace the changing role of women/men during historical (literary) time periods.	Describe the kind of person the next president (governor in your state) will be.
Describe a planet, moon, or star that contrasts sharply with our own.	What was the worst war in the history of the world?	Predict the country in which the next major war will occur.
Find and describe an animal (plant, rock, celestial object, culture, time period) with certain characteristics.	Make a list of the five best occupations suited to your skills and personality.	Predict the next five animals that will become extinct.

those higher-order thinking skills that help students understand and make judgments about the content they are learning.

✔ CHECKING YOUR UNDERSTANDING

11.1

At this point, these kinds of lessons are not packaged commercially with textbooks. Teachers must make their own lessons, and students sometimes must build their own databases. Building a database is not especially exciting, but neither is answering questions at the end of a chapter or doing worksheets. The added value for a student building a database is, once students have entered the facts into the database, they may manipulate them for analysis. This is not possible for students who have finished a worksheet or answered end-of-chapter questions except through class discussion.

Look back at the three introductory vignettes at the beginning of Chapter 10 and answer the following questions. The answers are listed at the end of this exercise.

Questions

1. In which vignette is an unknown described?
2. In which vignette is someone trying to make a prediction?
3. In which vignette is someone making a decision?
4. Re-read the database lesson on Native Americans. Was the assignment to describe an unknown, make a prediction, or make a decision?

Answers

1. The astronomy vignette
2. The marketing vignette
3. The insurance vignette
4. Make a prediction (Which culture would be best for me to live with?)

■ LEARNING WITH A DATABASE: DESCRIBING AN UNKNOWN

One useful purpose of databases is to help people get a picture of a location or thing that they have never seen and know nothing about. When NASA scientists send probes to distant reaches of the solar system, the information that comes back is not formatted in well-written paragraphs. Rather, it consists of numbers and other descriptors that can be formatted into tables something like the table (list) view of a database. After scientists have put this information into table format, they use it to describe objects that they have never actually seen. They do this by asking questions of the database and making inferences.

Astronomy is not the only topic that requires people to understand a thing, location, or idea that they cannot see. Social scientists also use similar data to describe cultures, populations, or locations. Our next field trip, Field Trip 11.1, is a database exercise for a unit in U.S. geography. Read through it carefully. Even though you might not ever teach this unit because you are a science teacher or English/language arts teacher, you can learn a great deal about how to create a database-supported lesson for the content that you teach. For example, if you are a science teacher, substitute the "Periodic Table of Elements" for the states. Bear in mind that the language and difficulty of the lesson always must be adjusted to the grade level that you teach.

Applying databases to classroom problems

FIELD TRIP 11.1

Solving a Mystery with a Database: The Mystery State

Mrs. Whiting began, "We learn about the world we live in many different ways. Sometimes we can see, hear, or feel what we need to know. Other times we must depend upon 'educated guesses' to know what is going on in the world around us.

"One way to make an educated guess is to compare what you know to what you don't know to find and describe the difference. This is what you are going to do in this lesson. You are going to choose the state that you think is different in as many ways as possible from the state in which you live.

Setting up the problem

"To do this you will be provided with a database of states, but the states, other than your own, will not be named. Your electronic database will look much like the example in Table 11.2. You will have to rely entirely upon your skill in asking your database good questions and interpreting the answers that the database gives you. When you have asked the database all of the questions below in addition to more that you will compose, you will write a travel brochure for people living in your state who might

TABLE 11.2 ■ List or Table View of States' Database

State	Highest Point (ft)	Lowest Point (ft)	Mortality (per 1000)	Population
A	5,000	0	5	10,000,000
B	12,600	565	12	6,000,000
C	8,320	30	8	25,000,000
D	12,000	265	4	1,500,000

want to take a trip to the Mystery State. Your goal is to write an article about the state that you pick. This article should be as accurate as an encyclopedia article and as interesting as a travel brochure.

Step 1

"The first thing you should do is get to know your database and think about how you might use it. Take a few moments to study the names of the fields below and think about the kind of information they provide for you. All of these fields are in your electronic database.

1. Mortality rate
2. Percent Hispanic, Caucasian, Black, etc.
3. Annual precipitation
4. Number of square miles
5. Population
6. Gross state product
7. Highest point
8. Lowest point
9. Highest temperature
10. Lowest temperature
11. Mean temperature
12. Number of sunny days
13. Percent of gross state product from agriculture
14. Percent of gross state product from mining
15. Percent of gross state product from fishing
16. Percent of gross state product from tourism
17. Major agricultural product
18. Number of lakes
19. Crime rate
20. Births per 1,000 people per year
21. Mean age
22. Number of people in the largest city
23. Number of towns above 50,000 people
24. Gross state product from manufacturing

"When you use a database to help you learn about something, you must ask questions. Usually, the more clever you can be about asking questions, the more information you can get from a database. For example, knowing the population of a state doesn't tell you much if you want to live there. You really don't want to know the population size so much as understand how the population will affect your quality of life. It is more important to know how crowded the state is than to know how many people live in the state. To find out how crowded a place is you must think about both the population and the amount of space in which people are living. Let's answer the questions on Worksheet 1 together."

Learning to ask questions

Worksheet 1

1. **If you wanted to find out how crowded a state is, what fields would you use and what would you do with them?**
    a. **What fields would you consider?**
        i. *Population*
        ii. *Number of Square Miles*
    b. **What facts would you gather?**
        i. *Fact: Descending sort on the states by population and find the state with the highest population.*
        ii. *Fact: Ascending sort on the states by population and find the state with the lowest population.*

Teaching students
to ask questions

    iii. Fact: Descending sort on the states by land area and find the state with the largest land area.

    iv. Fact: Ascending sort on the states by land area and find the state with the smallest land area.

    v. Fact: Find the record for my state and record the population and land area.

  c. What conclusions could you draw from the facts that you gathered?

    i. I will divide the population into land area for each state to figure out number of persons per square mile. The state that is most different from mine in population per square mile will be the answer to one question.

2. **The farmers in your state can't raise warm-weather crops and irrigate because there isn't enough rain. You want to find out what states can grow warm-weather crops without irrigation, which seems to you like a very different kind of agriculture.**

  a. What fields would you consider?

    i. Percent of gross state product from agriculture

    ii. Mean temperature

    iii. Precipitation

  b. What facts would you gather?

    i. Fact: I want to find names of states where agriculture is possible. States g, h, m, o, l, x, gg, and aa have the largest agricultural GSP.

    ii. Fact: States g, o, gg, and aa have the highest mean temperature

    iii. Fact: States g, o, gg, and aa have the amount of precipitation per year that warm-weather crops need.

  c. What conclusions could you draw from the facts that you gathered?

    i. Warm-weather agriculture is most feasible in state g, o, gg, or aa.

    "Below you will find more questions that will lead you to conclusions that you wouldn't come to if you just looked at the fields and records of your database individually. To answer these questions, you will have to use two functions of your database: sorts and queries. Sometimes you will have to sort on two or three fields at the same time. Sometimes you will have to use conjunctions like and/or in your queries to get the answer you want. The questions below are a "dry run" for you. They will help you understand how to write your own questions and analyze the information the database yields to you."

3. **If you wanted to find a state that had a lot of young people in it:**

  a. What fields would you consider?

    i. _____

    ii. _____

    iii. _____

  b. What facts would you gather?

    i. _____

    ii. _____

    iii. _____

  c. What conclusions could you draw from the facts that you gathered?

    _____

    _____

4. **If you wanted to find a state that had excellent ski resorts:**

  a. What fields would you consider?

    i. _____

    ii. _____

    iii. _____

    iv. _____

    v. _____

b. **What facts would you gather?**

    i. Fact: _____

    ii. Fact: _____

    iii. Fact: _____

    iv. Fact: _____

    v. Fact: _____

c. **What conclusions could you draw from the facts that you gathered?**

4. **If you wanted to find a state with many cultural attractions and activities like concerts and professional sports events:**

  a. **What fields would you consider?**

    i.   _____

    ii. _____

    iii. _____

    iv. _____

    v.   _____

  b. **What facts would you gather?**

    i.   _____

    ii. _____

    iii. _____

    iv. _____

    v.   _____

  c. **What conclusions could you draw from the facts that you gathered?**

_____

_____

Step 2

Mrs. Whiting continued, "Before you actually start asking your own questions of the database, you must decide which features of a state make it quite different from the one you live in. On Worksheet 2 below write down a list of items that you think would make a state very different than the one that you live in now.

    "Do not be concerned about the items in your list having the same names as the field headings listed above. As you have seen, you can sometimes get information from databases by working with several fields at the same time like you did when you figured out how to get data about crowding."

Worksheet 2

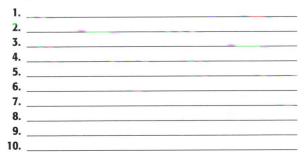

  1. _____

  2. _____

  3. _____

  4. _____

  5. _____

  6. _____

  7. _____

  8. _____

  9. _____

10. _____

Step 3

"Now that you have decided what would make a state very different from the state that you live in, it is time to use that information to build questions for the database on your computer.

"Some questions you ask will be very straightforward, like 'What is the most important agricultural product?' Other questions will have to be more clever, like the example questions in Step 2. Try to think about your questions like you thought about the questions above. **Ask a question, decide what fields are relevant, gather some facts, and make a conclusion.**

"Your work should look like the sample worksheet except for the number of facts that you gather. Sometimes you will gather only one or two facts and be able to make a conclusion. Other times you may need to find five or six facts before you can make a conclusion. Three facts are not the magic number. "Fact" is listed three times to help you remember that many times it will take more than one fact for you to reach a conclusion."

Step 4

"Now that you have spent some time gathering information and thinking about your Mystery State, it is time to describe it. Your goal is to write a report that is factually accurate as well as appealing. You want to convince your reader that this state would be a good place to vacation or even move to. If you do your report electronically, be sure that you include pictures of the Mystery State that look like the facts you have gathered. Be prepared to present your report to the class."

Step 5

Make a guess about the actual name of your mystery state and write it in the blank below.

_____

Mrs. Whiting finally provided the information that students had been anticipating. She said, "Now I will tell you the actual name of your Mystery State. Go to the encyclopedia or other reference work, look up, and read the information about your Mystery State. Answer the questions below."

Worksheet 3

What facts or observations did you include in your brochure that were not included by the encyclopedia?

1. _____
2. _____
3. _____
4. _____

What facts or observations in your brochure were different from those in the encyclopedia article?

1. _____
2. _____
3. _____
4. _____
5. _____

Go to another source and resolve the discrepancies you found above. Write the resolution in the spaces below.

1. _____
2. _____
3. _____
4. _____

Conclusion

Mrs. Whiting concluded by helping students step back and take a larger view of their work. "As you have worked with this exercise, you have thought about states many different ways. The database helped you process and analyze information very quickly and accurately. You could have done all of the research "by hand," but it would have taken you much longer because you would have had to look up answers for every state each time you asked a question. The database did that work for you. Databases are useful tools that help you organize and think about large quantities of information. Databases are good for studying other geographical topics besides states. Think about other geographical ideas a database might help you study and list them below. I will give you two hints. See if you can supply more."

1. Other economic systems
2. Other cultures
3. _____
4. _____
5. _____
6. _____
7. _____
8. _____
9. _____
10. _____

■ ANALYZING A LESSON PLAN

Below you will see a modified version of the "States Database Activity Plan." All of the blanks and some of the questions have been left out. You may need to look back to refresh your memory if you get lost. Using the steps described below, you can create a database lesson for any appropriate topic.

FIELD TRIP 11.2

A Lesson in U.S. Geography: Describing an Unknown

You learn about the world we live in many different ways. Sometimes you can see, hear, or feel what you need to know. Other times you must depend upon "educated guesses" to know what is going on in the world around you.

Step 1

One way to make an educated guess is to compare what you know to what you don't know to find and describe the difference. This is what you are going to do in this lesson. You are going to choose the state that you think is different in as many ways as possible from the state in which you live. To do this, you will be provided with a database of states, but the states, other than your own, will not be named. Your electronic database will look much like the example below.

> Set up the problem

　　You will have to rely entirely upon your skill in asking your database good questions and interpreting the answers that the database gives you. When you have asked the database all of the questions below in addition to more that you will compose, you will write a travel brochure for people living in your state who might want to take a trip to the Mystery State. Your goal is to write an article about the state that you pick that is as accurate as an encyclopedia article and as interesting as a travel brochure.

Step 2

Teach students to write questions

The first thing you should do is get to know your database and think about how you might use it. Take a few moments to study the fields below and think about the kind of information they provide for you. When you use a database to help you learn about something, you must ask questions. Usually, the more clever you can be about asking questions, the more information you can get from a database. It is one thing to state the population of a state and another thing to know what the population means to the quality of life of a person living in a particular location. Knowing the population of a state doesn't tell you much if you want to live there. What is more important to know is how crowded the state is. Whether or not a place is crowded is the result of the interaction between population and the amount of space in which people live. Knowing that, how would you answer the questions below?

Below you will find more questions that will lead you to conclusions that you wouldn't come to if you just looked at the fields and records of your database individually. To answer these questions you will have to use two functions of your database: sorts and queries. Sometimes you will have to sort on two or three fields at the same time. Sometimes you will have to use conjunctions such as *and/or* in your queries to get the answer you want. Try answering the questions below with your states' database.

Step 3

Encourage students to focus on a specific area to explore

Before you actually start asking questions of the database you must decide what characteristics of a state make it quite different from the one you live in. In the space below, write down a list of items that you think would make a state very different from the one that you live in now. Don't be concerned about the items in your list having the same names as the field headings listed above. As you have seen, you can sometimes get information from databases by working with several fields at the same time like you did when you decided how to get data about crowding.

Step 4

Teach students how to ask questions

Now that you have decided what would make a state very different from the one that you live in, it is time to use that information to build questions for the database on your computer. Some questions you ask will be very straightforward, like "What is the size of the gross state product?" Other questions will have to be more clever, like the example questions in Step 2. Using the list that you developed above to guide you, write your questions in the blanks below.

Step 5

Require a product of the student

Now that you have spent some time gathering information and thinking about your Mystery State, it is time to describe it. Your goal is to write a report that is factually accurate as well as appealing. You want to convince your reader that this state would be a good place to vacation or even live. If you do your report electronically, be sure that you include pictures that look like the facts you have gathered.

Step 6

Encourage students to resolve discrepancies

I will tell you the actual name of your mystery state. Go to the encyclopedia or other reference work, look up, and read the information about your mystery state. Answer the questions below.

1. What facts or observations did you include that were not included by the encyclopedia?
2. What facts or observations in your article were different from the encyclopedia article?
3. Go to another source and resolve the discrepancies you found above. Write the resolution in the spaces below.

Step 7

As you have worked with this exercise, you have thought about states in many different ways. The database helped you process and analyze information very quickly and accurately. You could have done all of the research "by hand," but it would have taken you much longer because you would have had to look up answers for every state each time you asked a question. The database did that work for you.

Databases are useful tools that help you organize and think about large quantities of information. Databases are good for studying other geographical topics besides states. Think about other geographical topics a database might help you study and list them below. I will give you two hints. See if you can supply more.

Encourage students to think about how to apply the process to other projects

■ UNDERSTANDING THE STEPS

The lesson plan just described applies not only to states and geography, but also to topics in the sciences, other social sciences, and language arts. A similar exercise could be constructed for mammals, short stories, or time periods in history. This model also applies to decisions and predictions as well. Whatever the topic, there is an underlying sequence of steps for building a lesson plan that uses databases efficiently. You will proceed a little differently for each step depending upon whether a prediction, decision, or analysis is your goal, but the steps themselves are the same.

Problems for content areas

Set Up the Problem

Setting up the problem is a key part of the process. It provides both motivation and structure for the student. The sample lesson, "Mystery State," was an exercise in describing an unknown. Other examples of exercises in which students might describe an unknown object or idea by comparing it to a known could be constructed of a database of animals, rocks, plants, cities, counties, countries, bodies of water, dinosaurs (for young students), or planets.

Doing an analysis or making a decision is very similar. You and your students could build a database of time periods in history and include fields ranging from number of wars, to the rights of women, to literacy rates. From such a database, students could extract a large number of ideas for writing and debate. The same kind of assignment would be appropriate in a literature class. This database might consist of literary periods, short stories, or some other genre. In the short story database, the class could explore everything from the changing role of women to the evolution of a theme from one literary period to another. On a more practical level for a class of students marginally interested in school, let alone databases, making a decision about which car to buy is a good topic for a database lesson.

Other examples of the kinds of topics that would be appropriate for using a database to make a decision would include the speed limit example discussed previously. In the case of the last two examples (the speed limit and buying a car), the decision is a practical one that directly impacts the lives of students. However, other scenarios can be set up that use making a decision as a focus. Picking a Native American tribe to live with is an example of this kind of decision. Picking a time to live in history is another example of interacting with content in an academic area to focus on making a decision.

Setting up problems requiring students to make a prediction is a very similar process. Other problems students could study that result in predictions include:

- Predicting the next president, senator in your state, mayor in your city, etc.
- Predicting the characteristics of the next down-turn or up-turn in business cycle
- Predicting the country or part of the world where the next war will take place
- Predicting which occupation will provide the best jobs in the year that your students would graduate from college

As you conceptualize a problem that you want your students to solve you will, no doubt, be concerned with more than just using a database. You will probably be worrying about exposing them to the information that they will need to pass an assessment that you have not created, such as an achievement test. You will be thinking about the actual resources available to your students to gather information to complete their assignment. You will also be trying to develop a problem to which your students can respond. Below are some guidelines and suggestions for writing problems:

1. Write your problem in the form of a story. Students and people in general respond positively to stories. If you write a story, your students will be able to visualize the characters and conflicts. They will automatically add detail from their own experiences and the problem will become more meaningful to them (Shank, 1997).

Set your problems up as a story

2. Define the problem clearly. If you do not define the question that you want your students to think about, they could select a different question and study a different set of information. If you need to have them assimilate certain information to prepare them for achievement tests, make sure that you define the problem they are to solve clearly enough to cause them to interact with the information that they need to know.

3. If the students must design and enter the data into the database themselves, be sure that you embed clues in your problem that will lead them to include fields that will contain the information you want them to study. Before your write your problem, decide if you want students to work alone or in groups.

✔ CHECKING YOUR UNDERSTANDING

11.2

Below you will find three short examples of problems. They have been written to give you examples of problems and to demonstrate the principles above. To help yourself identify some of the features listed above, answer the questions provided after each problem. Answers to each problem are listed after the questions.

Problem A: Building a Power Plant

You are a biologist working for a company that would like to build a coal-fired power plant somewhere in the world. Your company president is quite environmentally conscious and wants to build it in a biome where it will have the least impact. The company has located coal reserves in the tundra, northern coniferous forests, a deciduous forest, grasslands, several deserts, and a tropical rain forest.

Your job is to help her predict the impact of such a power plant on the plant and animal life in each biome. You have a database of biomes, their vital statistics (temperature range, precipitation, etc.) and common plant and animal life. You will need to find some information about the effects of coal-fired power plants on the environment. Use the sample environmental impact statement attached to this assignment to format your report.

Questions for Problem A: Building a Power Plant

1. Does this problem ask students to
   a. Analyze a problem
   b. Make a prediction
   c. Make a decision?
2. Underline all of the embedded suggestions for field names in this problem.
3. Who are the characters in the story?
4. How could you help your students personalize this story?
5. What mechanism does the teacher use to make sure that the students interact with the information she wants them to learn?
6. Right now, this problem is written for an individual. How could the teacher turn this problem into a group assignment?

Answers for Problem A: Building a Power Plant

1. The students analyze a problem. They do not make a decision; the company president does that. They do not make a prediction either. They simply present the facts.
2. Italicized below are words that will give the students hints about the fields they should include in their database.

   You are a biologist working for a company that would like to build a coal-fired power plant somewhere in the world. Your company president is quite environmentally conscious and wants to build it in a biome where it will have the least amount of impact. The company has located coal reserves in the *tundra, northern coniferous forests,* a *deciduous forest, grasslands,* several *deserts,* and a *tropical rain forest.*
   Your job is to help her predict the impact of such a power plant on the *plant* and *animal* life in each biome. You have a database of biomes, their vital statistics (*temperature range, precipitation,* etc.) and common plant and animal life. You will need to find some information about the effects of coal-fired power plants on the environment. Use the sample environmental impact statement attached to this assignment to format your report.

3. The characters in this story are the biologist with whom the student should identify and the company president.
4. To personalize this story, students identify the biome in which they live. They should also learn about the effects of coal-fired plants and consider how they would feel about living close to one. If they already live close to such a plant, how do they feel about living near it?
5. She makes sure that they interact with the proper information by requiring their report be framed as an environmental impact statement. Older students may actually fill out parts of a real environmental impact statement while younger students would be given an outline appropriate to their grade level.
6. This problem could be a debate between an energy production company and an environmentalist group.

Problem B: Buying a Car

You have been working as a grocery store bagger dreaming about having wheels for two years now. You have saved faithfully and have $3,500 for a down payment on a used car. Fortunately, you have a database listing every major make and model of car along with standard features like gas mileage, standard accessories, and manufacturer's price from 1980–1999. You are interested in making a good buy because you have worked so hard and waited for so long. You decide you are not going to make this decision on the spur of the moment. After you have made a list of features that you really want and calculated how much you can afford to pay each month, you sit down with the database and go to work. You know you must go to the loan company with your parents to justify your decision in order to get a loan for the remainder of the purchase price.

Questions for Problem B: Buying a Car

1. What does this problem ask students to do?
   a. Analyze a problem
   b. Make a prediction
   c. Make a decision
2. Underline all of the embedded suggestions for field names in this problem.
3. Who are the characters in the story?
4. How could you help your students personalize this story?
5. What mechanism does the teacher use to make sure that the students interact with the information she wants them to learn?
6. Right now, this problem is written for an individual. How could the teacher turn this problem into a group assignment?

Answers: Problem B: Buying a Car

1. The students *make a decision.*
2. Italicized below are words that will give the students hints about the fields they should include in their database.

   You have been working as a grocery store bagger, dreaming about having wheels for two years now. You have saved faithfully and have $3,500 for a down payment on a car. Fortunately, you have a database available listing every *major make and model* of car along with standard features such as *gas mileage, standard accessories,* and *price* for cars manufactured from *1980–1999.* You are interested in making a good buy because you have worked so hard and waited for so long. You decide you are not going to make this decision on the spur of the moment. After you have made a list of features that you really want and have calculated how much you can afford to *pay each month,* you sit down with the database and go to work. You know you must go to the loan company with your parents to justify your decision in order to get a loan for the remainder of the purchase price.

3. There is just one main character in this story, the student. However, the student is given some context and character.
4. You could personalize this story by changing the job to fit each student in your class. You could make the effort to find out what they do to make money and write a vignette for each one of them or have them fill in a blank with the name of their part-time job.
5. The student must go to the loan company to ask for a loan. This part of the assignment could be completed in class as role-playing, a speech, or as a written report.
6. "Problem B" might be an assignment to a team working for a simulated company to buy the best vehicle for a certain function.

Problem C: What Will the Next President Be Like?

You are in high school and you know that the person who is elected to be the next president will affect the quality of your life in many ways, such as the wages that you earn (or even if you have a job), whether you will be called to fight in a war, and the amount of taxes you pay. The two candidates running for office are very different. One is moderately liberal and the other is a hard-line conservative; one was a soldier in Vietnam, the other was never in the military; one is married and the other isn't; one has concerns about businesses using up the environment while the other says there are plenty of natural resources; one graduated from college, and the other didn't. The list of possible differences includes: voting records for civil rights, abortion, and the death penalty. You decide to look at a database of presidents to find out which of these two people is most likely to be elected based on the characteristics of past presidents. Once you decide who will win, you will write a letter to the editor of your local newspaper supporting the person whom you think should win.

Questions for Problem C: What Will the Next President Be Like?

1. What does this problem ask students to do?
   a. Analyze a problem
   b. Make a prediction
   c. Make a decision?
2. Underline all of the embedded suggestions for field names in this problem.
3. Who are the characters in the story?
4. How could you help your students personalize this story?
5. What mechanism does the teacher use to make sure that the students interact with the information she wants them to learn?
6. Right now, this problem is written for an individual. How could the teacher turn this problem into a group assignment?

Answers: Problem C: What Will the Next President Be Like?

1. The students make a *prediction.*
2. Underlined below are words that will give the student hints about the fields they should include in their database.

   You are in high school and you know that the person who is elected to be the next president will affect the quality of your life in many ways: the *wages* that you earn, or *even if you have a job, whether you will be called to fight in a war, the amount of taxes you pay.* The two candidates running for office are very different. One is moderately liberal and the other is a hard-line conservative; *one was a soldier in Vietnam, the other was never in the military;* one is married and the other isn't; one has concerns about businesses using up the *environment* while the other says there are plenty of *natural resources; one graduated from college, and the other didn't.* The list of possibilities for differences is long: *voting records for civil rights, abortion,* and the *death penalty.* You decide to look at a database of presidents to find out which of these two people is most likely to be elected based on the characteristics of past presidents. Once you decide who will win, you will write a letter to the editor of your local newspaper supporting the person whom you think should win.

3. There is just one main character in this story, the student. However, the student has real motivation to find out who might win the election. All of the underlined topics affect a person's daily life.
4. You could personalize this story by pointing out that if the next president provokes or enters a large war, young people are ultimately drafted. Or, if the economy gets bad because of poor decisions, the young who have the least skills and experience are often the first to go without jobs.
5. The student must write a letter to the editor on a specific topic.
6. This problem could be altered to become a debate on the worthiness of a candidate based on historical similarities to other good or bad presidents.

Teach the Nature of the Questioning Process

Until students have worked extensively with a database, they will not understand how to ask good questions. Most students only know how to ask a single-level question that yields a fact, for example, "What is the population of Ohio?" or "How tall are grizzly bears?"

The challenge is teaching students to ask questions that will yield facts from which they can draw conclusions. If they ask questions that lead to conclusions, not only will they be thinking analytically, but they will also be adding to the catalogue of facts they must learn anyway.

Take the question in the Mystery State exercise about crowding, for example. As you thought about the factors involved in crowding, you also practiced several different skills that are important for any literate person. You worked with the following facts and processes:

- Learning specific state populations
- Learning specific state land areas
- Practicing the mathematical problem-solving skills found in a story problem by generating the story problem yourself
- Practicing arithmetic skills as you did the division problem required to get the answer

Asking good question requires students to use many basic skills

When you finally extracted all of the facts you needed, you had to do three different division problems to form a basis for comparison. Although the division problems did not take place in the real world, it was nevertheless more meaningful for you than doing division problems "5, 6, and 7" at the end of a chapter in an arithmetic book. Furthermore, it was important to you for your calculations to be correct in order for you to draw a correct conclusion. To use a database effectively, students should learn that conclusions and reasoning are built on facts. This is the reason for the explicit requirement that students format their questions for databases as sequences of question/hypothesis or fact, fact, fact/conclusion sequences.

Classroom management is important in this phase of the process. To help students learn how to ask and answer more complex questions or for students just learning how to use databases, the activity designed to teach questioning should be done in pairs, in small groups, or as a class. Pairs and small groups should work at the computer. A teacher who decides to work with the whole class should use a computer projection device and ask a student to key in sorts and queries. The point of the exercise is not computer skills but rather problem-solving skills. If the students work in groups, one student can sit at the computer and type in the sorts or queries after the group has formulated a series of questions.

If students are still novice database users, the student who types in the problem can wait for explicit instructions for each keystroke from the group. In this way, students who do not know how to do sorts or queries see each step in the process. Also, the keyboarder can change for each series of questions. It does not take long for every member of the group to have an opportunity to participate at the keyboard.

Focus and Explore

In the case of the Mystery State project, students need to decide which qualities about a state make it different from their own. To do this they might look at the database's field headings for hints as well as brainstorm with each other. The teacher should encourage students to help each other think broadly because they are not in competition. The emphasis should be on ideas and a thorough coverage of the topic.

While working on the Mystery State project, students had to decide what would make a state most different (setting up a contrast). Furthermore, they grow to understand that to different people "most different" would mean different things. To a sports enthusiast, a state without skiing or professional sports might be very different, while to a rural person, a state with large population centers might be very different. In the case of the "biome" project, the students will ultimately have to come to the conclusion that the problem is "How can I help my boss decide where a coal-fired plant will do the least damage?" Then students will have to ask questions like, "What is damage—losing an endangered plant in one location or an endangered animal in another?" "Do such energy-producing plants destroy whole ecosystems?" "Which ecosystems are most fragile?" "What makes an ecosystem fragile?" Students will be able to use the database to answer some of the questions and will use other resources to answer others.

> Teaching students to use their answers to come to a conclusion

For the students who have to make a decision about a car, the question will be "What will serve my needs, be economical, and last until I can buy a different car?" Once students can focus on a problem (bearing in mind that all students may not choose to solve the same problem unless told to do so), then they are ready to ask questions.

Students Write Their Own Questions

Young or inexperienced students should write questions with each other. Experienced students may work alone at a location away from the computer in order to preserve computer time for those who have thought through problems and have written their questions down. The questioning process is iterative. Students can write a few questions, go to the computer, enter them, take their answers back to their work area, and work on their product for a while, or think of new questions. To help students write good questions and minimize time at the computer, the teacher should ask them to underline conjunctions and logical operators, mark field headings so they stand out, and indicate whether the question will be a sort or a query before they go to the computer.

One way to assist students who are learning to ask questions is to help them with steps of the process. Helping them involves giving them some of the answers to begin with and then withdrawing that support as students become more experienced. Students in grades 3 through 6 will always need prompts that older students do not need. Students who are learning content with a database for the first time will need more prompts than students who have studied several database-supported topics.

> Scaffolded learning experiences help students ask questions

Box 11.1 has an example of how a teacher might structure the "Mystery State Investigation" for young or novice database users. We will assume that you teach in Florida and you decide that focusing on finding out what states might have ski resorts would be a good problem for your students. Notice that your students do a series of queries and come to a conclusion. You could have asked them to provide the names of relevant fields. Or, you could have asked them to establish the parameters for where skiing is possible using the database itself rather than outside sources.

To provide such parameters they could have looked at highest points and decided how many feet above sea level a mountain should be in order to be both high enough

BOX 11.1   EXAMPLE 1: MYSTERY STATE INVESTIGATION

No one skis in Florida, so a state in which people can ski would be very different. Fields that will help you figure out where people might ski include highest point, low temperature, and annual precipitation. Next, you must decide how the information in these fields can help you make a comparison. To help yourself work this problem through, think of a place where you know that people ski. Go to the almanac and find the highest point, low temperature, and annual precipitation of that place.

Name of the place you selected_____

Your Approach

Find the identifying letters of all of the states in your database that have low temperatures equal to or less than the place you selected, annual precipitation greater than the place you selected, and highest points within 2,000 feet of the place you selected. What should you have the computer do?

(Answer: Query all of the states for low temperature close to or less than the place you selected.)

Fact: _____

Question: Which states have mountains high enough for skiing? What should you have the computer do?

(Answer: Query all of the states for mountains that have mountains nearly as high, as high as, or higher than the place you selected.)

Fact: _____

Question: Where is there enough moisture to make snow? What should you have the computer do?

(Answer: Query all of the states for precipitation with nearly as much, equal, or more than the place you selected.)

Fact: _____

Now make a list of the states that satisfy all three of your requirements for low temperature, highest point, and precipitation.

Conclusion (names of states):

_____

_____

_____

_____

and remain cold enough for skiing. To establish whether a place is cold enough, students could have looked at the lowest temperatures and the mean temperatures and picked the lowest third or fourth of the states as possible places for skiing.

If the Mystery State project were the second or third database project your students had done, the worksheet that the teacher hands out might look like the next one in Box 11.2. Note that the thinking represented in this example does not often happen the first or second time that students use a database to solve a problem. Young students may never achieve the ability to work as independently on assignments such this one. On the other hand, beginning in grade 7 or 8, some students are capable of this kind of independence, and by grade 12, most students should be able to engage in this kind of thinking with no prompts if they have had consistent exposure to lessons of this nature.

BOX 11.2   EXAMPLE 2: MYSTERY STATE INVESTIGATION

Being able to go to a ski resort would make a state very different from ours. You must decide which available fields will give you information about this problem. What are they? _____

Describe how numbers in the fields that you chose will show you that a state could support skiing

_____

Gather the facts you need from each field:

Fact: _____

Fact: _____

Fact: _____

Now that you have some actual ideas about states where people could ski, which ones do you think are most likely to have skiing?

Conclusion: _____

You will have to model these kinds of investigations to the whole class often, and perhaps start every database activity with some questions of your own to demonstrate and clarify important topics and trains of thought. Furthermore, many students may need to work in groups or with a peer in order to think through problems. It is safe to say that having students work in groups to formulate and enter questions for databases is always appropriate.

Another point to consider is that a complete database project will consist of many problems like the one in Examples 1 and 2. The number of problems that result in a product will depend on the size of the database (number of records *and* number of fields), the complexity of the product, and the age of the students. Table 11.3 lists very general guidelines by grade level for students who have been introduced to databases and use them regularly as a tool.

> Grade level appropriately assigned

When the students have a list of well-thought-out questions to start with, it is time for them to go to the computer. Again, this does not have to be a solitary activity. Two students can pool their questions and work together. Sometimes getting a query to work

TABLE 11.3 ■ Breadth of Assignments by Grade Level

Grade Level	Number of Problems or Questions	Size of Database	Size of Product
4–5	4–6	20–30 records 6–10 fields	3–6 paragraphs 3–6 page electronic report
6–7	7–15	50–75 records 10–15 fields	5–10 paragraphs 6–15 page electronic report
8–12	Number required to support a well-informed product	75+ records 10+ fields	The range of product size can vary from a simple five-paragraph position paper to a research report or electronic presentation.

requires some thinking and discussion, which necessitates several trips to the computer. This is one reason why your students should have cooperative learning experiences before you try database-supported lessons. It is hard enough to learn how to participate in a cooperative learning group. Adding the computer and databases to the mix can be overwhelming. Learning how to think with databases is a skill that improves with practice.

Require a Product

A conclusion or recommendation is the goal of a database assignment

Throughout the life of a database-supported unit, teachers should emphasize the database is only a tool and that the goal of the project is a product. These products can take many forms. They can be in a traditional report format, an electronic report done with presentation/hypermedia software, a speech with or without presentation software, a debate, or even a picture. If the object of the assignment is to describe an unknown, pictures and graphics may be very helpful, especially with younger children and those who do not write well.

Evaluating student products

Evaluation of the product is a key element of the database-supported lesson. The usual items (spelling, grammar, and organization) can be evaluated along with how well the student used the database information to shape the final product. If the students hand in all of the questions that they prepared for the database, the teacher can compare the questions to the product and make suggestions about how to improve database use.

Also, comparing the questions to the product will help prevent copying and pasting text from an electronic encyclopedia, throwing in a few pictures and calling the result a product. For example, the Mystery State project requires an accurate travel brochure. The Biome project requires a report based on the format ecologists use when they do an environmental impact statement. The car-buying project might require a sales speech in which the students try to sell the car that they have chosen to the class. The project described at the beginning of the previous chapter in which the student had to choose a Native American tribe to live with might be a journal, "A Day in the Life of a Nez Perce Boy," accompanied by a picture of a tribal village. One of the most important benefits of a good database-supported assignment is the original thinking students do.

Have Students Make Comparisons

Students should compare their findings to those of experts

Although having real world materials that enable students to corroborate their conclusions is not always possible, it is helpful when they are available. It should be a goal for teachers to create or obtain source materials so students can use them for comparing their analysis, description, or prediction to a similar case. This will help students remember the facts they have worked with as well as help them generalize about the ideas they have studied.

In the case of the Mystery State project, the teacher tells students the name of the state they have been working on and students go to encyclopedias and compare their article with the encyclopedia article. In the Biome project, the teacher could have some case studies of the effects of coal-fired power plants on the environment for students to work with. Students who were "buying" a car could go to a car dealership and talk to a car dealer, read newspaper advertisements, or talk to another adult about the purchase.

Encourage the Students to Resolve Discrepancies

Students should, again, create some kind of product that is a result of the comparison of their work to the work of others, even if it is only a brief paragraph, a two-minute presentation to the class, or a short discussion in a group. This activity provides closure to the unit and gives students a last chance to solidify the knowledge and relationships that they have come to understand.

> Students should learn to use a database

Encourage Students to Think About Using Databases to Solve Other Problems

This part of the lesson can also be very brief. It is the segment of the lesson that will help your students become life-long learners. No tool is useful to a person who does not know when it should be used. This piece of the lesson may be written down as a part of a worksheet as it was in the Mystery State project, or it may be the topic of a short, teacher-led presentation. The point for students is to generalize what they have learned so they can be proactive about their own learning in the future. Beyond the learning of a specific topic, a teacher's goal is to someday hear a student say, "I'll bet if I had that information in a database I could find the answer to that problem."

■ SUMMATIVE EVALUATION OF A DATABASE PROJECT

Evaluating a student's work with a database from beginning to the end of the project is a complex task. It is tempting to want to grade only the final product, with the justification that if the groundwork that the student has done is good then the final product will be good. This reasoning is faulty, however. Grading math papers is analogous to grading database assignments. Math teachers learned some time ago that just grading the final answer to a complex math problem does not give the teacher or the student accurate insight into the student's mastery of the information under study. In a database assignment, there are a number of visible products of student thinking that teachers can evaluate.

Each step that you complete in teaching the assignment has a student outcome. Table 11.4 lists each step and its associated student outcome. As students complete each of those steps, their work may be scored using a scoring rubric so that the whole grade for the assignment is not based on just the final product.

> Grade based on all work, not just project

Tables 11.5, 11.6, and 11.7 are simple rubrics adaptable to any grade level for scoring student work. Each column lists only a heading with the number of points available for that segment of the assignment. You will want to adjust these values to your scoring system. Notice that there is a column that allows for no points even though the student hands in something. Note that you will use the rubric in Table 11.5 only if you are having your students build their own database. You should also note that Table 11.7 does not include suggestions for scoring the format of the products. There could be

TABLE 11.4 ■ Steps in Database Lessons and Student Outcomes

Step	Student Outcome
1: Provide the students with a story or scenario that sets up the problem.	Students must formulate or restate the problem and break it into its components.
2: Teach students to write questions.	Students use the database to answer questions.
3: Have students focus on areas to explore.	Students decide on questions that will lead them to the answers they want.
4: Students write questions (Fact-Fact-Fact-Conclusion) for the database.	Students see beyond individual facts to logical sequences of ideas.
5: Require a product.	Students produce a written product, speech, or other summary and analysis of their findings.
6: Resolve discrepancies.	Students compare and contrast their conclusions with the conclusions of experts.
7: Generate new problems.	Students apply what they know about finding the answer to one question to finding the answers to other questions.

TABLE 11.5 ■ Scoring Rubric for Student-Planned Database (Design)

Criterion	2 Points	1 Point	0 Points
Design of Fields	The database contains all of the fields that the students will need to help them answer the question posed by the scenario.	The database is missing one or two key fields, but all fields are relevant.	The database is missing more than two key fields and has included irrelevant fields.
Ease of Use	Students assigned an appropriate common metric for each field.	There is evidence that students have thought about a common appropriate metric for each field, but some metrics that they have used aren't appropriate (i.e., 5'6" to measure height).	Students show no evidence of having planned how to express entries in appropriate common units.
Mechanics	All entries are spelled correctly.	Depending on the size of the database, there are a few spelling errors.	The number of spelling errors significantly affects the usability of the database.

TABLE 11.6 ■ Scoring Rubric for Student-Planned Database (Use of a Database)

Step	2 Points	1 Point	0 Points
1: Learning to write questions.	Can translate a teacher- or class-generated question into a database sort or query.	Knows whether a sort or query is needed, but lacks the skills to make the computer execute the sort or query.	Does not understand sorts and queries and cannot execute them on the computer.
2: Student focuses on the question and areas of exploration.	Translates the scenario into a question that can be explored with the database. Approach to the problem will be fruitful.	Translation of the scenario into a question is too broad or too narrow.	Student does not attempt to translate the scenario into a question or re-formulate it into a problem.
3: Students write questions to ask the database.	Writes questions that produce facts that lead to a conclusion (Writes Fact-Fact-Fact-Conclusion questions).	Writes questions that yield mostly unrelated facts. Produces only one or two Fact-Fact-Fact-Conclusion questions.	Writes questions that aren't related to the problem. Writes few or no questions.

TABLE 11.7 ■ Scoring Rubric for Student-Planned Database (Product)

Product	2 Points	1 Point	0 Points
Report, speech, discussion	Demonstrates both analytical and synthetical thinking; Has broken the problem into several parts; Has generalized series of Fact-Fact-Fact-Conclusion questions to reach conclusions.	Has applied the facts from the database to for-mulate new ideas; Has explained the relation-ships implied in Fact-Fact-Fact-Conclusion sequences.	Has recited a series of unrelated facts.
Resolving discrepancies	Finds more than one source for each piece of the problem and produces a logical discussion of differences and similarities.	Finds only one source for comparison, or Misses comparisons for pieces of the problem, or Comparison of differ-ences and similarities is not logical.	Finds only one source for comparison, and Misses comparisons for pieces of the problem, and Comparison of differences and similarities is not logical.
Generating new problems	Can generate more than one new associated problem that could be solved with database research.	Can generate one new, associated problem that could be solved with database research.	Cannot think of a related problem that could be solved using a database.

cells in this table where you provide students with standards for grammar, sentence mechanics, spelling, organization, and content.

✔ CHECKING YOUR UNDERSTANDING

11.3

Use one of the vignettes or ideas presented earlier in this chapter to build a database lesson. Make your lesson similar to the Mystery State project. Be sure that you explain and include each step. Remember what you learned about writing a scenario and be sure that you include complete instructions and examples for your students. Assume that your students know how to use a database, but this is the first time that they will actually do a complete lesson using a database to help them understand a topic. Include a cover page for your project that specifies the grade level for which you are writing the lesson and the kind of lesson it is (prediction, describing an unknown, or analysis/decision). After you have finished your lesson, include a one-page vignette at the end of your project modeled on the vignette based on the "Native American" project that describes the actual "look of the classroom" while the project is in progress. Also, include a scoring rubric that you would use to score the work students would produce as a result of this lesson.

Topics of the vignettes are:
- Buying and selling merchandise
- Choosing the next president
- Advisability of the 75-mile-an-hour speed limit
- Learning about another culture
- Biomes
- Studying novels, short stories, or poetry

Table 11.8 is a summary of activities associated with databases and their relationships to Bloom's Taxonomy. Notice that when students design, build, and use the database that every level of the taxonomy is represented. As you look at Table 11.8, try to match the "Database Activity" in the third column with the step for constructing a database-supported lesson that you learned earlier in this chapter.

TABLE 11.8 ■ Bloom's Taxonomy and Databases

Levels of Thought	Description	Database Activity
Knowledge	Name, locate, tell, list, repeat, point to	Looking up facts.
Comprehension	Define, summarize, infer, project, describe	Building question sequences.
Application	Use, solve, adapt, relate, perform	Drawing conclusions from related facts.
Analysis	Compare, classify, test for, screen, examine	Building a final product based on all of the conclusions drawn from the database.
Synthesis	Create, develop, compile, design, build, generate	Designing a database.
Evaluation	Judge, criticize, rate, rank, reject	Judging the merits of your work against that of others (the experts).

■ SUMMARY

Using a database to teach literature and language arts, social science, and science can be an extremely valuable and rewarding experience for both teachers and students. The current situation in classrooms is such that teachers will not be able to do this instantly. There are several hurdles to overcome.

1. Teachers must be sure that their students have the prerequisite skills to operate databases until that skill becomes a general part of the curriculum.
2. Databases and lessons using them have to be created by students and teachers.
3. Students and teachers need to work in a cooperative learning environment. If they don't have those skills already, then they must learn them before they tackle databases.

Once students and teachers have the resources and expertise to use databases to study topics, using databases becomes an extremely valuable teaching tool (See Box 11.3).

1. Databases assist student acquisition of facts and definitions.
2. When students use databases to think through a problem, they build relationships among related ideas.
3. Databases are "idea generators" when students use sorts and queries creatively.
4. After they have created their product, students compare what they have learned to what other people have said and thought about the same topic.
5. When they have compared their conclusion to the conclusions of others, students judge the accuracy of their own work.
6. In the questioning process, students start with an idea or theme (the problem) and build on it with increasingly complex concepts.

BOX 11.3 STEPS FOR CREATING A DATABASE LESSON

1. Set up the problem.
2. Teach the nature of the questioning process.
3. Encourage students to focus on a problem.
4. Have the students work with the database and get answers to the questions. Support young or inexperienced students by providing parts of the questioning process. As students become more adept, remove support gradually until they can work through the questioning process without guidance.
5. Require a product of the students.
6. Have the students compare their conclusions to the conclusions of other authors.
7. Ask the students to resolve any discrepancies between their work and the work of other authors.
8. Ask the students to think of other ways that a database could help them think about a problem in the content area.

7. When students are questioning a database, they receive immediate feedback about two items:

   ■ facts
   ■ accuracy (logic) of the questions they are asking.

8. Database software (the tool itself) is widely available and inexpensive. It runs on any kind or vintage of machine. Most machines that are sold to educational institutions have a "suite" of tool products including a database.

■ REFERENCES ■

Shank, R. C., & Cleary, C. (1995). Engines for education. Hillsdale: Lawrence Erlbaum Associates.

■ ANNOTATED RESOURCES ■

A Special Note About Databases in Mathematics

Mathematics and databases

Databases in mathematics are useful for giving students a large view of an entire topic. Although databases are not used in mathematics as frequently as spreadsheets are in science, nevertheless there are some appropriate moments. Databases are useful in mathematics for the same reasons they are useful in other content areas—they provide students another way to study a concept. What are some mathematical concepts for which useful databases could be built?

■ Number concepts—lower elementary
■ Shapes and formulas (geometry)—upper elementary through senior high school
■ Word problems (middle through high school)

To understand how a database for mathematics might be constructed and used, we will look at word problems in more detail. Mildred Johnson (1992) wrote *How to Solve Word Problems in Algebra: A Solved Problem Approach,* which summarizes different kinds of word problems and how they are solved. The problem is, given all of this information, how would we convert it to a database format that students could use to understand and learn how to work word problems better? The kind of database we will build using this information falls loosely into the category of "Describing an Unknown."

First, we will construct a table. To make our table clear for students, the kinds of word problems will come first in the table (coins, time, finance, mixtures, levers, age, numbers, work, plane geometric figures, digits, etc.). When we teach students how to do word problems we associate some fact or formula with the kind of problem that the student is solving. We also teach them how to sketch the problem. Finally, we provide them with examples and explanations of solutions. Given this information then, we can construct a table that will be the basis for a database (See Table 11.9).

TABLE 11.9 ■ Example of Some Fields for a Database on Word Problems

Name	Fact	Solved Example (problem statement)	Sketch of Solved Example	Unsolved Problem 1
Time, Rate, and Distance	Time × Rate = Distance Sketches are helpful.	The distance from Boston to Chicago is . . .	Time | Rate | Di — X | 45 | 900	A train leaves New York going 75 . . .
Mixtures	Amount of the mixture times the percent of pure stuff equals the amount of pure stuff. Sketches are helpful.	You are getting your car ready for winter and discover that you need to add antifreeze to . . .	6% + 12% + 15%	A cook is making a large batch of soup which requires a mixture of milk and . . .
Levers	$W_1D_1 = W_2D_2$ Sketches are helpful.	A weight at one end . . .	60 | 130 — 8 ft | X	Using a crowbar . . .
Plane Geometric Figures	1. The perimeter of a rectangle = its width × 2 + its length × 2 2. The sum of the angles of a triangle = 180° 3. The area of a rectangle. . . . 4. The sides of a square are. . . . 5. Sketches are helpful.	A rectangle is three feet less than four times its width. The perimeter . . .	2x – 3	One angle of a triangle is 3 times the next angle and . . .

This database could become more complex. For example, there are different kinds of time, rate, and distance problems (two trains meeting versus how long it takes to get from one place to another). There may be more than one row for each kind of word problem. Your database may have eight or ten different examples of time, rate, and distance problems. Also note that the complex sorts and queries that are possible with other example databases in this book are not possible for this database. The only column that may be sorted or queried meaningfully is the first one, which holds the names of the different kinds of word problems. Your students could simply use the database as a reference—or you could modify it and leave out information in some cells, asking students to provide it. The construction and use of such a database puts word problems into a larger context and allows students to see that there are patterns for solving word problems in general as well as patterns for the solution of individual word problems.

CHAPTER

12

Acquiring Data

OBJECTIVES

- Know where to look for electronic sources of data.
- Know how to transform the data to a usable format.

Acquiring data for a database is one of the biggest challenges for teachers who use database-supported lessons. Classes can construct some databases themselves, but database construction is a time-consuming process and not always the best use of a student's time. During the past several years, the number of datasets available on the Internet has increased significantly. Knowing where to find them is difficult.

Once you do locate a dataset it is useful if you know how to change the format of the information for use with a database engine. Once you have reformatted data into a comma- or tab-delimited format you may use it not only for databases but also for spreadsheets, the topic of the next chapter. The skills you should know or learn as you study this chapter include:

- Use an Internet search engine
- Download a file to a floppy drive or hard drive
- Use a word processor to convert data to a comma or tab delimited text file
- Use a database

■ HOW DO TEACHERS ACQUIRE DATASETS?

Teachers and their classes do not always have to make their own databases. More and more often an Internet search will turn up a database that is appropriate for some unit of content. Science and social studies teachers are most fortunate in this area. To the extent that students study the historical context of the works that they read, literature teachers also find databases that are helpful. In the social sciences, the U.S. Census and state and county records are available as databases on the Internet. In the sciences, NASA maintains a large number of databases on astronomical objects, and other branches of the government maintain databases on the weather, ecological studies, health, and nutrition.

Data on the Internet: Examples of Some Good Sites

Internet addresses change often, so there is no point in providing a long list of Internet data resources. However, there is a short list of sources that have had a relatively long life, electronically speaking. Each has its own quirks and peculiarities. Following are comments and Table 12.1 with the name of the site and an accompanying address. What you can take from the sites as much as data is an understanding of the variety and amount of data available to anyone with a computer.

The Data and Story Library (1996) is an excellent location for finding data related to a large number of content areas. Although this database is meant for students of statistics, the data for the problems is available in tables. The tables cover the following content areas:

Archeology	Education	Finance	Miscellaneous	Social science
Astronomy	Energy	Food	Nature	Sociology
Automotive	Engineering	Geography	Nutrition	Sports
Biology	Environment	Government	Physics	Weather
Consumer	Europe	Health	Psychology	Zoology
Economics	Famous datasets	Medical	Science	

These tables are not supported by a database engine, but can be copied and imported into a database engine as tab delimited data. What distinguishes this site from

TABLE 12.1 ■ Summary of Sample Databases and Their Internet Addresses

DASL Project (1996). The Data Story Library. [On line]	http://lib.stat.cmu.edu/DASL
Federal Interagency Council on Statistical Policy (2000). FEDSTATS. [On line]	http://www.fedstats.gov/
National Climatic Data Center (2000). Publications [On line]	http://www5.ncdc.noaa.gov/pubs/ publications.html
U.S. Census Bureau (2000). Statistical Agencies (International). [On line]	http://www.census.gov/main/www/stat_int.html
Journal of Statistics of Education (2000). JSE Data Archive. [On line]	http://www.amstat.org/publications/jse/archive.htm

the government sites that you will see listed below is the variety of data not connected to topics that the government wants to know about.

National Climatic Data Center

The National Climatic Data Center has a huge library of up-to-date statistics on local, national, and world climate. However, the site charges for its data. The charges are not large, but if you plan on using the site, you must plan ahead. Some of the data that you can get include the following:

■ Monthly climatic data for the world
■ Storm data
■ Local climatological data, edited
■ Climatological data
■ Hourly precipitation data
■ Climatography of the United States: monthly normals
■ Heating and cooling degree day data
■ Climates of the world; wind climatology
■ Freeze/frost data for the United States

FedStats

FedStats (2000) is an agency that collects statistics from over seventy government agencies. Not only does this site provide links to the data, but it also provides tools to access the data. That is to say, the data is supported by a database engine so that you do not have to download and convert it. Some of the major agencies that FedStats links to include: Bureau of the Census, Bureau of Labor Statistics, Energy Information Administration, Environmental Protection Agency, National Agricultural Statistics Service, National Center for Health Statistics, National Science Foundation, Bureau of Justice Statistics, and the National Center for Education Statistics.

U.S. Census Bureau

The U.S. Census Bureau (2000) has an enormous site with free data on every question asked by the census and more. From this site you may get national data as well as regional and state data. Buried in the U.S. Census Bureau Site is the Statistical Agencies (International) site, which lists statistics on approximately one hundred countries beginning with Algeria and ending with Yugoslavia. The countries themselves maintain these sites, and often the listings are available in both English and the language of the country listing the statistics. Not only would these sites be good places to obtain data for a social studies class, but they also serve as a valuable resource for foreign language classes.

Journal of Statistics in Education

The Journal of Statistics in Education, much like the DASL project, is aimed at providing data and analyses of that data for students studying statistics. However, like DASL, this project provides data on topics that the government is not typically interested in. To give you a flavor for the variety of information on this site, titles of some of the data sets and accompanying articles include: Population at Risk and Death Rates for an Unusual Episode (data on the sinking of the Titanic); What Does It Take to Heat a New Room?; Time of Birth, Sex, and Birth Weight of 44 Babies; The Draft Lotteries of 1970, 1971, and 1972; Fitting Percentage of Body Fat to Simple Body Measurements; Sexual Activity and Lifespan of Male Fruit Flies; Galileo Motion Data; U.S. Senate Votes on Clinton Removal; Normal Body Temperature, Gender, and Heart Rate; and The Statistics of Poverty and Inequality.

■ FORMATTING DATA FOR USE IN A DATABASE

Making downloaded databases useful is a challenge. Sometimes you can find a great database, but it is in a large table with no database engine to support it. Hence, students are unable to do sorts and queries; all they can do is look at the facts, which is not the point of a database at all. However, in many cases, it is not too difficult to download a table from the Internet and convert it to a format that a database engine can use. The other possibility is finding a database that is supported by a search engine on the Internet. Let us first look at how to make online databases usable.

> Much data on the Internet must be reformatted to work with a database engine

Technique 1: Making Raw Internet Data Usable

Take, for example, a database found on the NASA website called the "Planetary Factsheet" (NASA, 2000). In Figure 12.1, you see the screen as it is displayed on the NASA site. The database is an HTML table with no database engine to support it. But what if you wanted your students to manipulate those numbers and find the largest, smallest, most distant, least distant, fastest, slowest, coldest, hottest, and do some comparisons? You need to make this information accessible to a database engine. More recent versions of word processors and database engines make this possible. The examples that you will see are in Microsoft Word and Microsoft Access.

To make the file in Figure 12.1 accessible to Access, you should use the following procedure:

1. Download the HTML file (what you see in Figure 12.1) and save it.
2. Open Word.
3. Open the HTML file that you downloaded and saved in Word.
4. Click on the Table menu and click on Convert Table. Choose Table to Text. Then choose either comma-delimited or tab-delimited format. This table will look ugly, like Figure 12.2. But don't worry. Things will get better.
5. Save the downloaded file as a text file. Save it as "Text with line breaks."
6. Open Access, and open the text file you just saved.
7. Access will ask you whether it is tab- or comma-delimited when you try to open it. Choose the correct option box, and the table will open in Access and look just like Figure 12.3. You are almost there.
8. Now you must format each field (remember that column headers are the field names) so that it reflects the kind of data in the field. In this case, you will want to make sure that the computer sees these fields as "numeric" fields.
9. Now your database is ready for your students to use. Once you have gone through the process a few times, you will find that it takes less than fifteen minutes from the beginning of the download to the appearance of the usable table in the database.

Products other than Microsoft Office offer similar features. Every major database and spreadsheet manufactured allows the user to import tab- and/or comma-delimited data. Many, but not all, word processors allow users to convert tables to text.

> Converting HTML tables to text is the critical step in using Internet data

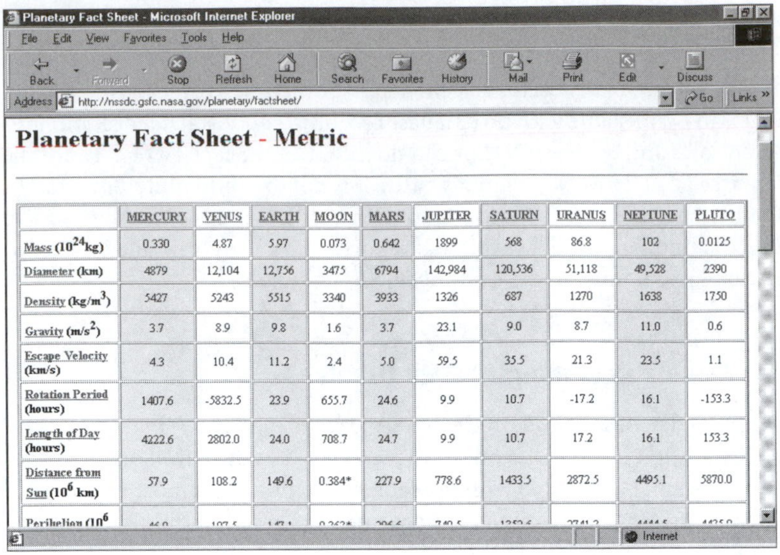

FIGURE 12.1 ■ First Half of Planetary Fact Sheet from NASA Web Site

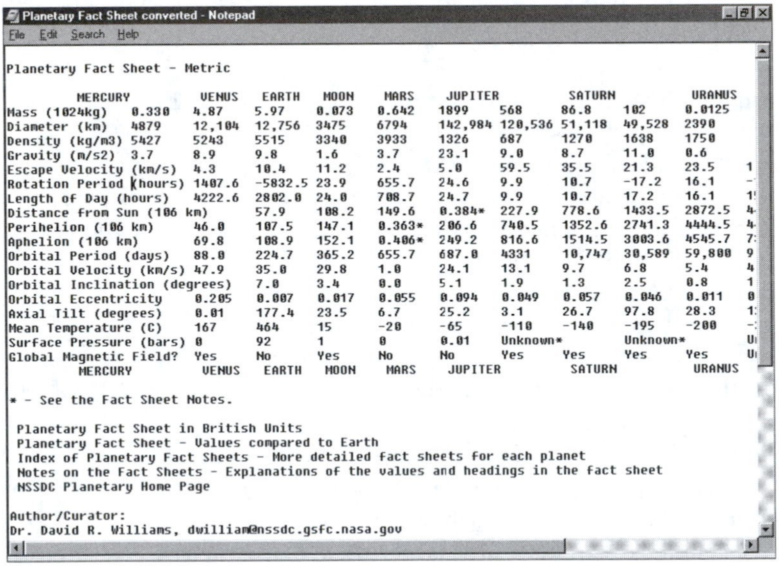

FIGURE 12.2 ■ Internet Planetary Fact Sheet Converted to a Tab-Delimited Text File

If your school does not use the Office suite or uses an older version, you may need to request a copy of either Office or other software that does convert HTML tables to text. This is the critical step in using much of the data that you can retrieve from the Internet.

Microsoft Access - [Planetary Fact Sheet converted : Table]

File Edit View Insert Format Records Tools Window Help

Field1	Field2	Field3	Field4	Field5	Field6	Field7	Field8	Field9	Field10	Fie
Planetary Fact Shee										
	MERCURY	VENUS	EARTH	MOON	MARS	JUPITER	SATURN	URANUS	NEPTUNE	PLUTO
Mass (1024kg)	0.330	4.87	5.97	0.073	0.642	1899	568	86.8	102	0.0125
Diameter (km)	4879	12,104	12,756	3475	6794	142,984	120,536	51,118	49,528	2390
Density (kg/m3)	5427	5243	5515	3340	3933	1326	687	1270	1638	1750
Gravity (m/s2)	3.7	8.9	9.8	1.6	3.7	23.1	9.0	8.7	11.0	0.6
Escape Velocity (km	4.3	10.4	11.2	2.4	5.0	59.5	35.5	21.3	23.5	1.1
Rotation Period (hou	1407.6	-5832.5	23.9	655.7	24.6	9.9	10.7	-17.2	16.1	-153.3
Length of Day (hours	4222.6	2802.0	24.0	708.7	24.7	9.9	10.7	17.2	16.1	153.3
Distance from Sun ('	57.9	108.2	149.6	0.384*	227.9	778.6	1433.5	2872.5	4495.1	5870.0
Perihelion (106 km)	46.0	107.5	147.1	0.363*	206.6	740.5	1352.6	2741.3	4444.5	4435.0
Aphelion (106 km)	69.8	108.9	152.1	0.406*	249.2	816.6	1514.5	3003.6	4545.7	7304.3
Orbital Period (days)	88.0	224.7	365.2	655.7	687.0	4331	10,747	30,589	59,800	90,588
Orbital Velocity (km/	47.9	35.0	29.8	1.0	24.1	13.1	9.7	6.8	5.4	4.7
Orbital Inclination (d	7.0	3.4	0.0	5.1	1.9	1.3	2.5	0.8	1.8	17.2
Orbital Eccentricity	0.205	0.007	0.017	0.055	0.094	0.049	0.057	0.046	0.011	0.244
Axial Tilt (degrees)	0.01	177.4	23.5	6.7	25.2	3.1	26.7	97.8	28.3	122.5
Mean Temperature ('	167	464	15	-20	-65	-110	-140	-195	-200	-225
Surface Pressure (ba	0	92	1	0	0.01	Unknown*	Unknown*	Unknown*	Unknown*	0
Global Magnetic Fiel	Yes	No	Yes	No	No	Yes	Yes	Yes	Yes	Unknow
	MERCURY	VENUS	EARTH	MOON	MARS	JUPITER	SATURN	URANUS	NEPTUNE	PLUTO
* - See the Fact She										

Record: 14 ◀ | 1 | ▶ ▶I ▶* | of 50

Datasheet View   NUM

FIGURE 12.3 ■ The Finished, Working Database—Not So Ugly Anymore

Technique 2: Internet Databases with Their Own Search Engines

Another fortunate find on the Internet is a database with its own search engine. An example of such a site is the "Valley of the Shadow" (Ayers, 1998a) that is dedicated to helping students understand the Civil War from the perspective of the average citizen of the North and the South. The site provides parallel information about two small towns, one northern and one southern. Included are letters between soldiers and their families. There are many graphics, pictures of the people from the two towns, and of the war. In addition, the site has extensive databases (Ayers, 1998b). These databases include U.S. Census records, military records, church records, and local government records. The interface for the search engine that accesses these records looks like Figure 12.4. Notice the fields with the "greater than" (>) sign in front of them. This sign means that all of the comparison operators are available for the search, which allows for much fine-tuning. The Personal Estate Value field shows this drop-down box extended, allowing the user to choose a symbol.

"The Valley of the Shadow" is an excellent example of a site that includes not only databases but also other material prepared specifically for use in teaching. You will find other databases with their own search engines on the Internet as well, though supporting materials aren't included, and they are not designed for classrooms. Some of the database search engines that you will find have their own quirks and operational differences that will require you and your students to learn how to use the interface before you can proceed with queries. Usually figuring out how to use a new search interface takes no longer than ten or fifteen minutes, and often there are instructions. The more search engines you use, the easier it will be to learn new ones.

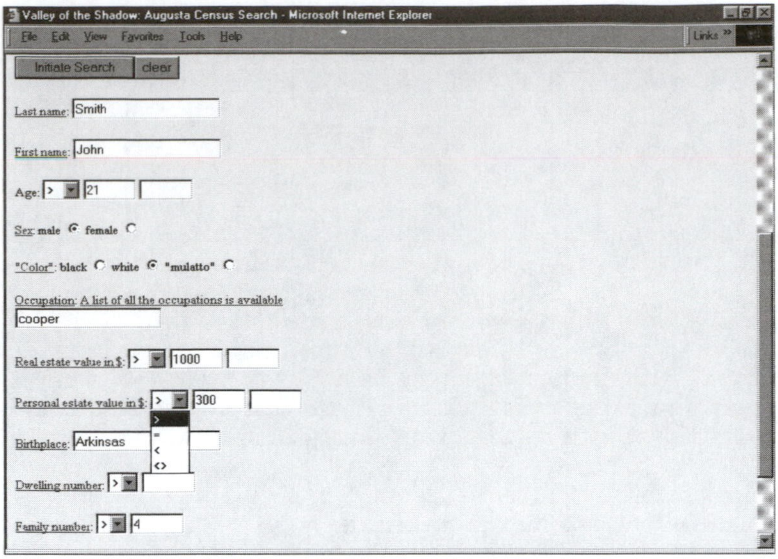

FIGURE 12.4 ■ A Sample Search of the "Valley of the Shadow" Database

Technique 3: Building Your Own Database

The lack of a prepared database for a topic that a class is studying should not stop a determined teacher from using databases as a tool for teaching. Students can make their own databases. In making the database themselves, students are looking up facts and working with them. Having students create their own database is no more tedious or meaningless than the practice of having students look up and memorize definitions, do work sheets, and answer questions at the end of the chapter.

In fact, the difference between doing these activities and building a database is significant. When students are building a database, they are doing it with a goal in mind—building a tool that will help them think more clearly. They must think about information and enter it accurately, because their carefulness will affect the usability of the database they create. A second benefit of building a database is that students must design the database themselves. They must decide which fields to include and how to format the information in each field. Before they commit themselves to their design (their decisions about which fields to include), they will run some trial sorts and queries to determine whether the design is adequate. Ultimately they will use the dull, fact-finding work and precise requirements of building a database to formulate creative, thoughtful questions and skillful queries that give them answers to difficult questions with fuzzy edges. Furthermore, building a database gives some purpose to the tedious part of learning that everyone must endure. In order to reason and think analytically, people must have a base of accurate, available facts. Building a database is one way of acquiring these facts. A database can be graded for accuracy and completeness just like worksheets, end-of-chapter questions, and pages of terms and definitions.

From a practical standpoint, having students build their own databases means that for the first few years you teach with databases you will be building one almost every time you want to do a database-supported lesson. Therefore, for the first year you

> Students use both low- and high-level thinking skills when they build their own databases

may only build one per quarter or even less. Nevertheless, you will start the next year with four ready-made databases and will be able to add to your repertoire. Furthermore, if other teachers in your subject build databases, you will soon have databases for every topic for which they are appropriate. Then, you and your students will simply need to maintain the databases you have.

There is another reason why your students might build a database other than the fact that a database does not already exist for the topic your class is studying. You may want to have your class build a database as they collect data. For example, a class studying plant growth under various conditions may want to build a database in which they record their observations. Or, your class may do a survey and put the data that they collect into a database. In either case, your class would have to design the database and develop a form for entering the information that they collect.

Building a database
takes time

■ SUMMARY

Acquiring a database is a key part of building a database lesson. There are three different methods for obtaining them:

1. Downloading them from an electronic source and converting them into a format that a database engine can read
2. Finding data on the Internet or on a CD that has its own database engine
3. Having your class build databases based on the information that they are studying

If there is time, your students can learn at several levels by building their own. They must find facts and transfer them accurately to the database. They must understand the structure of the information that they are studying in order to design the database, and they must decide whether they have designed a useful database before they commit themselves to entering all of the data they need.

Building a database covers the lowest and highest levels of Bloom's Taxonomy (Table 12.2). It provides students a point of contact with elemental facts at the lowest level. On the highest levels it provides students a way of organizing single facts in such a way as to help them understand the structure of an entire topic.

✓ CHECKING YOUR UNDERSTANDING

12.1

1. Using one of the Internet resources listed in this chapter, find and convert an electronic database. Write a topic for research, writing, or discussion for students at a grade level that would use this database. Write ten sample queries that would shed light on this topic.

2. Using "The Valley of the Shadow" databases, design a lesson. Provide a writing topic for students at your grade level of interest. Write ten sample queries you would do which would shed light on your writing topic.

3. Think of a topic that is appropriate to a grade level that you will teach. Design a database to support that topic. List the fields you will use. Write ten sample queries.

TABLE 12.2 ■ Bloom's Taxonomy and Building Databases

Level of Thought	Description	Database Activity
Knowledge	Name, locate, tell, list, repeat, point to	Locating and entering information into the database
Comprehension	Define, summarize, infer, project, describe	
Application	Use, solve, adapt, relate, perform	
Analysis	Compare, classify, screen, examine, test for	
Synthesis	Create, develop, generate, build, compile, design	Designing the database
Evaluation	Judge, reject, criticize, rate, rank	Doing some practice queries and sorts to determine if the database design is adequate

■ REFERENCES ■

Ayers, D. R. (1998a). *The valley of the shadow.* [On line]. Available: http://jefferson. village.virginia.edu/vshadow2/choosepart.html.

Ayers, D. R. (1998b). *The valley of the shadow.* [On line]. Available: http://valley. vcdh.virginia.edu/govdoc/au.census1860.html.

DASL Project (1996). Data and Story Library [On line]. http://lib.stat.cmu.edu/DASL. [Retrieved Feb. 3, 2001].

FedStats (2000). Federal Interagency Council on Statistical Policy. http://www. fedstats.gov/. [Retrieved Jan. 18, 2001].

Journal of Statistics in Education (2000). JSE Data Archive [On line]. http://www. amstat.org/publications/jse/archive.htm. [Retrieved Dec. 15, 2001].

NASA (2000). "Planetary Factsheet," National Aeronautics and Space Administration [On line]. Available: http://nssdc.gsfc.nasa.gov/planetary/factsheet. [Retrieved Feb. 8, 2001]

National Climatic Data Center (2000). Publications [On line]. http://www5.ncdc. noaa.gov/pubs/publications.html. [Retrieved January 15, 2001].

U.S. Census Bureau (2000). Statistical Agencies (International). Available: http://www. census.gov/main/www/stat_int.html. [Retrieved February 4, 2001]

■ ANNOTATED RESOURCES ■

Lockard, J. & Abrams, P. D. (2001). *Computers for 21st century educators.* 5th ed. New York: Longman. On pages 199–122 the authors discuss research on databases.

They state "relatively little research has appeared concerning measurable impacts of learning with databases, and so one must be cautious about generalizations."

They have, however, found some older studies (1992, 1991, 1990, 1991, 1988) that support some general conclusions. Sources that Lockard and Abrams summarized include:

Ehman, L., Glenn, A., Johnson, V., & White, C. Using computer databases in student problem solving: A study of eight social studies teachers' classrooms." *Theory and Research in Social Education*, Spring 1992, 20(2), pp. 179–206.

Problem solving strategies, constructing fields, learner characteristics that prevented maximum use of a database lesson, appropriate size of a database, evidence of higher order thinking, the role of the teacher, length of time for teaching a database supported lesson, structure in a database lesson, and grouping.

Maor, D. Development of Student Inquiry Skills: A constructivist approach in a computerized classroom environment. Paper presented at the Annual Meeting of the National Association for Research in Science Teaching (Lake Geneva, WI, April 7–10, 1991). ERIC (ED 336 261).

This is about inquiry-based science teaching and the use of a computerized database on birds of Antarctica.

Kern, J. F. (1990). Using "Readers' Guide to Periodical Literature" on CD-ROM to teach database searching to high school students. Ed.S. Practicum Report, Nova University, Ft. Lauderdale, FL, 1990. ERIC (ED 328 291.)

This is a comparison of student database searching of both computerized and print databases in an English class.

Collis, B. The best of research windows: Trends and issues in educational computing. Eugene, OR: International Society for Technology in Education, 1990. ERIC (ED 323 993.)

This is a summary of six database studies addressing the ability of students to formulate appropriate questions when they query a database.

Gaffuri, A. (1991). Expanding third graders' vocabulary using a data base, individual thesauri and brainstorming strategies. Ed.D. Practicum I Report, Early and Middle Childhood Program, Nova University, Ft. Lauderdale, FL, 1991. ERIC (ED331 035.)

This is a study on using a database to help third grade students improve their vocabularies.

Rawitsch, D. (1988). The effects of computer use and student work style on database analysis activities in the social studies. In *Improving the use of technology in schools: What are we learning*. Research Bulletin #1. St. Paul, MN: MECC/University of Minnesota Center for the Study of Educational Technology, November 1988, pp. 1–3.

White, C. S. (1990). Access to and use of databases in the social studies." *International Journal of Social Education*, Spring 1990, 5(1), pp. 61–73.

These studies yield some empirical evidence that database use improves students' higher order thinking skills. Other conclusions resulted from this study as well.

CHAPTER 13

Using Spreadsheets to Think about Numbers

OBJECTIVES

- Describe when the use of a spreadsheet is appropriate in science, social studies, mathematics, and language arts.
- Be able to explain mean, median, mode, and standard deviation.
- Use descriptive statistics to describe phenomena about which you have found or gathered data.
- Know how to make graphs and charts using computer software.
- Know how to use charts and graphs to visualize information.
- Know how to use pivot tables to tease out patterns in information.
- Design a pivot table.
- Use formulas and "Goal Seek" to ask "what if" questions.

■ NUMBERS AS TOOLS BEYOND MATH

Numbers are among humankind's oldest friends. Cuneiform tablets in the Middle East, examples of our first writing, were engraved with numbers. These numbers recorded business transactions. Do you recall the reason for the development of the first electrically powered computer? Numbers were, again, at the root of this development. The United States military needed to make complex calculations quickly during World War II. It needed to calculate the trajectory of artillery shells.

Although one could not say that our we are in love with numbers (in fact, numbers scare many people), numbers and the ability to manipulate them quickly and accurately are the basis for everything that makes modern medicine, science, and business viable. Knowing how to use and think about numbers is one reason for our metamorphosis from hunter-gatherer to information worker.

Our society is based on our ability to use numbers effectively

A criticism of our educational system is that children only learn the mechanics of working with numbers instead of learning how to apply numbers to practical situations. At some level, this may be true in many classrooms but for a number of reasons other than teacher negligence or district apathy. From the point of view of a classroom teacher, the task of helping children think with numbers is quite daunting.

For example, one challenge lies in children's skill level in working with numbers compared to the kinds of problems that are interesting and useful for them to solve. It is only interesting to figure out where two cars, boats, or trains that are going different speeds meet between points A and B once or twice. The reason most students learn how to solve this problem is for practice in identifying and practicing the steps leading to its solution. Once students find a solution, they know nothing more about the world than they did before they learned how to solve the problem.

Another challenge lies in our perception of where numbers fit in the curriculum. Many teachers, as students themselves, struggled to understand numbers. Because so many people lack confidence with numbers, they see them as obstacles rather than useful tools that help us think well. Students study history, social studies, and science diligently. They learn the meanings of words. For example, when they study government they learn the definition of an oligarchy. In science, they learn the definition of a mitochondrion. Moreover, they learn to attach words to pictures like recognizing the tundra from an unlabeled picture or recognizing countries on a map in geography. They use words and pictures as tools to understand our world.

Numbers are tools too, and like words they have meaning both as text and as pictures. However, we use them less frequently than words or pictures to help students make sense of the world. Very few social studies teachers have had the training and tools to show students how to analyze social and historical problems and trends with numbers. Young science students are limited to using numbers they know how to manually calculate as they study complex problems. They must learn facts and theories on faith from those who do know how to work and think with numbers derived from complex calculations.

The goal of this chapter is to raise the level of understanding of the contribution of spreadsheets to the learning process for those who teach science, social studies, and to some extent mathematics. The purpose of this chapter is not to focus on mathematics or tools for mathematics. That is a book of its own, especially for high school-level mathematics. Rather, the aim here is to provide some examples where spreadsheets have helped students explore common science and social studies topics that are taught from elementary school through high school. You must use your imagination as you read about the different possibilities and use your creativity and experience with children to generate lessons that will work in your classroom.

Spreadsheets provide answers to the same kinds of problems as databases: analysis, prediction, and description of an unknown, but they are designed to work with numbers rather than text. They even provide tools for performing sorts and queries, as well. Furthermore, spreadsheets require a very similar instructional model to the database though there is some variation. First, there must be a problem. Second, the students must choose and/or acquire the data they need to solve the problem. Third, students must figure out how to set up the problem on the spreadsheet and decide which tool(s) to use. Finally, students must analyze and present their results as well as check their results with an outside source.

Spreadsheets help students think about the concepts behind numbers

Numbers are a tool like text that helps us understand our world

Teachers in many content areas can use numbers to help students learn concepts

Methods for using spreadsheets are similar to those for databases

Managing the classroom using spreadsheets is very similar to managing the classroom using databases. In the one computer classroom, the teacher uses an LCD projector and works through the problem with the whole class using the spreadsheet to stimulate class discussion. Another approach is to set up the computer as a center and require groups to work through the problem together while other groups work at other centers. For five-computer classrooms, spreadsheets, like databases, are especially suited to group work because of the interactive question generating process they stimulate. In addition, students working together can generally decide on the keystrokes they need to get their problem solved while students working alone sometimes are utterly lost. To begin our exploration of spreadsheets, let us look at the kinds of problems spreadsheets solve.

Choosing the Problem

At this point in the book, you will know without being told that the first step in using a spreadsheet is choosing and describing the problem. The focus in this chapter is on choosing problems for which the solution involves only simple arithmetic that we have all learned by upper elementary school: using formulas, elementary statistics, and percentages. Table 13.1 is a list of some possible problems and the kind of elementary mathematics that people use to think about them. As an expert in what you teach, you can probably generate more if you think about it.

Table 13.2 lists further topics that you can explore if you wish to read the articles that they reference. K–12 teachers wrote all of these articles and the lessons have been executed in classrooms. Some of the problems described in Table 13.2 involve different mathematical concepts than formulas, statistics, and percentages and are for specific scientific and mathematics topics in high school. If high school mathematics or science is your specialty, these resources will provide you with some valuable insight into uses for spreadsheets in your classroom.

■ THE VERSATILE SPREADSHEET

Spreadsheets are a tool made of many tools. They are like a Swiss Army knife. If you need a screwdriver, it is available. If you need a knife, saw, or bottle opener, those tools are available as well. Some tools are more complex than others.

The remainder of this chapter will be devoted to a study of some simple and intermediate tools available in spreadsheets. Not every tool is appropriate for every age level or every problem. For example, tools used on a regular basis in the ninth grade may be used for enrichment in the fifth or sixth grade. Nor can this chapter capture every possible use for every spreadsheet tool. As you read, you must think about the curriculum you teach or that you will teach someday.

Easy Spreadsheet Tools

A spreadsheet is a grid that consists of cells with columns designated by letters and rows designated by numbers. The spreadsheet at its most simple level allows the user

TABLE 13.1 ■ Examples of Problems for Which Spreadsheets Are Useful

Problem	Spreadsheet Tool
Use demographic data for populations (human, animal, plant) to track change in their (numbers, locations, health, wealth) over time. Use the data to explain the changes.	Charts and graphs; Elementary statistics
Determine the monthly payment on a loan using different repayment amounts, terms, and interest rates.	Formula
Measure the speed and distance objects move over different lengths and heights of inclined planes.	Formula
If the sun were the size of a basketball, what would the relative sizes and distances be for objects in the rest of the solar system?	Percentages
Given the history of change in my city (country, hemisphere), what will my city be like in 50 years when I am getting ready to retire? In 10 years when I will start looking for a job?	Creating a formula; Charts, graphs
Given the rate of extinction of plant and animal species over the last fifty years, how many more species will be extinct by the time I am 20? 30? 40?	Creating a formula; Charts, graphs
Using the equation e=mc^2, how much matter would I need to run my refrigerator, my house, our city) for a year?	Formula
How would a change in the minimum wage affect the businesses in my city? How would it affect me as a young worker?	Percentages
What happens to the number of bacteria in a bean infusion over time? (Cuevas, 1994)	Charts, graphs
Measure the temperature change of water in different colored containers that are standing in the sun.	Charts, graphs
How are population growth, land area, and irrigated land related to a country's wealth and to each other?	Percentages, charts, graphs
How do prices change when there is a shortage or surplus of a commodity?	Percentages, charts, graphs
Is there a relationship between the accumulation of national debt and national income?	Charts, graphs
Compare the effect of acid rain to ordinary water on sprouting seeds. Compare the sprout rate of weed seeds to food seeds (Cuevas, 1994).	Elementary statistics; Charts, graphs
What are the effects of natural disasters and the weather on national economies?	Charts, graphs
Analyze voting patterns to determine how diverse populations affect politics in the United States.	Charts, graphs

to type numbers into the cells and then add, subtract, multiply, or divide them. Once a series of numbers has been computed or acquired, the spreadsheet user then builds a chart or graph to visualize this data. The chart is created with a pop-up menu and either displayed on the worksheet with the numbers or on a sheet by itself. Furthermore, the chart and all of the numbers may be cut and pasted into a word-processed document or **dynamically linked** to a presentation. Simple arithmetic problems that

dynamically linked
If the student changes the chart in the spreadsheet, then the copy of the chart that was put in the presentation will reflect those changes.

TABLE 13.2 ■ Examples of More Problems, Their Content Areas, and Grade Levels

Topic	Grade Level	Subject
• Understand the stock market (Whitmer, 1992)	7, 8, 9	Math/Economics
• Set up and solving word problems (Verderber, 1990)	7, 8, 9	Math
• Explore the composition and amount of marine debris (Lynch & Walton, 1998)	9–12	Science
• Teach area and perimeter (Widmer & Sheffield, 1998)	5–12	Math
• Compare average yearly concentration of carbon dioxide to average midtropospheric temperature for a lesson on greenhouse gasses (Slattery, Hundley, Finegan-Stoll, & Becker, 1998)	11–12	Science
• Trend analysis of weather (Slater, 1998)	8–10	Science
• Model population growth (Slater, 1998)	10–12	Science
• Explore the history of convicts in Australia (Lloyd, 1998)	10–12	Social studies
• Set up and solve equations (Niess, 1998)	7–9	Math
• Calculate ratios and proportions of the human body using their own and classmates' measurements as the data. Compare these calculations to Leonardo da Vinci's calculations based on his drawing "The Proportions of the Human Figure" (1492) (Morgan & Jernigan, 1998)	7–12	Art, science, Math
• Track expenses on a virtual trip (Bitner, Wadlington, Austin, Partridge, & Bitner (1999)	4–8	Social Studies
• Understand probability (Pugalee, 1999)	7–9	Math
• Understanding how batteries work (Albrecht & Firedrake, 1999)	2–12	Science
• Teach matrices and geometric transformations (Feicht, 1999)	7–12	Math
• Understand exponential population growth and patterns (Drier, 1999)	3–9	Social science, Math
• Model graphs and functions	7–11	Math

yield elementary statistics (mean, median, range, mode, and standard deviation) and resulting charts are powerful tools to help children see the relationships numbers have to each other and the real world.

Another mathematical tool that children use at an early age is the formula. Examples of mathematical formulas that children learn early include:

Distance = Rate × Time

Interest = Rate × Principal

Perimeter = S1 + S2 + S3 . . .

Area of a rectangle = Length × Width

Percentage = N1 / N2

Spreadsheets are built to allow people to enter a formula and then ask "what if" questions. When you are using a formula in a spreadsheet, it is easy to solve more than one problem. Consequently, students can see what the formula means in many problems rather than looking for an answer to just one problem.

■ DESCRIPTIVE STATISTICS

Example: Understanding How Soil Affects Plants

We will continue now by looking into two classrooms where the students are studying topics that involve descriptive statistics. These two upper elementary science classrooms are studying soil composition and plant growth. The reason that the students are using a spreadsheet is to help answer the question, "What do these numbers we are collecting mean?" The question the two teachers have given their students is, "Do different soils affect how fast plants grow?" Although the teacher in the first classroom is trying to do a good job with what she has, she could be doing more to help her students realize the potential that numbers have to help us understand our world better.

FIELD TRIP 11.1

The Mean Bean

Picture in your mind Ms. Clayton's fifth grade students, who are growing twenty bean plants in different kinds of soil—humus, clay, and sand. The beans all received the same sunlight and the same amount of water. The students measured the growth of the beans at the end of three weeks. Then they calculated their averages by hand, and none of the groups' averages matched the others. Ms. Clayton finally told the students that their averages were pretty much "in the same ballpark" and since they were studying science, not math, they didn't have to go back and recalculate one more time to see whose math was wrong. Her real reason for saying this is that she just didn't have time to have the students redo the calculations. Furthermore, she knew that some of her more challenged students would just get frustrated and not redo their averages anyway. The point was that the beans grown in humus were taller according to everyone's calculations, even though the numbers didn't exactly match.

In creating such a lesson, the teacher may *feel* like she or he has encouraged students to use numbers to analyze and solve a problem. She may take some pride in the fact that she didn't let the students get so bogged down in arithmetic problems that they lost sight of the real goal: to study soil types. But, in fact, a lesson conducted this way encouraged the development of some misconceptions on the part of students, all having to do with numbers and how to use them to solve problems.

■ She ignored "precision of measurement" issues.
■ She has led the student to believe that because one average is different from another average, the two populations they represent are always different.

In contrast, let us look at Ms. Hull's fifth grade classroom doing the same experiment but using a spreadsheet. In this classroom, the experiment was the same but keeping and analyzing records was different. At the end of the experiment, the students measure the beans and enter their measurements into a spreadsheet. Mrs. Hull had students work in groups at the five computers in her classroom. The teacher asked the students which soil grew the tallest beans. The students determined the average height of the beans in each group. There is no need for them to do the calculations by hand when a spreadsheet calculates quickly and accurately. She reminded students of the importance of accuracy as they entered the numbers they had obtained from their measurements. She asked each group to check their work against the work of the other groups. The averages that the different groups calculated didn't match, but not because of inaccurate math. Each group found that its average was slightly different than the average of other groups because the students weren't able to be precise in their measurements. Ms. Hull used this activity to generate a discussion about errors in measurement. After the "error of measurement" discussion was over, each group concluded that the beans grown in humus were the tallest, while beans grown in sand were a very close second. The beans grown in clay were much shorter than the beans in either of the other two samples.

Ms. Hull's next exercise for the students was to send them back to their five computers to create a chart illustrating the growth rates of beans in the three different kinds of soil. Students took some time getting their chart right. It was not clear to them whether to use the height of the beans or whether they should use three averages that they calculated. They had to argue and experiment before they completed their charts correctly (Figure 13.1).

Then Ms. Hull said, "Our calculations and charts show that the beans grown in humus are, on the average, one centimeter taller than beans grown in sand and four centimeters taller than beans grown in clay. What would happen if we changed the scale of the charts from 10 centimeters to 64 units?" The children re-created the chart after changing the scale of the chart from 10 to 64 (Figure 13.2). Ms. Hull then asked them why the two charts were so different. She also asked them whether, if they saw only the chart based on 64 units, they would think that the beans grown in clay are very much shorter than the beans grown in humus. As the children worked through this exercise, they learned how people could lie to them using statistics (Huff, 1982). Their teacher concluded this part of the lesson by asking if it is

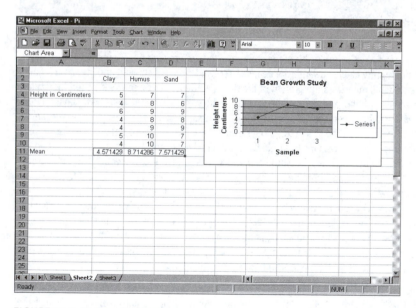

FIGURE 13.1 ■ Bean Problem

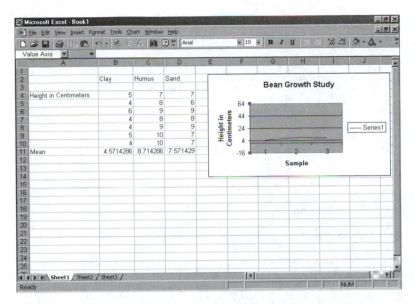

FIGURE 13.2 ■ Bean Growth Problems Using Different Scales on the Y Axis

right to try to influence people by changing the units on a chart or graph to make it say what they want it to say. In this way, she was not only teaching them science but also the ethics of science.

Then Ms. Hull made another observation. She said, "Look! Here is a bean growing in sandy soil that is taller than some of the beans growing in humus. How can we really know that beans grown in humus are generally taller than beans which are planted in sandy soil? According to our averages, all beans grown in humus should be taller than beans grown in sand."

The children did not know how to explain this, so Ms. Hull proceeded to introduce standard deviation to her class. She explained that there is a mathematical way of determining how likely it is that beans grow in humus better than they grow in sand. Using an LCD to display the spreadsheet of bean measurements that students have entered, she showed them how to find the standard deviation for each group of beans.

First she went to the Insert menu item and chose Function (Figure 13.3). She said, "This can seem very intimidating because none of the words on the list mean anything to you because you have never studied statistics. Nevertheless, if you just persevere and click on Statistics first and then STDEV, you will get a dialogue box (Figure 13.4). In this dialogue box, enter the range of cells (in this case B:4 to B:10) for which you want a standard deviation. Click on OK and the standard deviation (the measure of how closely individual scores approximate the mean) will appear in the cell where you left your cursor. After doing this, you can either repeat the process for the other two columns of bean measurements or simply select the cell where you have the completed standard deviation and drag your cursor across the next two rows. When you have finished, the worksheet will look like this." She showed them Figure 13.5.

Because this is a fifth grade classroom, none of Ms. Hull's students understands the mathematics or mathematical theory behind a standard deviation. Nevertheless, they do understand "average." They can also understand that the "mean" does not describe any one bean. Each bean is a little taller or shorter than the "mean bean." What they did

The spreadsheet helps students understand what the data mean

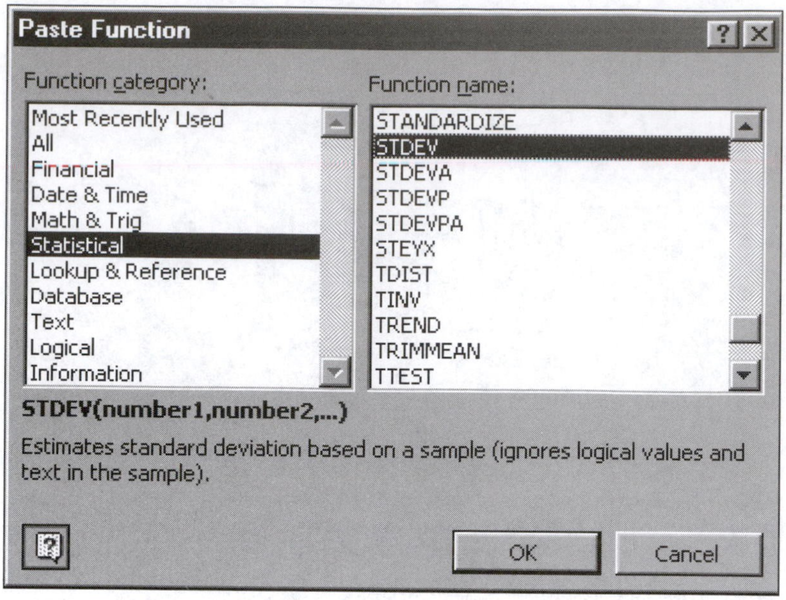

FIGURE 13.3 ■ Choosing to Calculate a Standard Deviation

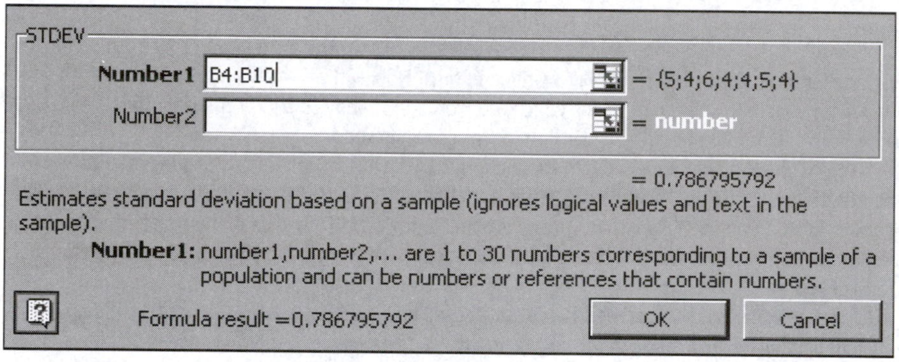

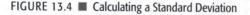

FIGURE 13.4 ■ Calculating a Standard Deviation

not understand until this lesson is that even though one average is higher than another average, the two averages do not necessarily represent statistically different populations.

What does this mean? The standard deviation of clay-grown beans is .73 centimeters, for humus-grown, 1 centimeter, and for sand-grown, 1 centimeter (rounded). Now look at the heights of the clay-grown beans: 5, 4, 6, 4, 4, 5, 4 (centimeters). If you added .73 centimeters to any of the clay-grown beans, none of them would be as tall as either the humus- or the sand-grown beans. In other words, the beans grown in clay are really different than the beans grown in sand or humus. On the other hand, if you look at the heights of the humus- and sand-grown beans and add or subtract one centimeter (the standard deviation of both groups) to the height of any of the beans in the

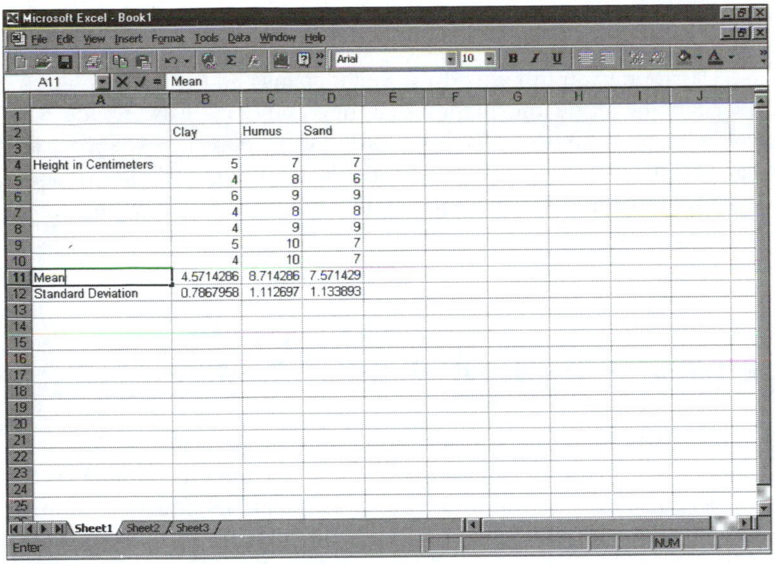

	A	B	C	D
1				
2		Clay	Humus	Sand
3				
4	Height in Centimeters	5	7	7
5		4	8	6
6		6	9	9
7		4	8	8
8		4	9	9
9		5	10	7
10		4	10	7
11	Mean	4.5714286	8.714286	7.571429
12	Standard Deviation	0.7867958	1.112697	1.133893

FIGURE 13.5 ■ Standard Deviation of Bean Heights

other group, you can see that there are many overlaps between the two groups. It could be that in a different test, the mean height of the beans grown in sand might be greater than the beans grown in humus. Students in the second fifth grade classroom are learning some important lessons:

- You can't always believe what you see.
- Sometimes charts or graphs help you understand what numbers mean, but you have to be clever about reading them.
- There are ways to test numbers that can help you make difficult judgments.

Why should students learn to apply descriptive statistics to the problems they study?

Before going further with Ms. Hull and her students, we must come to an understanding about a philosophical question. The question is, "Should a class of fifth graders be introduced to a difficult statistical concept like a standard deviation?" These children cannot understand or do the math behind this statistical test. What purpose is there in introducing such an idea? The premise behind many examples in this book is that the teacher is not teaching mathematics but rather science and social science concepts and methods. Advanced math teachers in high school have students use graphing calculators to free students from the tedium, distraction, and possibility of error created by doing pencil and paper calculations. Similarly, science and social studies teachers can free students of similar distractions by using spreadsheets. In the example of Mrs. Hull's class, the concept behind the standard deviation is not difficult to grasp. That a student doesn't understand the mathematics behind a standard deviation makes no more difference than the same student not knowing the chemistry behind a pH test strip. Both the standard deviation and the pH test strip are *tools.* When a skilled teacher uses them effectively, they can help students better understand the concepts and events that they study.

We have just looked in on two teacher's classrooms, Ms. Clayton who did not use spreadsheets and Ms. Hull who did. You have a general idea of how a spreadsheet might work in a classroom. You can see how it might change and amplify children's conceptual understanding of the information that they study as well as provide a basis for a constructivist approach to developing a lesson plan. To further whet your appetite for using spreadsheets, we will back up and take a more global view of some spreadsheet-assisted problems involving statistics that other teachers have integrated into the work of their classrooms.

■ DESCRIPTIVE STATISTICS: WHAT DO THEY MEAN?

Understanding the implication of a number

We are going to talk about four different statistical terms: mean, median, mode, and standard deviation. Mathematically, they are quite easy to compute. A third grader working at grade level can calculate the first three by hand and the fourth with three clicks of a mouse in a spreadsheet. Meaning is more difficult than computing. There are two stages through which students progress as they learn what these statistics mean. In the first stage, students can understand the implications of a mean or a median for a data set if a teacher or another student explains it. At another level, the student says, "Oh, if I could just compare the mean and the median for this data set, I could understand why x happened instead of y."

Descriptive statistics are derived from a range of data. Let us return to the bean study. In Figure 13.6, you see the mean, median, and mode for each group of beans.

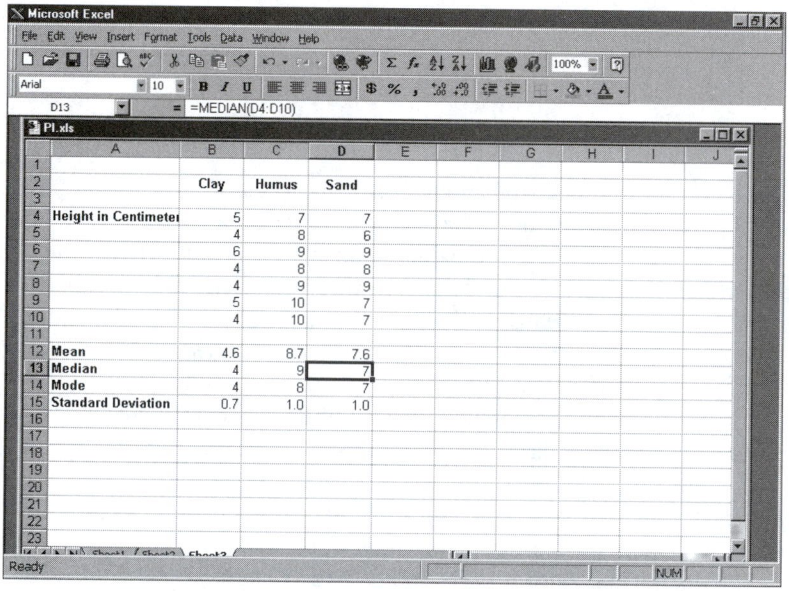

	A	B	C	D
1				
2		Clay	Humus	Sand
3				
4	Height in Centimeter	5	7	7
5		4	8	6
6		6	9	9
7		4	8	8
8		4	9	9
9		5	10	7
10		4	10	7
11				
12	Mean	4.6	8.7	7.6
13	Median	4	9	7
14	Mode	4	8	7
15	Standard Deviation	0.7	1.0	1.0

FIGURE 13.6 ■ Descriptive Statistics for the Bean Study

Notice also the formula in the formula bar. The spreadsheet does the math. All you have to do is indicate the range of cells for which you want one of these measures of **central tendency.** While we were on our field trip, we did not look at the medians and means of the three types of beans. However, they are easily calculated. Each of these statistics gives us slightly different information about a data set.

Mode

The mode is the most frequently occurring score in the distribution or group. Although mode is the least reliable of the three measures of central tendency, it nevertheless provides information. For example, if you knew that in Africa the most common (mode) gross national product is $7 billion dollars per year but the average (mean) gross national product for the continent is $32 billion dollars, you might guess that there are many poor countries and a few rich ones. Likewise with the bean study, you know that the mode for beans grown in sand is 7 centimeters and the mean is 7.6 centimeters. There are a few beans that are shorter than the "mean" bean.

> The mode is the most frequently occurring number

Median

The median is the middle score—the point above and below which an equal number of data fall. It is the most stable measure of central tendency. That means that if there are outliers in the data (extremes), these outliers do not influence the median nearly as much as the mean. A classic example is a data set of salaries. In Figure 13.7 you see a list of salaries with both the mean and median salary for the data set. Note the median

> The median is the middle number

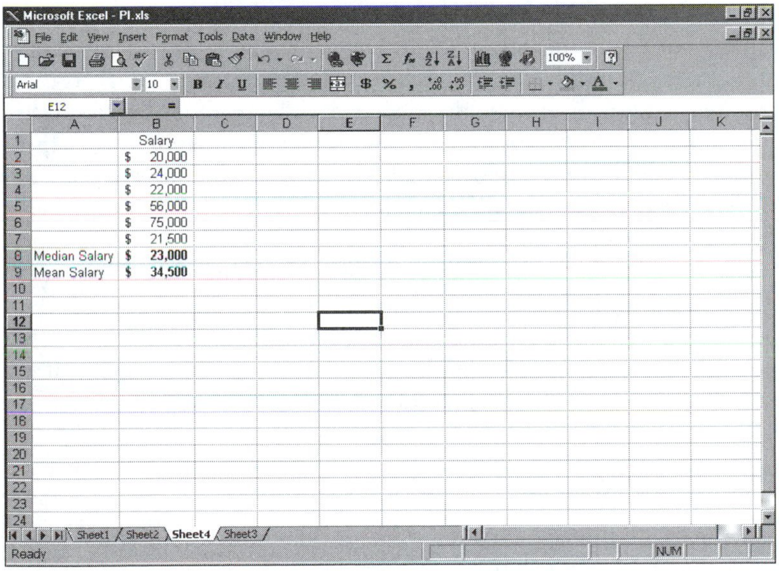

FIGURE 13.7 ■ Mean and Median Salaries

central tendency
What the "middle" of the data looks like. The **mean** is the arithmetic average that students are familiar with because grades are often based on students' mean scores. The **mode** is the most frequently occurring number, and the **median** is the middle score.

distribution
The group of scores that you are working with. For example, all of the heights for the beans grown in clay are one distribution.

reflects the more common salary, not the mean. The outliers are $56,000 and $75,000. These two people may represent management, while the rest of the salaries may represent clerical or professional staff. If someone wanting to get a job with this company had noted only the mean salary in the company, not the median salary, she would be disappointed with the company's offer. Similarly, if the bean study had had outliers, our impression of the "average" height of the beans would be far different if we looked at the mean rather than the median. Looking again at Figure 13.6, you can see that the mean and median are similar because there are no outliers. This is an important concept to teach children. Viewed from one perspective, using a mean when a median is more appropriate is another way that people can lie to them using statistics. From another perspective, understanding the concept of computing a median rather than a mean when there are outliers will give them a better understanding of what a "middle data point" of a data set is.

Mean

> The mean is the arithmetic average of a group of numbers

The mean is the measure of central tendency with which most of us are most familiar. For example, when teachers compute student grades, they get a mean by adding each score and dividing by the number of scores. It is most helpful for data sets where the distribution of data points is normal. "Normal" means that they reflect a symmetrical curve—the proverbial "bell shaped" curve. An example of a set of data points describing a roughly normal curve would be 50, 60, 60, 70, 70, 70, 80, 80, 90. It is the same concept as grading on the curve—that is, constructing standards based on the highest and lowest grade. It is reflected in the assumption that on any test the fewest students will get As and Fs while the most will get Cs, with a fewer number of students receiving Bs and Ds. Look back a few lines at the data points describing a normal curve. This could be a set of scores on a test.

> The mean, median, and mode give no different information about a range of numbers

The mean is a very useful measure of central tendency, but its flaw is the disruption caused by outliers. For this reason, it is important that students learn to report and reason with not only the mean, but also the median and the mode. You have already read one example in the previous section about how the mean is misleading when there are outliers in a distribution. Just to reinforce that point, let us try another, this one from *How to Lie With Statistics* (Huff, 1982). If the Oklahoma City Chamber of Commerce wanted to attract people to come to Oklahoma to live, they could advertise a comfortable average (mean) temperature of 60.2 degrees between 1890 and 1952. The temperatures actually ranged between –17 and 113 degrees. We didn't even have to look at the median to catch the flaw in this use of the mean. We simply looked at the *range* of temperatures. You never have the whole picture of what a data set means unless you can see and explain the mean, median, mode, and range of the numbers in a dataset.

> Using descriptive statistics to interpret a survey

Mean, Median, and Mode and Scales of Measurement

Not all measurements are the same. If your students do a survey, for example, they could collect information in several different formats. Not all of these formats are appropriate for use with all measures of central tendency (mean, median, and mode).

Suppose you are working as a team with a group of history and English teachers who have assigned their students to do an oral history of your community. Your students visit a retirement home to collect stories from residents, and as a part of the project ask residents a series of demographic questions to provide context for the oral histories. Some of the questions include the following.

1. Sex (1 = male, 2 = female)
2. Year born
3. Age you began your first full-time job
4. Preference on a scale between 1 and 4 for watching television
5. Preference on a scale between 1 and 4 for going on a walk
6. Actual hours spent watching television each week
7. Actual hours spent walking outside each week.

The first three questions represent different kinds of numbers; (questions 4 through 7 represent the same kind of number). Table 13.3 provides examples for each kind of number. With Table 13.3 in mind, think about the following statements:

1. The mean sex at the retirement home is 1.7
2. The mode for sex at the retirement home is 2
3. The median age for first full-time job at the retirement home was 15.5 years
4. The mean age for first full-time job at the retirement home was 13 years
5. The mean preference for watching television was 1.5; the mean preference for taking a walk was 3.5
6. The mean hours spent watching television each week was 30; the mean hours spent walking outside each week was 1

What does this all mean? Before you read the answers below, on a sheet of practice paper write your own interpretation of the survey results.

1. This finding is meaningless unless you believe that the nursing home is full of hermaphrodites in transition. Finding the mean of nominal results is a meaningless conclusion.
2. This finding is quite meaningful. It tells us that more women than men live at the retirement home.

TABLE 13.3 ■ Measurement Scales

Scale of Measurement	Example	Appropriate Measure of Central Tendency
Nominal	1 = Male 2 = Female 1 = Yes 2 = No	Mode
Ordinal	1 short 2 medium 3 tall Height	Mode
Interval	30 31 32 22 34 35 36 37 Degrees, Celsius	Mean, Median, Mode
Ratio	10 20 30 40 50 60 70 80 Miles, Watts, People, Cattle	Mean, Median, Mode

3, 4. Three and four are interesting. If the mean age for first job is 15.5 years and the median age is 13 years, some of those old folks are outliers and must have started working when they were very young.

5, 6. Preferences for walking versus television were revealing and meaningful. The number of hours is interval data and thus meaningful when a mean, median, and mode are computed. Residents would rather be out walking, but instead they are sitting in front of televisions.

The Standard Deviation

During our field trip where we observed students growing beans, we learned something about the standard deviation. It is probably the most commonly used measurement of *variability* because it is so stable. It is important to know how variable scores or other values are because it helps you understand whether you are really dealing with real difference between two groups or just chance variation. Standard deviation also helps us decide whether two groups of people or objects ("populations") are the same or different. Just to reinforce the concept of standard deviation, let's look at it again in a different context. You just looked at a portion of a survey taken by a group of high school students working on an oral history of elderly residents at a nursing home. One part of the project was to compare their demographics with students' demographics to learn more about what causes the differences of viewpoints and life styles that exist between the generations. If, for example, the mean hours spent per week watching television at the retirement home is thirty and among high school students it is twenty-five, are retirement home dwellers and these high school students members of two different populations or members of the same group whose mean hours varied simply by chance? If the standard deviation for retirement home residents was six hours, the difference is most likely chance rather than genuine. If the standard deviation for high school students were six hours, the same would be true.

There are other more precise methods for determining how likely it is that different means indicate different populations. At a basic level, however, this technique can begin to help students understand how to think about data. It is one more tool to help move students' interaction with information to the higher levels of Bloom's Taxonomy. If this kind of analysis moves from the math teacher's classroom to the classrooms of the history teacher, science teacher, and English teacher, it will become second nature to our children early in their academic careers.

> Understanding how to judge whether two groups of data are really different

■ USING SIMPLE ARITHMETIC OUTSIDE THE MATH CLASS

Simple arithmetic means using addition, subtraction, multiplication, division, and percentages to solve problems. One way of using these spreadsheet functions is to allow students to check their math problems with spreadsheets. If they do their problems once by hand, they focus on knowing their math facts, such as what is "5–3"? If they use the spreadsheet to check their computational skills, they focus on process—for example, how to set up a subtraction problem.

variability
The amount of dispersion of scores about a central value, such as the mean (Borg & Gall, 1998).

Using arithmetic in social studies

However, there are many other ways to use simple arithmetic outside of math class. Since we have already looked at a science problem, let us take a social studies problem and use a spreadsheet to think about it.

Suppose you are studying the Middle East in current affairs and you would really like your students to know more about the demographics of the countries and the relationships of the demographics to the turmoil in that area of the world. You have your students go to the CIA World Factbook on the Internet and make the worksheet shown in Figure 13.8. Think about how students might work with these numbers to learn more. Given the numbers they have, they can ask the following questions:

1. What is the differential between the birth and death rate for each country? What are the implications of this differential? What do the countries with the largest and smallest differentials have in common?
2. How many people are there per square kilometer in each country? What are the implications of these numbers?
3. What is the differential between imports and exports in each country? What are the implications of this differential? What do the countries with the largest and smallest differentials have in common?
4. What percentage of the population of each country are men of military age? Why is it larger in some countries than others? Are countries with more men of military age more aggressive than others?

Students can use the spreadsheet to quickly acquire the answer to the questions in italics. Using their reasoning skills, data in their texts and on the Internet, they can synthesize the answers to the other questions listed above as well.

Microsoft Excel - Middle East

	Population	Area****	Birth Rate	Death Rate	Military**	Imports	Exports***
Iran	65,619,636	1,648,000	18.29	5.45	10,545,869	13.8	12.2
Iraq	22,675,617	437,072	35.04	6.4	3,176,826	8.9	12.7
Israel	5,842,454	20,770	19.32	6.22	1,226,903	30.6	23.5
Egypt	68,359,979	1,001,450	25.38	7.83	11,766,949	15.8	4.6
Lebanon	3,578,036	10,400	20.26	6.42	592,264	5.7	0.866
Libya	5,115,450	1,759,540	27.68	3.51	841,039	7	6.6
Syria	16,305,659	185,180	31.11	5.29	2,358,973	3.2	3.3
Saudi Arab	22,023,506	1,960,582	37.47	6.02	3,225,809	28	4.8
Gaza Strip	1,132,063	360	43.14	4.31	0	2.5	1.17

http://www.odci.gov/cia/publications/factbook/fields/population.html

* Per 1,000 Population
** Men between 15 and 49
***In Billions
****In Square Kilometers
*****Per square Kilometer

FIGURE 13.8 ■ Middle Eastern Demographics

> Different kinds of charts and graphs are useful for different purposes

The categories in Figure 13.8 are only a few of the categories the students could be working with. In addition, there are other demographic categories (see Figure 13.5) along with accompanying text information on such topics as religion and kind of government. With some imagination, a student could ask and answer many questions using simple addition, subtraction, division, multiplication, and percentages.

■ CHARTS AND GRAPHS

Once you or your class has gathered numbers on a topic, entered them into a spreadsheet, and calculated means, medians, modes, and percentages, there is more that you can do to help your students understand the significance of their findings. They can turn their numbers into pictures with charts and graphs. Not all charts and graphs do the same thing. Spreadsheets typically offer many different kinds of charts. Excel, for example, offers fourteen different kinds of charts and graphs with subsets for formatting associated with each. The rest of this section will be devoted to explaining the major kinds of charts and the kinds of information for which they are most useful.

Bar Charts and Column Charts

First, let us look at the anatomy of a chart. In Figure 13.9, you see data with labels that indicate how those numbers are represented on a chart. In Figure 13.10, you see a chart representing one data series. In Figure 13.11, you see a chart representing two data

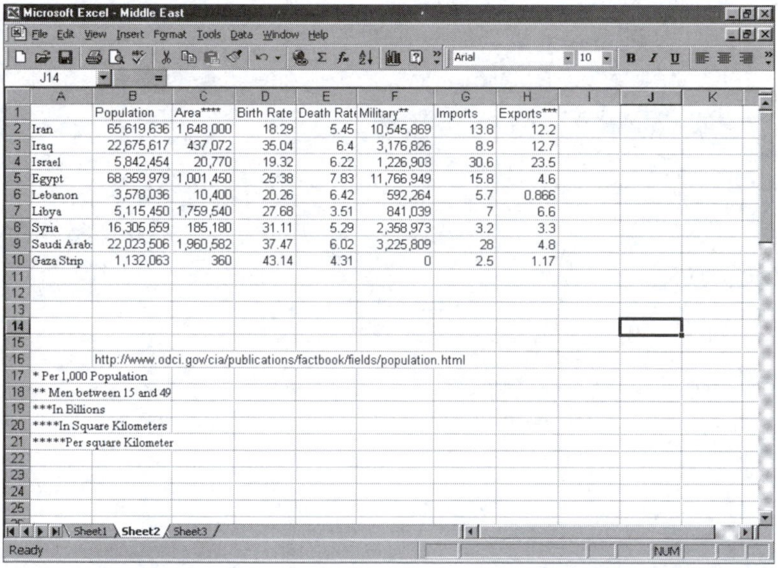

	Population	Area****	Birth Rate	Death Rate	Military**	Imports	Exports***
Iran	65,619,636	1,648,000	18.29	5.45	10,545,869	13.8	12.2
Iraq	22,675,617	437,072	35.04	6.4	3,176,826	8.9	12.7
Israel	5,842,454	20,770	19.32	6.22	1,226,903	30.6	23.5
Egypt	68,359,979	1,001,450	25.38	7.83	11,766,949	15.8	4.6
Lebanon	3,578,036	10,400	20.26	6.42	592,264	5.7	0.866
Libya	5,115,450	1,759,540	27.68	3.51	841,039	7	6.6
Syria	16,305,659	185,180	31.11	5.29	2,358,973	3.2	3.3
Saudi Arab:	22,023,506	1,960,582	37.47	6.02	3,225,809	28	4.8
Gaza Strip	1,132,063	360	43.14	4.31	0	2.5	1.17

http://www.odci.gov/cia/publications/factbook/fields/population.html
* Per 1,000 Population
** Men between 15 and 49
***In Billions
****In Square Kilometers
*****Per square Kilometer

FIGURE 13.9 ■ Anatomy of a Chart

TABLE 13.4 ■ Examples of Usable Data for Spreadsheets

Geography

Location	Coastline	Elevation extremes	Irrigated land		

Demographics

Population	Age structure	Population growth rate	Birth rate	Death rate	Net migration rate
Sex ratio	Infant mortality rate	Life expectancy at birth	Total fertility rate		

Economy

GDP	GDP—real growth rate	GDP—per capita	GDP—composition by sector	Population below poverty line	Household income or consumption by percentage share
Inflation rate (consumer prices)	Unemployment rate	Budget	Industrial production growth rate	Debt—external	Economic aid—donor
Economic aid—recipient	Exchange rates				

Energy

Electricity—production	Electricity—consumption	Electricity—exports	Electricity—imports		

Communications

Telephones—main lines in use	Telephones—mobile cellular	Radio broadcast stations	Radios	Television broadcast stations	Televisions

Transportation

Railways	Highways	Waterways	Pipelines	Ports and harbors	Merchant marine
Airports	Airports—with paved runways	Airports—with unpaved runways	Heliports		

Military

Military manpower—availability	Military manpower—fit for military service	Military manpower—reaching military age annually	Military expenditures—dollar figure	Military expenditures—percent of GDP	

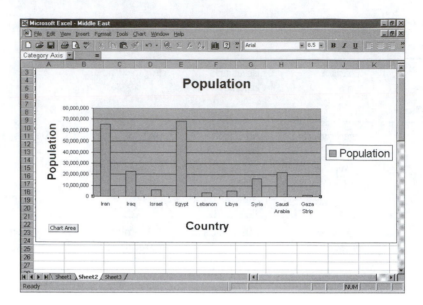

FIGURE 13.10 ■ Chart for One Data Series: Population

Bar charts for comparisons series. You can see that this graphic representation brings the numbers to life. The name for what you are looking at is "a bar chart representing two data series." Look again at the data in Figure 13.10. Would it make sense to add a third series to this chart given the data available in Figure 13.9? The answer is "probably not," unless you would

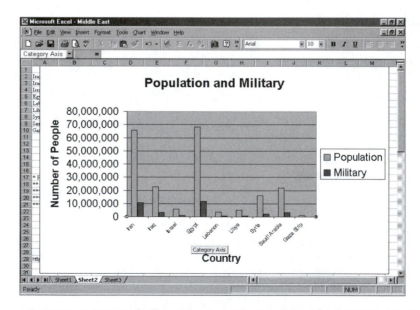

FIGURE 13.11 ■ Men of Military Age Compared to Population—Charting Two Data Series

want to add a series that compares land area for each country. The units for birth rate, death rate, imports, and exports are very different and would not even show up on a chart measuring other series in the millions.

Pie Charts

Pie charts are always used with only one data series. They give the viewer a sense of how the parts relate to the whole. See Figure 13.12.

> Use pie charts to see a relationship of the parts to the whole

Area Chart and Bar Charts—Looking at Data Over Time

One activity that is common in both history and the sciences is looking at data over time ("trends"). Charts are quite helpful because they make relationships between numbers quite clear. Read the following numbers: income per household in 1990 and 1995 ($29,606 and $32,606) and retail sales per household in 1990 and 1995 ($16,645 and $25,309). Having just glanced at these numbers, what could you say about them? Now read the chart in Figure 13.13 and make a relevant comment about the numbers. Your students will experience similar epiphanies.

> Use area and bar charts to look at trends

Pivot Tables

Pivot tables are one more way to help students summarize information. This time, let's take our example from a biology class. In your biology class you may have had students count the number of certain kinds of birds that visited the area outside of the classroom window at a certain time of day during the months of December

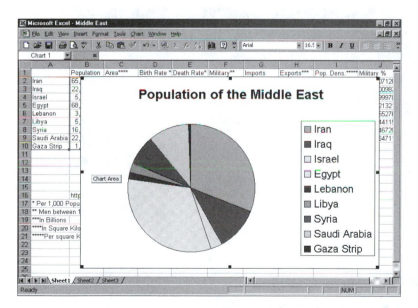

FIGURE 13.12 ■ The Pie Chart—Looking at the Whole

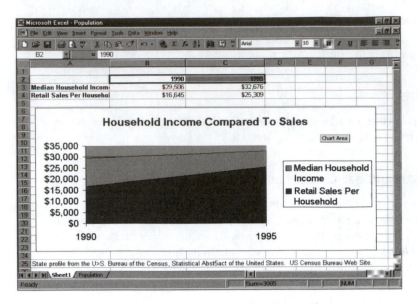

FIGURE 13.13 ■ Comparison of Income and Spending

Use pivot tables to
get different perspectives
on data

and April. At the end of April, your students have a table that looks like Figure 13.14, only much longer. Now they need to summarize and interpret the data that they have collected. This is where the pivot table is quite helpful. Look at Figure 13.15. Even without the help of a chart, patterns emerge when students read the totals columns

FIGURE 13.14 ■ The Data for a Pivot Table

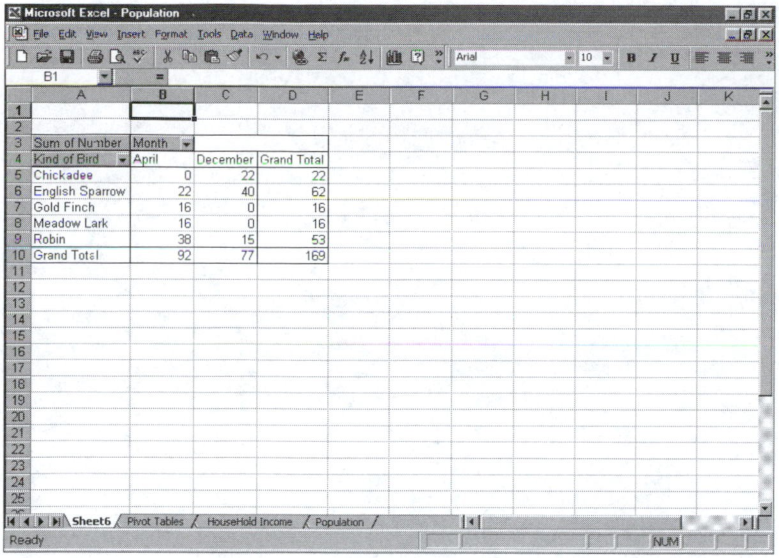

FIGURE 13.15 ■ The Pivot Table

and rows. For example, it is clear that chickadees are winter birds and goldfinches and meadowlarks are spring birds. Not only can students read this pivot table, but they may also turn it into a series of charts and graphs, depending on the questions they are asking.

Formulas

Finally, we will look at the formula, a way of using the spreadsheet to do "what if" exercises with students. The spreadsheet function that we will use for this exercise is "Goal Seek." First, let us start with a simple problem, understanding the relationships among distance, rate, and time.

Suppose you would like to investigate how long it will take to get between two cities driving a car at different speeds and how that might compare to flying in an airplane. You simply set up the formula on a spreadsheet as you see it in Figure 13.16. Now you want to ask a "what if" question. Simply by changing numbers in the cells D7 and E7, you can get a variety of combination of rates and times. Try it.

The "Goal Seek" dialogue box (Figure 13.17) is another tool for asking "what if" questions. An example of a goal seek question is, "How fast would I have to go if I wanted to go somewhere 60 miles away in a half an hour?" (Figure 13.17). The answer is 119 miles per hour in the Rate cell (Figure 13.18). To change the time to three-quarters of an hour, invoke the goal seek dialogue box and replace ".5" with ".75." You may change the kinds of questions you ask the formula by changing the cell that contains the base formula for the problem. In other words, any time the content you teach

> Use formulas to answer "what if" questions

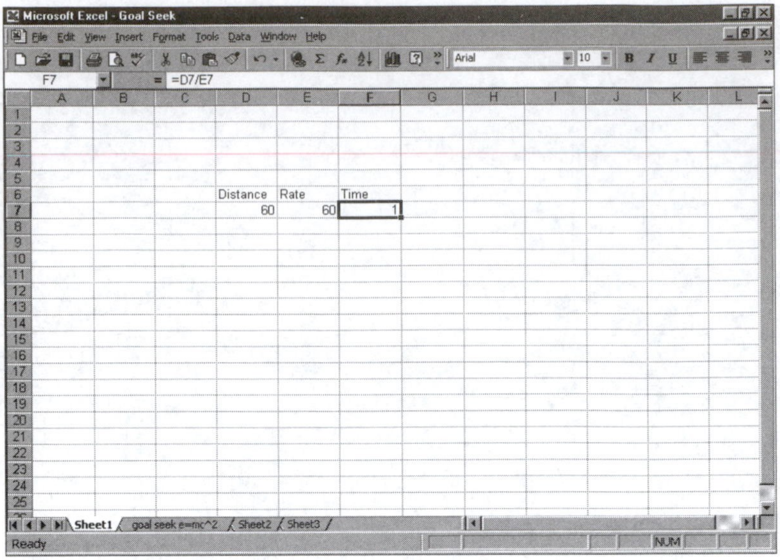

FIGURE 13.16 ■ Distance, Rate, and Time

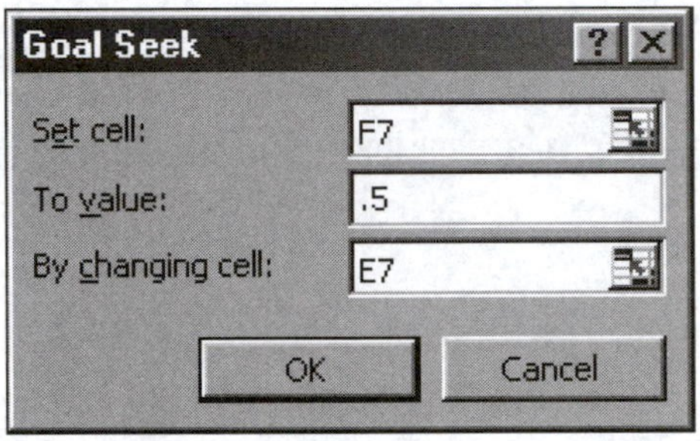

FIGURE 13.17 ■ Looking at Alternatives

contains a formula, you may design problems that encourage students to ask "what if" questions to explore the meaning and implications of the concept they are studying. The trick with this exercise, as it is with all spreadsheet functions, is providing a meaningful scenario or context from which students can work.

■ BLOOM'S TAXONOMY AND SPREADSHEETS

Spreadsheets are tools that challenge students to work at the middle and higher levels of the taxonomy (Table 13.5). Because spreadsheets assist students in thinking about

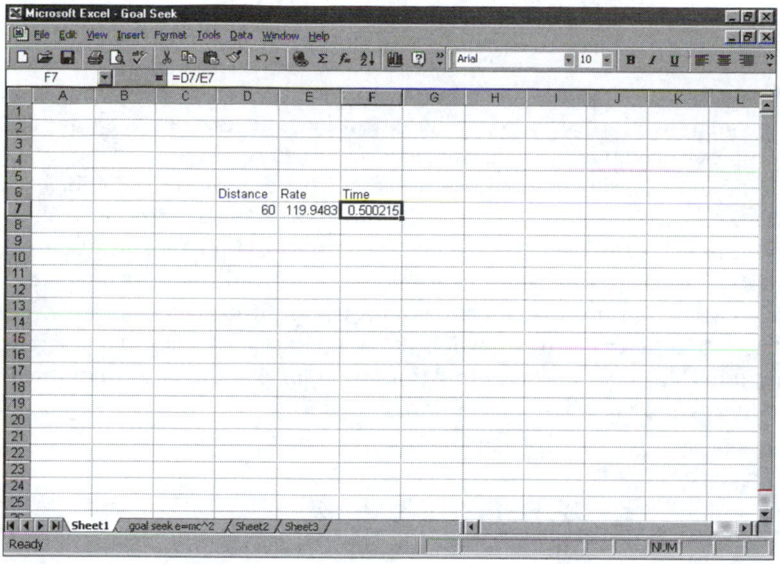

FIGURE 13.18 ■ The Solution

and using numbers to solve problems (as opposed to teaching them to manipulate numbers) the levels of the taxonomy that are addressed are different. As you make an effort to teach to all levels of the taxonomy, you will find that spreadsheets will assist you in filling in the middle and upper levels with meaningful exercises.

TABLE 13.5 ■ Bloom's Taxonomy and Spreadsheets

Level of Thought	Description	Spreadsheet Activities
Knowledge	Name, locate, tell, list, repeat, point to	Identifying relevant chunks of information on a chart.
Comprehension	Define, summarize, infer, project	Using descriptive statistics: mean, median, mode, standard deviation
Application	Use, solve, adapt, relate, perform	Using formulas and pivot tables
Analysis	Compare classify, screen, examine, test for	Using formulas and the goal seek function to ask "what if" questions.
Synthesis	Create, develop, generate, build, compile, design	Designing a chart or graph
Evaluation	Judge, reject, criticize, rate, rank	Judging the meaning of charts, graphs, and descriptive statistics.

■ SUMMARY

Spreadsheets are to numbers what databases are to text. Both are collections of tools that help users analyze information. With the spreadsheet the user can do simple calculations, complex calculations, and use spreadsheet functions to do calculations that are either too time consuming or too difficult to do by hand. While they do not assist students with their knowledge of math facts, they do allow students across disciplines to think about problems and concepts that involve numbers. Using the spreadsheet to calculate simple, descriptive statistics students may analyze their own experiments and surveys. Using charts, they may visualize their data. Using pivot tables, they can organize their data into different formats, which allows them to look for patterns. Using formulas and tools like the "Goal Seek" function, they can experiment with numbers to look for patterns and ask "what if" questions.

■ REFERENCES ■

Albrecht, B., & Firedrake, G. (1999). Flashenlightenment. *Learning and Leading with Technology, 26*(7), 36–39.

Bitner, N., Wadlington, S., Partridge, E., & Bitner, J. (1999). The virtual trip. *Learning and Leading with Technology, 26*(6), 7–9.

Borg, W., & Gall, M. (1989). *Educational Research.* New York: Longman.

CIA (2000). CIA world factbook. Found on the Internet at http://www.odci.gov/cia/publications/factbook/fields/population.html.

Cuevas, M. (1994). *Holt physical science.* Austin: Holt, Rinehart and Winston.

Drier, H. (1999). Do vampires exist? *Learning and Leading with Technology, 27*(1), 7–9.

Feicht, L. (1999). Creating a mathematical laboratory. *Learning and Leading with Technology, 26*(7), 46–51.

Huff, D. (1982). *How to lie with statistics.* New York: W. W. Norton & Company.

Lloyd, M. (1998). The problem cycle: A model for computer education. *Learning and Leading with Technology, 26*(3), 7–13.

Lynch, M., & Walton, S. (1998). Talking trash on the Internet. *Learning and Leading with Technology, 25*(5), 26–31.

Manouchehri, A., & Pagnucco, L. Julio's run. *Learning and Leading with Technology, 27*(4), 7–13.

Morgan, B., & Jernigan, J. (1998). A technology update: Leonardo da Vinci and the search for the perfect body. *Learning and Leading with Technology, 26*(4), 22–25.

Niess, M. (1998). Using computer spreadsheets to solve equations. *Learning and Leading with Technology, 26*(3), 22–27.

Pugalee, D. (1999). Rolling the dice. *Learning and Leading with Technology, 26*(6), 19–21.

Slater, T. (1998). Collecting science in a net. *Learning and Leading with Technology, 26*(2), 28–36.

Slattery, W., Hundley, S., Finegan-Stoll, C., & Becker, M. (1998). Collecting science in a net. *Learning and Leading with Technology, 26*(1), 25–30.

Whitmer, J. C. (1992). *Spreadsheets in mathematics and science teaching.* Bowling Green, OH: School Science and Mathematics Association.

Widmer, C., & Sheffield, L. (1998). Modeling mathematics concepts. *Learning and Leading with Technology, 25*(5), 32–35.

United States Census Bureau. (2000). Found on the Internet at http://www.census.gov/hhes/poverty/povanim/pvmaptxt.html.

Verderber, N. (1990). Spreadsheets and problem solving with Appleworks in mathematics teaching. *Journal of Computers in Mathematics and Science Teaching, 9*(3), p. 51.

■ ANNOTATED RESOURCES ■

Lowery, L. How new science curriculums reflect brain research. *Educational Leadership,* November 1998 (v56, (3), p.26).

One point that I have repeatedly made in the chapters on data analysis tools is their importance in helping children perceive and understand relationships. This article provides another perspective on this. Even if you do not teach science, you will take much from this article with respect to the importance of helping students construct their own knowledge.

Constructivism and perceiving relationships

Albrecht, B., & Davis, P. (2001). Model the movements of the planets. *Leading and Learning With Technology.* Volume 28(8), p. 33.

Morgan, T. (2001). DigStats: A web resource for statistics and data analysis. *Leading and Learning With Technology.* Volume 29(1), p. 32.

These resources appeared too late to be included in the text of this chapter. However, they are excellent references for both methods for using data in science and math and sources for that data.

More data sources

Enderson, M. (2001). Marking time with math. *Leading and Learning With Technology.* Volume 28(5), p. 28.

One software tool math teachers use that I have not mentioned is Geometer's SketchPad. This software title is a tool used to build geometric shapes. Once they have defined a shape, the tool allows them to study the many properties (angles, distances) of the shape as well as the theorems associated with the shape. This recent reference will help you understand how this tool works.

Geometer's Sketchpad

APPENDIX

A

Your Network

Before you begin learning about how to use the tools we discussed briefly in Chapter 1, you need to know a little bit about the infrastructure that supports those tools. How well your infrastructure works for you will have either an enabling or disabling effect on everything you do. You may design a wonderful lesson based on presentation software and find that the network is down the day you had planned to have your students search the Internet for graphics. Or worse, they may have done their Internet search for graphics and lost them all somewhere on the network. Or worst of all, some child may have finished the assignment and deleted it because s/he doesn't know how file management works. You expect your students to know how to use a pencil sharpener to keep their pencils sharp and to store their papers in notebooks and folders where they can find them when they need them. Similarly, you will develop a set of expectations for them about their work with computers.

Your Intranet (your school network) is both a giant filing cabinet and your connection to the world beyond your classroom. It provides you with storage space, effortless file transfer among computers, and a pipeline to the Internet. Knowing just a little bit about how it works and its capacity will help you use the computer tools that you have more efficiently. Just what should you know about your Intranet to be an effective advocate for and teacher of your children? Some terms that you should be familiar with are server, router, hub, host, client, bandwidth, and modem. If you know these terms you can talk knowledgably with your technology coordinator or technician. You may be cynical about having to know such technical-sounding terms. To help you understand why you are learning this new vocabulary, I am providing some statements that your technology coordinator might say to you. If you can understand what s/he is saying, you will be able to make an informed decision about how to respond. If you don't understand, you and your students will be at the mercy of someone who does not know you, your students, or your instructional objectives. Now, to the statements:

- "Your class can't add any more information to your web site—the server is full."
- "We can't put another computer in your classroom. The hub is full."
- "We don't want you to try using Internet video in your classroom. There just isn't enough bandwidth."

- "No wonder that takes you so long to download at home. You only have a 28K modem."
- "The name of our web server is Plato.K12.edu. You will need to know that name in order to upload the web site you just finished."
- "You need to either archive your email or delete it. You are taking up too much space on the server."
- "No wonder your email isn't working. Your client isn't configured correctly. You have the wrong name for the host."
- "The network is down."

As you can see, the statements that a technician might say to you someday will affect you at a very practical level in your classroom. What if you don't want to delete all of your email? What are the alternatives? What if there isn't room on the hub for another computer—is that the end of the world or can it be fixed? If the server is full, what are the alternatives for the kids and the web site that they built for their project on Central America? So the client isn't properly loaded—what should be done? How long will it take to fix? When will the class have email again? What do you mean the name of the web server is Riverside? I thought you just put a web site in a directory and everyone sees it. If the network is down, what can't you do and what can you do?

Imagine if your school network administrator said all of these things to you in the same week. If you had made your lesson plans around the belief that all of the bad things listed previously weren't going to happen to you and then they did, your classroom would be chaos. If, on the other hand, you understand what is going on, you can make contingency plans, understand timelines, ask intelligent questions, and even argue a little. So let's go to work figuring out how the computers in your classroom communicate with other computers in the school and ultimately to the outside world.

Figure A.1 is a diagram of some computers that reside at Riverside High School. Although we are looking at a high school, such a configuration would be just as common at an elementary school. We see four classrooms, each with three computers. We see the server room with a variety of different kinds of servers. We can also see downtown Riverside where the local Internet service provider has offices, and not far from there to the west we see Mr. Tibbs' house. Let us do a tour of the server room first.

FIELD TRIP A.1

A Tour of the Server Room

Server 1, the district email host, provides email service to all of the students and faculty in the Riverside district. The server has a name, Riverside, and address, Riverside.K12.edu. Mrs. Frederick's email address is, for example, frederik@riverside.K12.edu. Mr. Smith's email address is smith1@riverside.K12.edu. Email gets to and from all of the teachers' rooms when their computers send or receive it through the hub in the wiring closet outside of Mr. Jones's room. From there it goes directly to or comes from the server. If the email is being sent out of the district, the server sends it to the server of the school's Internet provider downtown (Server 5) where it is routed on to its destination. If the email is going to remain in the district, then

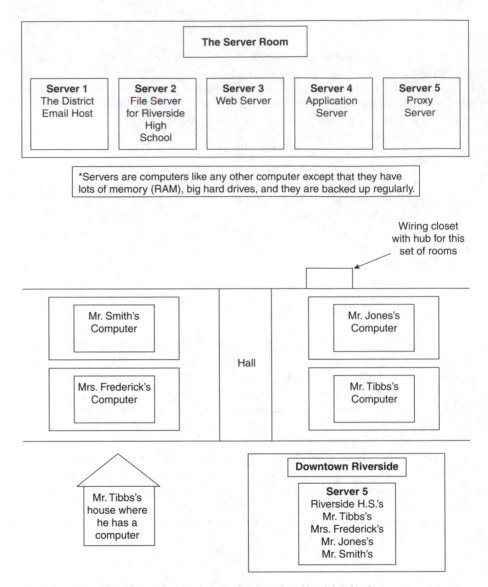

FIGURE A.1 ■ Floor Plan, Center Section, South Wing, Riverside High School

the Server 1 deposits it in the box of the recipient named in the address where it waits until that person decides to open it. There are nearly 10,000 students and teachers in Riverside School district who each send several messages a day. The district had to make a rule about leaving email on the server. Each person is allowed to accumulate 1 megabyte of information. After that the person's email account will not receive any more messages. This makes it hard for students and teachers to send attachments, especially graphics files. They had to learn how to use compressed .JPG files to exchange graphics using email.

Server 2, the file server, serves only the students and teachers at Riverside High School. This server does many different tasks for students and teachers. One important function of the file server is to provide a place where students and teachers can store their work. The hard drives of the computers in the classroom are not large enough to store all of the text and graphics files that everyone uses for the many ongoing projects in each classroom. Each student and each teacher has a secure folder which only he or she can access. There they can make their own subdirectories where they store drafts of documents that they are word processing, presentations they are making, graphics files they have downloaded or scanned, and email messages they have had to delete from the mail server. In addition, there are public directories. All of the teachers share a folder where they can exchange files. Mr. Smith, for example, has just downloaded a wonderful series of graphics on cloud formations that he found on the Internet and wants to share it with Mr. Jones who is just starting his unit on weather. Mr. Smith simply needs to copy these files to Mr. Jones' public folder and Mr. Jones will have them. All of the teachers provide public folders for their students as well so that they can just drop files into a student's folder. They use this to provide electronic materials and curriculum that are often a part of their assignments. The teachers also provide a special assignments folder for each student. When a student finishes an electronic assignment, s/he may simply drop it into the appropriate folder. Only the teacher and the student have the rights to access this folder. When the teacher has graded the assignment, s/he drops it back into the student's folder where the student may open it, read comments, and see the grade. This is especially helpful for files that are too big to fit on a floppy disk. But even if the files aren't too big, it saves the teachers and students from having to deal with keeping track of a floppy disk while they are keeping track of so many other more important things as well.

All of this activity to and from File Server 2 in the diagram goes through the hub on the other side of the wall of Mr. Jones' classroom. The network administrator named this server Socrates. Since it is not connected to the Internet, it doesn't have an address. Another way of saying that information goes back and forth between classroom computers and the server is, "Information that goes from a client (a computer in one of the classrooms) to the server goes through the hub." The hub is a small box with holes for network cables. When a computer is on a network, it has a network card that has a plug-in for a network cable. That cable goes to a hub that then directs the information to a server through a larger cable. Each of the computers in each of the four classrooms has a network card with one end of the cable plugged into it and into the hub at the other end. Soon each of these classrooms will have five computers instead of three. Before these new computers will be able to communicate with any of the servers, they will have to plug into a hub as well. The hub that the four teachers are using now only has 15 ports (the holes where the network cable is attached), so when the school ordered the new computers, they ordered a new hub as well. Mr. Tibbs asked the network administrator to order a hub large enough to handle another five computers above the 20 because he is writing a grant and thinks that he will get an additional five computers for his classroom. His network administrator, a sometimes parsimonious person, told him to write an extra hub into his grant and take care of it himself. Mr. Tibbs is just grateful he knows what a hub is, and he is not so sure he is going to write a hub into his grant. This may be a matter for the principal to decide. It seems to Mr. Tibbs that if he is willing to write a grant for the district that the district should be willing to chip in $200 for a hub to help him with the matching money his grant requires. Technology is such a new item in the district that traditions and procedures regarding who pays for what have not yet been established, and oftentimes getting things done is a matter of negotiation and compromise.

But back to the server room—we are now gazing at the web server, Server 3. Its name is Aristotle, and its address is Aristotle.Riverside.K12.edu. It is a large, sleek machine that hums with the sound of constant activity. Like the other machines it looks like a wire farm with cables leading to a tape back-up drive, the network, and the Internet service provider downtown. On this web server each teacher maintains a homepage so that parents, students, and others can see a picture and get some background on that teacher's education, interests, and accomplishments. Each class also maintains a web page. On the web page are assignments for each day as well as pictures of each member of the class. In addition, the teacher has posted the syllabus for the class and the learning objectives for the semester and year.

Server 4, named Dewey and the last machine in the row of servers on our tour, is the application server. This server really just serves one application. It is a large integrated learning system that provides computer-based instruction (CBI) in language arts and mathematics. Teachers use it for kids who have trouble keeping up with the rest of the class or in situations where a particular concept is hard for a whole class. Mr. Tibbs, for example, uses it when he teaches fractions to his general math class. Not only does the machine display the lessons, but it also keeps track of each student's score on the exercises and quizzes and the amount of time that the student is logged on. To use this CBI, Mr. Tibbs had to go to a special two-hour workshop and learn how to enter students' names and passwords into the course management system, assign lessons, and get reports on student work.

Server 6, the proxy server, came as the result of much debate and a "precipitating incident." A proxy server filters Internet sites, allowing students to access sites that do not contain objectionable content. Some companies that provide software for proxy servers provide a basic set of filters and also allow districts to add additional filters. One mechanism for setting up these filters is to type in a list of words that will block a site from being downloaded. There are disadvantages to proxy servers. The primary disadvantage is that they slow down the user's ability to move from page to page. Some even require teachers to bookmark sites ahead of time so that they can be searched. Because of these inconveniences, there was a lively debate among teachers, parents, and administrators in Riverside about whether to install a proxy server. Many did not want the additional baggage of having to deal with a proxy server. Instead, they wanted each student to sign an "Internet Code of Honor" in which they promised not to go to sites with violent or sexual content. Neighboring Arlington School District had successfully implemented such a program. Students in that district all signed the Code of Honor. Of course, within six weeks of school starting a student was discovered in violation of the code and his computer privileges were revoked for a semester. After that, things settled down and there were no more violations.

However, the whole situation played out differently at Riverside. Before the issue had been decided, four fifth-grade boys secretly downloaded a bomb-making manual and went to work on a homemade bomb in the basement of one of the boy's houses. Since they were more curious (and dumb) than malicious, their parents discovered the plot, extracted the story about downloading the manual at a school web site, went to the principal, superintendent, and school board about the evils of unprotected web sites, and Riverside School District installed a proxy server the next month. The presence of a proxy server in a district is a reflection of local values and how a community wants to buffer and protect its young people from the dangerous and unsavory side of life. A truly determined and skillful student can find his or her way around anything, and the best protection is the watchful eyes of a caring teacher and parents as well as a lot of discussion and problem solving about right, wrong, and the Internet.

The final stop on our tour of servers is in downtown Riverside, where "Speedo Internet Services" maintains Server 5, the equipment that Riverside School District uses to connect to the Internet. It is important to understand that in order to be connected to the Internet, anyone—individual or a school district—must use an Internet provider (gateway). The quality of the service to the individual or district depends upon how much bandwidth the individual or organization buys.

Riverside has one "T1" line running from Speedo to the district. Information runs through wires much like water runs through pipes. The amount of information that gets through a wire depends on its size. T1 is a size of cable and is one of the most common kinds of large "pipes" that Internet Service Providers (ISPs) use for school districts and other large customers. In the beginning that was enough, but as more students and teachers began using the web to get information and graphics for assignments, web pages began loading more and more slowly. The district is now trying to figure out where it is going to find another $500 per month to pay for an additional T1 line.

One of the real problems the low bandwidth has created in the district is the inability of teachers to video conference with other schools and experts across the country. Mr. Smith received a grant from the National Science Foundation (NSF) for money to buy a fast computer, a special video card, and a camera so that his AP biology class could consult experts in various biological sciences during the school year. The first time Mr. Smith and his class used the system, traffic on the school network slowed to a crawl. Web sites took minutes to load, and Internet lessons and work in other classes came to a standstill. Mr. Smith was embarrassed, the network administrator was cranky, and the school administrators had to explain to the teachers why they evaluate teachers on their creative and innovative use of technology in their classrooms when the infrastructure does not support it. The short- term solution to the problem came as the result of negotiation and compromise. Mr. Smith and his AP biology class, who had to use the equipment to keep the grant, agreed to do some of the interviews after school. On days when interviews could only be conducted during school hours, the rest of the school was informed and teachers tried to keep Internet usage to a minimum while the biology class conducted an interview. This was a patch. The real answer to the problem was to get more bandwidth from the Internet service provider (Speedo).

Notice that Mr. Tibbs's house is also in the diagram in Figure A.1. He has a computer there that he bought because he has found that he really can't keep up with his work at school without having a computer at home. When he is at school he rarely has time to sit at a computer and try things out, and he definitely has no time to look for new and interesting web sites. He hardly ever has access to the computers in his room because the kids are always using them. When he bought his computer, he knew that he wanted access to the Internet. For that, he had to buy a modem along with his computer and contact an Internet service provider to give him a logon to an Internet server. Since he gets his Internet service through his telephone line, Mr. Tibbs knew that his connection would probably be slow. Nevertheless, he bought the fastest modem available and hoped for the best. Although Mr. Tibbs could have chosen a national company like AOL, he chose Speedo instead. Mr. Tibbs was set up with both an email account and Internet access that would allow him to get to any Internet site in the world. Since the server at Riverside High School is a POP3 server, Mr. Tibbs can access his school email account at home along with his email account provided by Speedo. He uses his Speedo account to send and receive personal messages from friends and family and does business on the school account. Nevertheless, he can configure his home email program that he downloaded for free from the Internet to access both accounts. Some email software does not allow email readers POP3 access to their comments. These closed systems can only be read with their proprietary software. If your technology coordinator tells you that your district has a POP3 server, that means that you can use non-proprietary email software, such as Pegasus or Eudora (both are downloadable free on the Internet), to access your school email at home.

The story you just read is typical of the thousands of schools across the country. If you are a preservice teacher, the classroom technology configuration and the political problems that you step into when you have finished your training will be similar to the ones that you just read about. If you are already teaching, you will recognize both the hardware and the political problems.

To make this information your own, you must now find out (if you do not already know) the specifics of the network and Internet providers where you are. "Checking Your Understanding A.1" will help you find out about your local resources. It will provide you with the right questions to ask and the right words to use when you ask them. Once you open a dialog with a network administrator and Internet provider and try using language that you have just learned, you will be able to use all of the resources that you have more effectively. One of the best ways you can help yourself is to use key words we have learned so far with other people who know more about this than you do. Do not be afraid of using the wrong word. You will only sound silly once (as we all have at one time or another) and then you will gain the power that comes with knowledge.

✔ CHECKING YOUR UNDERSTANDING

A.1

1. Survey your network by answering the following questions. Take notes. These questions are just the minimum. As you ask questions, you will generate more questions. As you get answers, you will probably get more information than you asked for.

   a. With your instructor's help, use your computer's file management system to learn the names of the computers on your network.

   b. With your instructor's help, use your computer's file management system to learn how the file server in your lab is set up. Which folder on which drive belongs just to you? What is the procedure for getting a folder where you can make sub-folders for your whole class? How do you request a folder that you and other teachers can share?

   c. What is the name of the Internet provider for your school district or university? How much bandwidth does your school district or university buy every month? Name three local Internet providers and answer the following questions about each.

      i. How many hours of service does the provider give you per month and at what price?
      ii. What is the highest speed modem that the provider will support?
      iii. Name the hours per week that technical support is available?
      iv. How often has the provider's service been down in the last year (they should be able to tell you)?
      v. When they were down, how long were they down on average?
      vi. How much space will the provider give you to store your email?
      vii. Will the provider allow you to put up a web site for free? If they will, how much space will they give you for your site?

   d. Find out if there is an application server on your school or university network. Which applications does it serve?

   e. Where is the server room in your university or school? Ask your instructor or network administrator for a brief tour.

   f. Where is the wiring closet in your school or university for your lab? Ask the network administrator to open the door and let you look at the hub(s) for your floor or wing. Are there extra ports? How many?

   g. If there are 3 extra ports on the hub that serves your wing or your floor, what does this mean?

2. With the information that you have collected from the questions you just answered, complete two of the following three activities and present your work to the class:

   a. Write and present a presentation (Hyperstudio, PowerPoint, Web) to your (future) school board outlining why you need more network resources.

   b. Write and present a presentation (Hyperstudio, PowerPoint, Web) for the class that you teach on the new file management system that you have set up for them that will allow them to have:

      i. Their own private directories.
      ii. Directories where they can share information with other students.
      iii. A private directory where each student may hand in electronically generated work.

      Note: You should present this to the class that you are in first. You should have screen shots (captured pictures of the screen) of the folders you have created for your students and walk them through the process of submitting, copying, and pasting work to and from those directories.

   c. Using a word processor, write a comparison/contrast paper of 300 words, discussing the following topic: Of the three Internet providers that you investigated, which would you choose? Why?

File Management

Before each semester starts, you will want to take an inventory of the storage space available for both you and your students. You will want to check out the hard drives of the machines in your classroom and clean off unnecessary folders and files left by last year's students or last semester's students. These hard drives are not good places for students to store everything that they collect electronically, because of space issues. However, local drives are good places for students to back up items they are working on so that they will be available if the network goes down. You should make folders for students ahead of time so that when students first sit down to the computer their space will be ready for them. You should do the same thing on the network. To do this you will work with your network administrator to establish a network drive where you can create folders for your students. You will want to create several different kinds of folders including:

- A private folder as a workspace for each individual student
- A public folder where students can share files
- An assignments folder that is a private drop box for each student

You should also understand how many megabytes of space the network administrator will allow for your class. If you plan on students creating presentations that will require extensive graphics and audio/video, you should tell the network administrator and negotiate something workable for both of you. To help you understand how much you will need for each student, you should look at the size of electronic presentations that are about the size and complexity that you will expect your students to make. Then double the space because the students will be working on other projects as well—word processed documents, spreadsheets, and databases. Your class will probably only have enough room to work on one presentation per person at a time. Once the class is finished with their presentations, you might then have to upload them to the web server in order to display to parents and others for a while, and save them on a "zip" disk of some kind or press them to a CD for storage. It is important to understand that since you and your class are sharing computer space with many people, you need a plan to move work through the storage space on the server so that once an assignment is complete you and your students can clear out the space and begin a new project.

This moving around of information brings us to an important skill that you and your students should acquire early: file management. Understanding where files go when they are saved will save you many hours of either searching for one you have misplaced or redoing lost work. If many of your students are constantly misplacing their files, you will spend countless valuable hours helping them track down their work. One of the first activities you will want to provide for your students is a refresher on how to get around your school network and a tour of the folders you have set up for them. Although some will understand immediately, others will be lost.

An always popular activity that will get your students started is called "The Fruit Files." To get students used to moving among folders and drives on their local computers' network, create folders and subfolders named for fruit or animals or other groups of objects for easy identification. An example of such a folder with its subfolders appears in Figure B.1. In each of these folders, place a text file with a joke or interesting fact and directions about where to go next. Require students to find and open each of these files in a word processor, saving each file that they find to the next folder they must visit. So, for example, if their first visit is to the Apple directory, they will copy a file and place it in the next directory that might be the Banana directory. Then they will copy and paste both files to the next directory to which they are instructed to proceed, and so on until they reach their destination. Success on the assignment means having collected all of the files into a single destination folder. A good destination folder is a folder labeled Assignments, to get students used to the idea that they should drop their finished assignments into a folder.

This skill is typically not learned in one sitting but over several different attempts. It is always helpful to provide your students with a physical analogy. Figures B.2 and B.3 are some simple diagrams that you can copy and display as you introduce the concept of folders to your students. For very young students you might actually put files in a real filing cabinet and have them walk through the physical process before they attempt the virtual process. Another way to ease into this process if your students are really new to file management is to put all of the Fruit files on a floppy disk and have students solve the problem in groups. Once the students have solved the problem in groups, give each student a fresh disk and have him or her solve it alone. If the student is still confused,

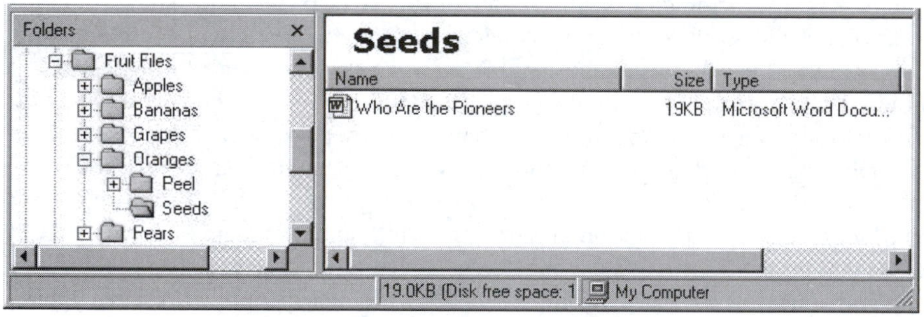

FIGURE B.1 ■ A Simple Fruit File Folder Structure

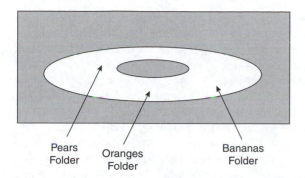

Pears
Folder

Oranges
Folder

Bananas
Folder

Information is stored on discs inside of disk drives that are part of your computer. Some discs are removable, like floppy discs, and others stay inside your computer.

FIGURE B.2 ■ Where Do My Files Go?

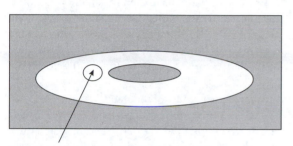

Let's magnify this spot (the Oranges folder) on a disk drive to see what it might look like.

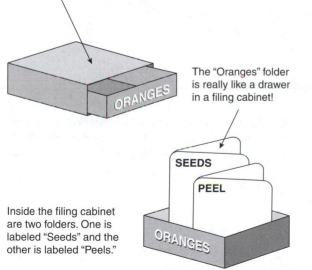

The "Oranges" folder is really like a drawer in a filing cabinet!

Inside the filing cabinet are two folders. One is labeled "Seeds" and the other is labeled "Peels."

FIGURE B.3 ■ The Disk Drive as a Filing Cabinet

have the student work with a peer or mentor who is good at getting around on the computer. Once you are satisfied that students can find and save files on a floppy disk, you can then show them the network, explain about different drives and drive letters, show them where their private and public spaces are, and have them complete the next Fruit File assignment. For the final assignment, use the following locations to place your fruit folders and files: the student's directory on a classroom machine, several public directories on the network drive, and the student's assignment folder.

There is one thing that can go wrong with this assignment. When you place a file in a directory where many students can get to it, someone invariably moves it or cuts and pastes it rather than copying it. You will want to point this difference out to your students and also be ready to replace files in public directories at a moment's notice while the exercise is in progress.

Another item that always comes up is the skill differential in the class. By the time the class has finished doing this exercise on the network, some of your students will be experts, many will be OK, some will still be really fuzzy, and others still utterly lost.

As soon as you find two or three students who really understand the process, rather than having them complete this exercise again, have them create more of these exercises for students who are still having a hard time understanding file management on the computer. Although you will not be able to give these students the rights that allow you to access student's private directories, they can still make very good searches using a floppy disk, the hard drive on a class computer, and the public directories on the network drive.

One of the most difficult concepts for some people to understand, young and old, is that of the virtual filing cabinet—the hard drive, floppy drive, and network drive. Without that understanding, working on a computer is extremely frustrating and time consuming for the student and the teacher. You can never be too sure that your students have this fundamental skill. After all of your preparation, explanations, and exercises you will still often find one or two who still don't understand and frequently misplace their work. With these students you must spend individual one-on-one time until they understand this very basic but essential process.

✔ CHECKING YOUR UNDERSTANDING

B.1

Build a file search exercise for your students like the Fruit Files exercise discussed above. Design it to work on a floppy disk. When you submit your assignment, be sure that you submit a cover sheet that specifies the grade level for which your exercise is intended and the visuals that you will use to introduce this first lesson in file management.

Chat and Internet Conferencing

As the Internet becomes more available in each classroom, live chat will evolve into another tool that teachers and students will use to communicate with people at a distance. When people engage in chat over the Internet, they type in text that is immediately seen by someone in a remote location. This person may answer immediately, and a conversation ensues. Some chat utilities are very helpful in that they not only display the text, but also tell the participants in the conversation whether the other person is actually typing in an answer at any given moment. NetMeeting, CuSeeMe, and MSN network are examples of applications that enable chat.

On the open Internet there are chat rooms that are, for the most part, dangerous places for children. These are sites where strangers congregate to have virtual discussions, sometimes on a specific topic or maybe just general conversations. Most schools filter these locations. Unless you come upon a chat room built by educators for a specific purpose and monitor student use carefully, you should keep your students away from these sites. Furthermore, you should warn them that some people go to these sites to try to find others who are vulnerable, and warn them to beware of anyone who tries to make live personal contact with them after a visit or series of visits in a chat room.

The dangers of chat aside, there are some uses for chat in the classroom. Speaking with an expert and speaking to children from a different culture are two possible ways to use chat with your children. Figure C.1 is an example of a distance connection to an expert. In this case, a high school math class exploring careers in mathematics is talking to a college student majoring in computer science (CS). The teacher is projecting the chat session with an LCD projection panel and the class is asking questions.

■ WHITE BOARD

Some chat software not only allows a text conversation but also allows a "white board" in which participants may jointly view and operate a virtual whiteboard upon which they may both draw and make notes. Further along in the chat session with the CS student, the student mentioned that he was currently taking a class on parallel comput-

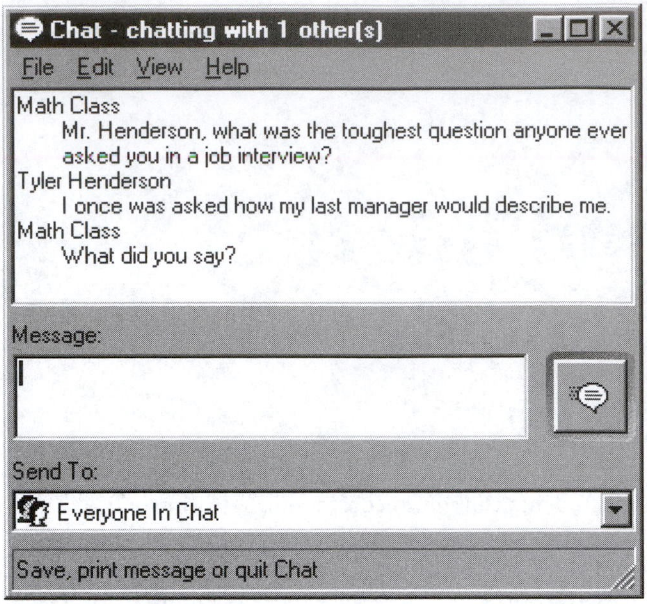

FIGURE C.1 ■ Example of a Chat Session

ing. The math class asked him to draw a parallel computer, and he sketched a diagram of the CPU arrangement that he was building with a team of computer scientists and students at his university (see Figures C.2 & C.3). Notice the spelling error. This happens during chat sessions. Students should understand that they should try very hard to communicate clearly so that how they write doesn't interfere with communication. However, sometimes in the rush of trying to communicate, mistakes happen. In this case it was the expert who made the mistake.

■ APPLICATION SHARING

One further useful tool attached to chat applications is application sharing. The tool is activated when one of the conversants starts an application, a database, for example. The chat dialogue box remains visible, but in addition, one or all of the parties in the conversation may control the application. Several users may be discussing "what if" questions, for example. During the chat session, anyone may compose sorts or queries for the database and everyone sees the results. Or, the person who launched the database (to keep things orderly) may not allow others in the chat session to control the database and retain control of the application. You can see an example of a dialogue box that launches an application in Figure C.4. In this case the user is getting ready to share a spreadsheet named "Pi" with other members of an on-line discussion.

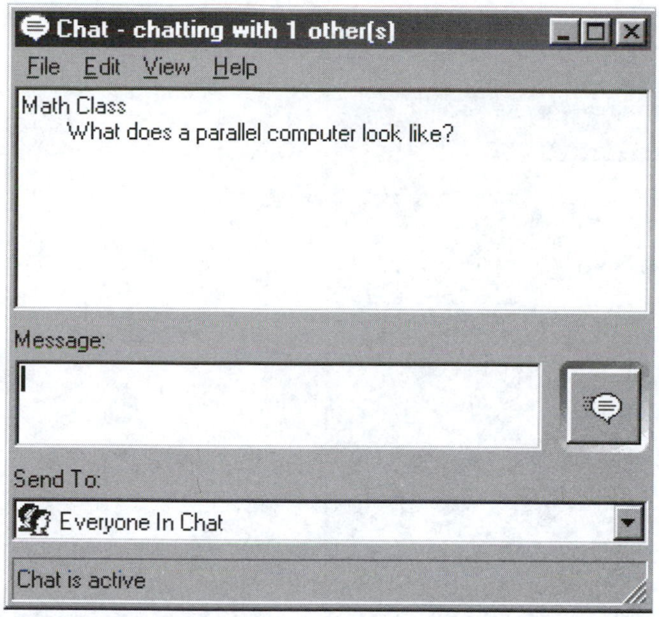

FIGURE C.2 ■ Asking the Question That Requires a White Board

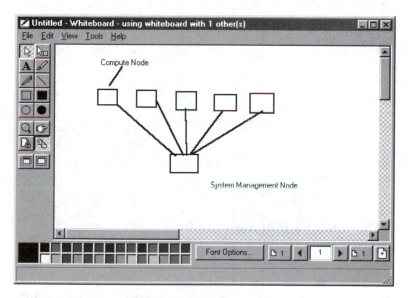

FIGURE C.3 ■ Using the White Board

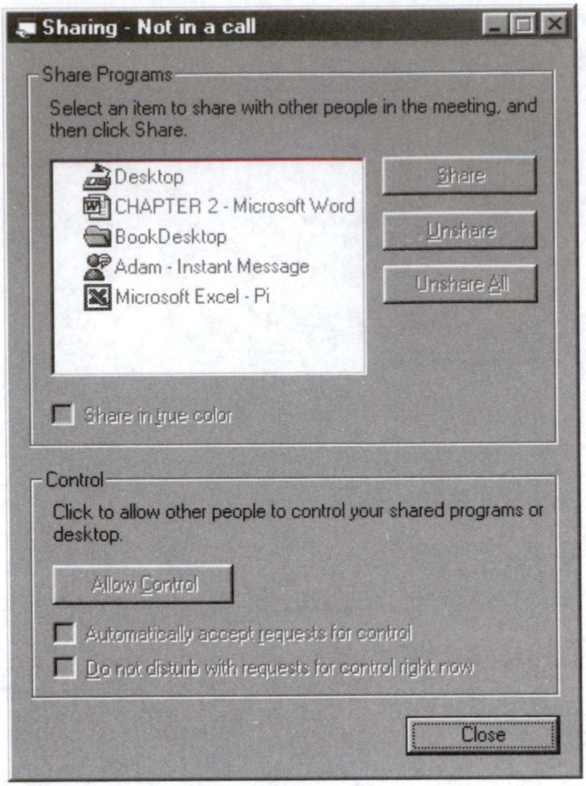

FIGURE C.4 ■ Example of Application Sharing

■ FILE SHARING

A fourth tool offered by most computer communications interfaces is file sharing. With this tool you may send and receive files from the people with whom you are in communication. This is not an especially remarkable advantage since people may also send files to each other using email attachments. However, it is sometimes convenient during a conversation to send a file that someone forgot to send or to send a file that becomes important because of the conversation without having to leave the conversation and send an email to do it.

■ ADVANTAGES AND DISADVANTAGES

Chat requires very little bandwidth. In a classroom with no telephone line, it is the only way to have a conversation with a remote expert or other person of interest. You can be confident that if you decide to use chat, you will not impact your school network significantly, and even on a bad (slow) Internet day, chat will function as quickly and effectively as on a good day.

Some days on the Internet are better than others. Some times of the day are better than others depending on where you live. If every computer in your school is simultaneously accessing the Internet, it will probably be slower than if just half of them are using the Internet. The effect is the same at each level of the network. If all of the computers using your district's T1 line are on the network, the whole district will be slow. Or, if someone is doing live video over your school's Internet connection and your school doesn't have enough bandwidth to support it, everyone's access will be slower.

As for disadvantages, chat is text-based. Consequently, students can huddle around a monitor, five at a time, or the teacher must set up an LCD projector for the whole class to see the conversation. Or, students may engage in their chat sessions one at a time. But then it is difficult to find an expert who is willing to give that kind of time. One-at-a-time chat is more feasible if students are connected with other students for some reason, such as a cultural exchange. One-on-one sessions are successful for foreign language students, for example. Slow readers or slow writers are at a disadvantage. Watching a second grader attempting chat with another second grader is excruciating because of its slowness. One questions the actual instructional benefit of such an exchange.

Application sharing is also slow on the open Internet. The graphic of the complete application is transmitted across the Internet each time the screen is re-drawn (for example, moving from one screen to the next with presentation software). On a bad Internet day it is easier for each person to bring up their own application and run it locally and then talk about the results. If one of the members of the chat group does not have the specific file that people are working with (i.e., a database, spreadsheet, or word processor file) it may easily be transmitted using the file sharing tool discussed previously.

■ AUDIO AND VIDEOCONFERENCING

Live videoconferencing will soon come of age in the public school classroom. Supported by the same software that enables chat (NetMeeting and CuSeeMe, for example), videoconferencing enables the same kinds of interactions that chat does except the computer provides a video image of the participants with accompanying audio. A small camera typically attaches to the computer's parallel or Universal Serial Bus (USB) port, or, in the case of Macs, is built-in. Cameras range widely in quality and price. Modest but usable cameras and supporting software cost under $100, while others with zoom or wide-angle lenses and special microphones cost as much as $800 to $1,000.

When the Internet connection is activated, the user may simply launch the camera's software, enter another user's IP address, and begin the session. An IP address is an Internet facility that allows computers to identify themselves and be found by other computers. Think of it as your computer's "telephone number." You can find your own IP address on a PC by clicking on "Run" in the Start menu and typing *winipcfg*. Sometimes, computers have "static" IP addresses. That means they stay the same. However, it is more likely that you have a dynamic IP address and will have to look it up every time you log on. When people who have dynamic IP address want to videoconference and need each other's IP addresses, they most often contact each other by email first, exchange the IP address of one machine or the other, and then begin the conference.

Videoconferencing over the open Internet is not yet very reliable. On a bad Internet day, the video is slow and jerky (even with a T1 connection if people are using it for functions other than video) and the audio breaks up. On a good day, the picture is small, but it works and the audio is tolerable. The size of a typical video image looks like the one in Figure C.5. If you make it larger (which is possible), it becomes quite grainy. Notice that from this box all four of the tools (chat, application sharing, file transfer, and white board) are available for simultaneous use. Once our local and national infrastructure provides us with the bandwidth that we really need to use these tools in a practical way, they will begin to have an impact on classrooms.

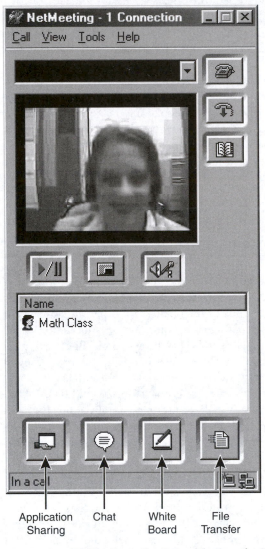

FIGURE C.5 ■ Video Image Size, Transmitting over the Open Internet

All of this points to one conclusion. Videoconferencing is only coming of age. For now it is an unpredictable adolescent that is sometimes moody and a little uncontrollable. You will want to think very carefully before you invest in the time and effort to use this technology. If, instead of spending all of the time that it would take you to set up and test the videoconferencing equipment for one thirty-minute videoconference, you use that time instead to prepare a great email lesson, you may be far ahead in getting content into kids' heads. On the other hand, if you have an opportunity to show your class some historic moment or provide them the opportunity to talk to a world-famous expert, you might want to consider the videoconference.

There is another option for videoconferencing that might be more useful, and that is the "web cam" observation site. For example, zoos place web cameras in the pens of baby and adult animals and you simply need to log on to the Internet site to observe. You do not have to set up a camera of your own. Such a site might be a center in a biology class, for example, if you have found a site that matches your curriculum and you have a specific objective for your students' observations. It is impossible to list sites here, since they come and go on a daily basis. If you visit educational sites regularly (such as "The Global School House"), you will see addresses of these sites and leads to where you can find more addresses. An example of one site that is a directory for web cameras is www.Earthcamforkids.com.

Audioconferencing is a very viable alternative to videoconferencing. Although it is sometimes "broken sounding," audio without video usually transmits quite well even through connections with low bandwidth. The same applications that provide for videoconferencing include audio-only conferencing. The connection is made the same way, with an IP address. For best quality on both ends of the connection, participants should use headsets because speakers produce feedback. If, however, your class is consulting an expert, you will want to have the expert's voice come from speakers for the whole class to hear. This means that the expert must put up with the feedback. It is always best to set up the system and do a trial run with the person your class will connect to first. A speakerphone would be a better alternative if your classroom has a telephone line. The drawback to the telephone line is the long distance charge. With an Internet connection there is no charge. You can talk to anyone in the world for as long as you want.

> 30 minutes is about all that people care to spend on a rough, jerky videoconference

✔ CHECKING YOUR UNDERSTANDING

C.1

Using chat and audio- and videoconferencing is notoriously tricky and fails when you least want it to. Chat is the most reliable, audioconferencing is second, and videoconferencing comes in as a distant third. Before you attempt to execute a lesson with a class using any of these technologies you should be very familiar with them. The only way that you will be able to diagnose and fix a problem that occurs while your class is trying to use one of these technologies is to have run into it before. As a part of training yourself, you should set up chat and audio- and videoconferencing sessions with another person and run through the checklist of items to practice that are listed below.

Chat Practice Items

1. Make a connection with another person using an IP address.
2. Conduct a conversation.

3. There is usually an item listed somewhere in the menu structure called "options." Find this in the software you are using. See Figure C.6 for an example. As you conduct your conversation, practice changing the options and observe the effects. For example, if you are projecting a chat session with an expert with an LCD projector for the whole class to see, how would you change the font size of the text to make it more readable for your students?

Audioconferencing Practice Items

1. Set up an audio conference with a partner using a headset and microphone. Plug in the headset and microphone yourself so that you know where the plugs go.
2. Use an IP address to connect with your partner.
3. Spend a few minutes conversing to get used to the sound quality as well as the delays that occur after you speak and before your partner hears you.
4. Find the audio options dialogue box and open it. Practice with the settings. Find out what each one does. Be sure that you make note of the default settings so that you can return your computer to its original state when you have finished practicing or in case you change a setting and the audio stops working.

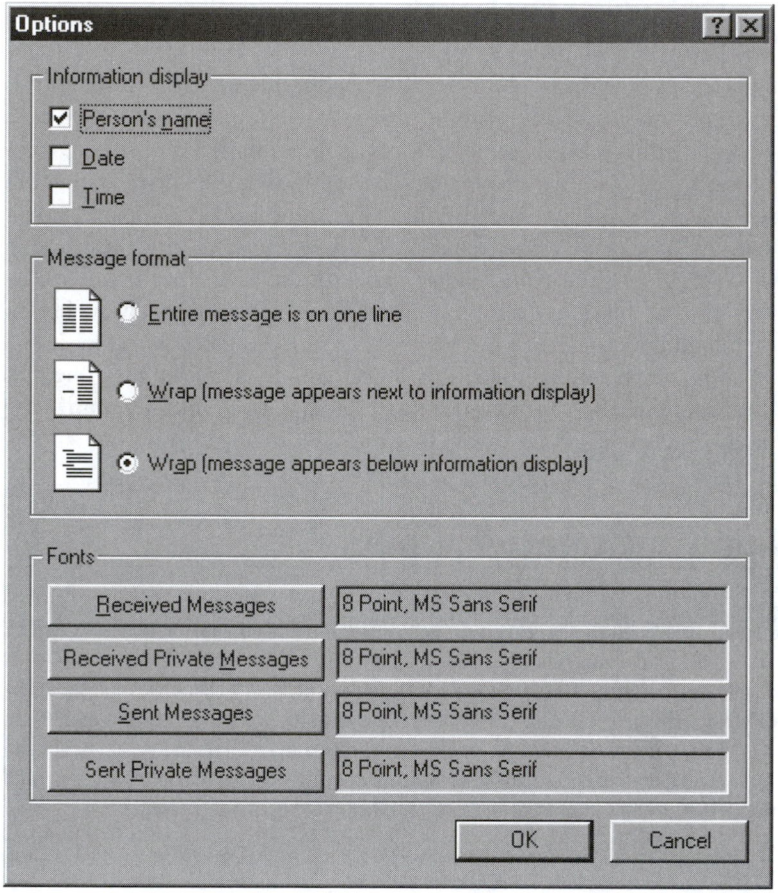

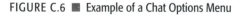

FIGURE C.6 ■ Example of a Chat Options Menu

Videoconferencing Practice Items

1. Set up a videoconference with a partner using a headset and microphone. Plug in the headset and microphone yourself so that you know where the plugs go.
2. Use an IP address to connect with your partner.
3. Spend a few minutes conversing to get used to the sound quality as well as the delays that occur after you speak and before your partner hears you.
4. Practice turning the video off, leaving the audio on. This is sometimes helpful on a bad Internet day. You can see a picture of the person with whom you are conversing for a while, but when the connection is too slow you can turn off the video and talk more comfortably using only audio.
5. Find the video options dialogue box and open it. Practice with the settings. Find out what each one does. Be sure that you make note of the default settings so that you can return your computer to its original state when you have finished practicing or in case you change a setting and the audio/video connection stops working. See Figure C.7 for an example of a video settings dialog box.
6. Practice speaking without using earphones. Note the feedback and how it affects your conversation.

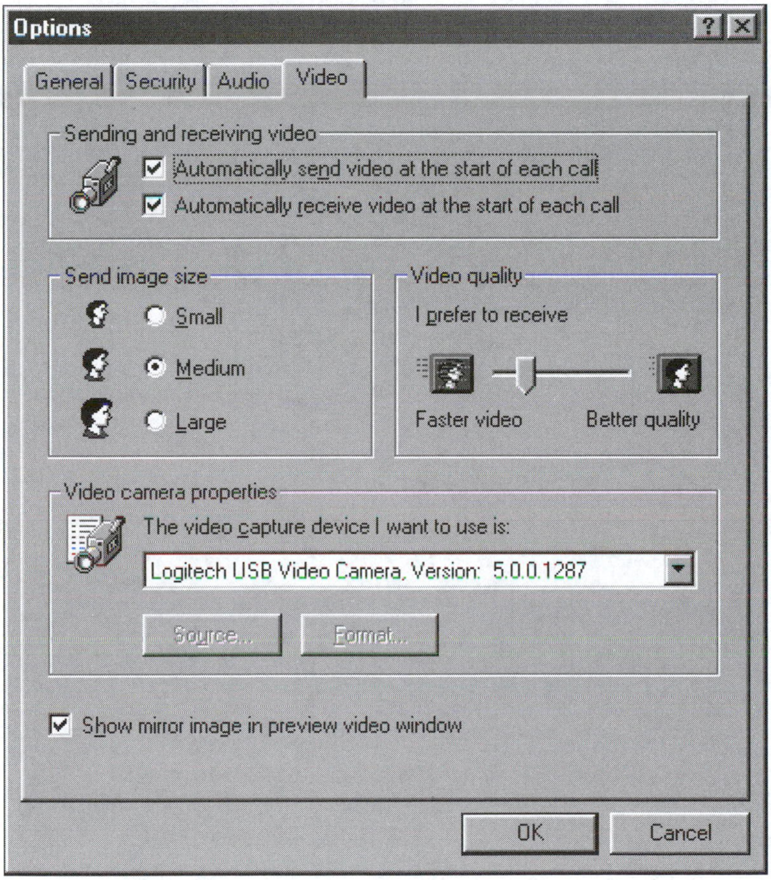

FIGURE C.7 ■ Example of a Video Options Menu

C.2

You should complete this exercise at least once each for chat and audio- and videoconferencing. Have your instructor or your partner disable some element of your conferencing software or hardware without telling you what she or he has done. Using the familiarity with the hardware and software that you acquired in "Checking Your Understanding C.1," fix the problem. As you or you and your partner debug the problem, speak out loud explaining your problem-solving strategies as you proceed. This will help you become more familiar with the language associated with this genre of hardware and software.

Concept Maps

There is a variety of different kinds of idea maps for organizing concepts. *Visual Tools for Constructing Knowledge* by Hyerle (1996) is a well written, in-depth book on the subject. Since this book is about computer tools, we will not cover idea mapping in the depth that it deserves, but rather encourage you to look at other books and articles to help you develop your skills with these thinking tools. Our goal is to help you understand a few basic mapping techniques very well.

> Different kinds of knowledge are expressed with different kinds of idea maps

Let's begin with brace and tree maps, ideal tools for knowledge that you want students to classify. If you look carefully at the brace map in Figure 7.2 and the tree map in Figure 7.3 of Chapter 7, you can see that they could show one of the following relationships for any concept:

is part of	is contained in
comprises	includes/is included in
is an example of	

All of the categories in this idea map may contain categories below them. For example, most countries contain states or provinces (which were explored), and states or provinces usually have smaller units, like counties. It would be easy to list all of these levels on a tree or brace map. The following topics would yield good tree or brace maps: polygons, plant, animal or insect classifications, and language groups (for example, Indo-European languages > Romance Languages > Spanish).

Brace maps and tree maps are best for classifying examples of concepts because concepts often exist in hierarchies. However, you cannot completely explain a concept by listing its examples. You must also list its properties or descriptors. Properties are qualities that define concepts (categories). Human beings have many properties in common with mammals (i.e., warm-blooded, young are born, etc.). Properties do not arrange themselves in hierarchies as examples do. They appear in clusters or webs. To compare and contrast the difference between examples and properties, observe Figure D.1. Template idea maps for concepts and their examples are on the left, and maps for concepts and their properties are on the right.

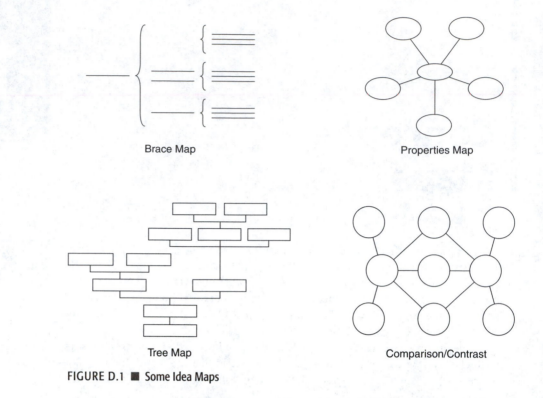

FIGURE D.1 ■ Some Idea Maps

Now look at the "Properties" map in Figure D.2. Notice that there is a central idea (concept), "Plant Organ Systems." It is surrounded by and connected to circles labeled with words that describe it. In the case of "Composition" there are additional properties. The map in Figure D.3 is the beginning of a web. Properties maps are concerned with descriptive information rather than levels of detail. They do not have examples. Plant organ systems in this idea map are defined by function, composition, and location. Function would never be below composition or location in a hierarchy. No matter how you think about it, there simply is no hierarchy. Connecting lines and circles to each of the properties (function, composition, location) will add detail to this map. For example, you could draw additional lines out from function that would further ex-

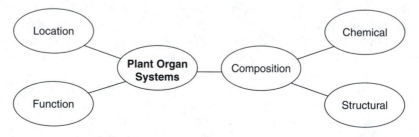

FIGURE D.2 ■ Properties Map for Plant Organ Systems

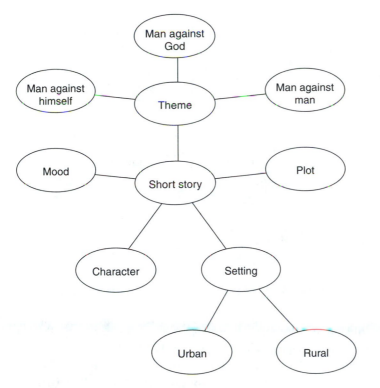

FIGURE D.3 ■ Properties Map of the Short Story

plain the function of an organ, such as the chemicals it produces and its relationship to other organs.

Thinking of a different example, let us look at a properties map for a short story. Short story is the concept. Theme, setting, character, and mood are its properties. When we look at each of those properties, we find that they themselves have properties. See Figure D.3 for a properties map of the short story. Properties for mood and character are missing, but you get the idea. Using this properties map as a basis for planning, consider how you would develop the navigation for the presentation about a short story based on this map. If the presentation that is a basis for this map were a simple explanation of the short story, then the first ring of ovals around "Short Story" would probably represent a menu page. The second set of ovals around each property of short story would represent an information page with explanations and examples of the different ideas that the ovals represent.

As you remember from the preceding paragraphs, you were able to classify examples of concepts using two kinds of idea maps (tree and brace). Properties are no different. There are many ways to draw pictures of properties. Once you start thinking about concepts as either properties problems or classification problems or a combination, you will find that your abilities to express them graphically will become more diverse. For example, one common activity in language arts and social science classes is to compare and contrast. Comparing and contrasting is really a properties problem.

Examples of properties

Using properties in language arts and social science

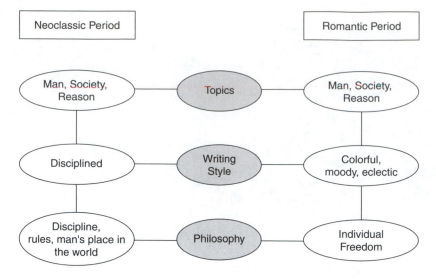

FIGURE D.4 ■ Comparison/Contrast Map of the English Neoclassic and Romantic Periods

You are asking the students to tell you how the properties of some concept are alike and different. This activity can be mapped, and the map can then be used to provide your students with the beginnings of a navigational structure for a presentation.

For an example, let's use a comparison/contrast problem commonly assigned in a senior high English literature class—"Compare and contrast the Neoclassical period in English literature with the Romantic period." Look at Figure D.4, an example of a comparison/contrast map. The gray ovals in the center name the properties that are the basis for the comparison. They are also those ideas that each literary period had in common; each period had a writing style, a set of common topics, and a philosophy. The white circles provide the space where differences (the contrasts) are displayed. Now think about how this map would translate to the design of a presentation. It is clear that the dark gray ovals could represent a menu page, while the light colored circles would represent the content of the destination pages on the menu.

✔ CHECKING YOUR UNDERSTANDING

D.1

Activity 1

Let's see if you can match an idea with its corresponding kind of idea map. You will be able to choose among the four kinds of idea maps you have just read about. Use a sheet of paper to cover each answer. Write your suggestion before you look at the answer. You will be using the concept map templates in Figure D.1. Which concept map would be most helpful for thinking through the following concepts and the relationships they represent?

Parts of the human body

(*Tree map*)

Similarities and differences between two cultures

(*Compare/contrast map*)

Description of a character in a short story or novel

(*Properties map*)

Illustrating the different levels of government in America

(*Tree map*)

Kinds of clouds

(*Properties map*)

The composition of the solar system

(*Tree map*)

Similarities and differences in characters, settings, theme, and mood in short stories, poems, and novels

(*Comparison/contrast map*)

Activity 2

Choose two of the concepts from the list above: one for which you would use a properties map and one for a tree map. Draw the maps.

■ IDEA MAPS FOR EVENTS

Events are a second kind of knowledge that we have about the world. Unlike concepts, events usually have steps or stages. They are mapped and presented differently than concepts. Events can be chains with a beginning and an end, or they can be cycles with no beginning or end. Figure D.5 is a tree map illustrating how events are classified and Table D.1 provides examples of each of these kinds of events.

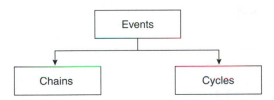

FIGURE D.5 ■ Tree Map of Events

TABLE D.1 ■ Examples of Events Classified by Type

Chain	Cycle
Tornado	Farming
Development of a disease	Maintaining a car
Circulation of blood through the body	Tying a shoelace
The seasons	Working a long division problem

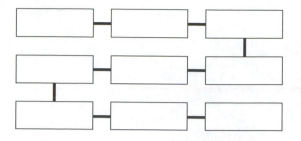

FIGURE D.6 ■ Plot As a Procedure Represented As a Chain

Idea maps for events

Figure D.6 is an example of how a chain is diagrammed as a map. It could be a description of the steps leading to the birth of a hurricane or the writing of a short story. There is a beginning step and an ending step, and at a low-to-middle level of detail, the steps are quite straightforward. Looking at a chain with content, such as the one in Figure D.7, you would think that building a presentation from a chain diagram would be quite simple. Such a presentation would go from the first page to the last, each page describing each step with some text in a box and perhaps a picture or appropriate audio or video clip.

Such an approach, however, is probably a waste of time and computer resources. As an English teacher, I would rather have the students describe plot with a word processor if this is all they did with the topic when they wrote a presentation. If they wrote a paper with a word processor, at least they would get practice organizing and writing good paragraphs to form a coherent whole. It is important to recognize that a simple event, either chain or cycle, can be made into a richer presentation than a mere recitation of steps. The reason is that within every step there are embedded concepts, each of which has properties and examples. Embedded concepts are the ideas basic to a procedure or process. For example, if you are trying to describe the process that creates a thunderstorm and you don't know what barometric pressure means, then you can't fully understand the process because barometric pressure is an embedded concept in the process of the formation of a thunderstorm.

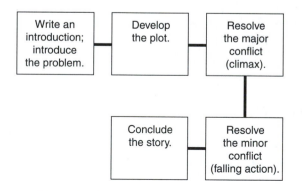

FIGURE D.7 ■ Chain

In the short story example, step one involves introducing a problem or conflict. The student could easily elaborate on this step by linking to a screen that explains that problems are based on themes. This screen could lead to another screen explaining prototypical themes (man against man, man against God, man against society, etc.) that usually form the basis for the problem or conflict. In other words, each step in the chain is really the basis for providing for a rich web of branches to embedded concepts, depending upon the students' age and the complexity of the finished product.

Another example of enhancing an explanation of an event by using concepts embedded in each of its steps is provided for you as a map of a hurricane in Figure D.8. Notice that the steps of the event are described in boxes, while the associated concepts appear in ovals. The boxes are connected with arrows to indicate the flow of the event.

The next four figures are examples of how such a chain diagram might develop into a presentation. Spend some time looking at Figure D.8 and then at Figure D.9,

> Adding embedded concepts to a map that describes an event

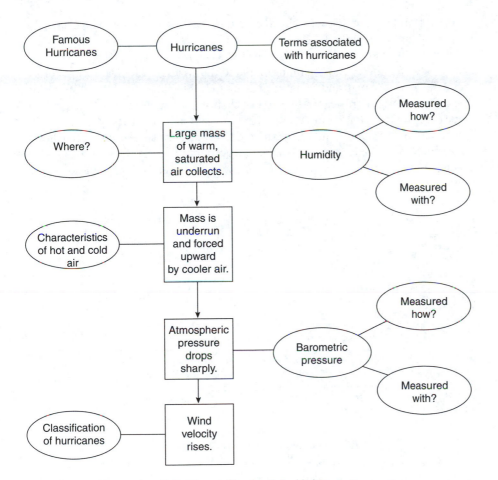

FIGURE D.8 ■ **Process in a Chain Diagram Showing Embedded Concepts**

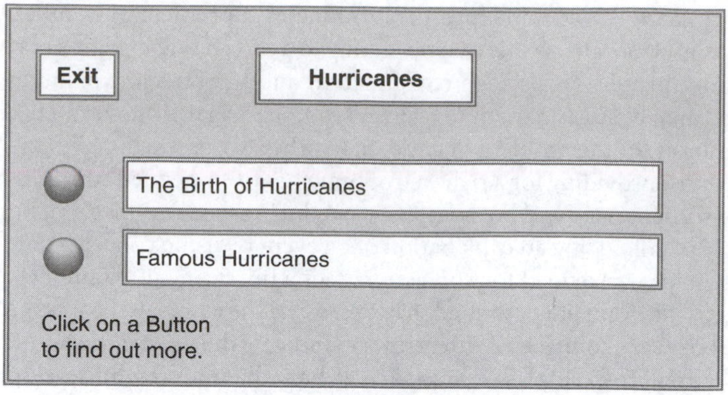

Exit   Hurricanes

⬤   The Birth of Hurricanes

⬤   Famous Hurricanes

Click on a Button
to find out more.

FIGURE D.9 ■ Hurricane Main Menu Screen

D.10, D.11, and D.12. Associate each screen in these figures with a box or an oval in the chain diagram in Figure D.8.

Now, back to events. The cycle is similar to a chain, in that it is a series of steps or stages. However, there is no beginning or end to the cycle. Now look at Figure D.13, a template for a cycle map and at Figure D.14, an example of a map of the Evaporation Cycle. Cycles may be treated very much like chains in a presentation. They, too, have embedded concepts. For example, if you look carefully at Figure D.14, you will see the embedded concepts *vapor* and *precipitation*. These terms are surely worth branches in a presentation. There is an added twist in the evaporation cycle. There are also other events embedded in the Evaporation Cycle. Note the terms *evaporate* and *condense*.

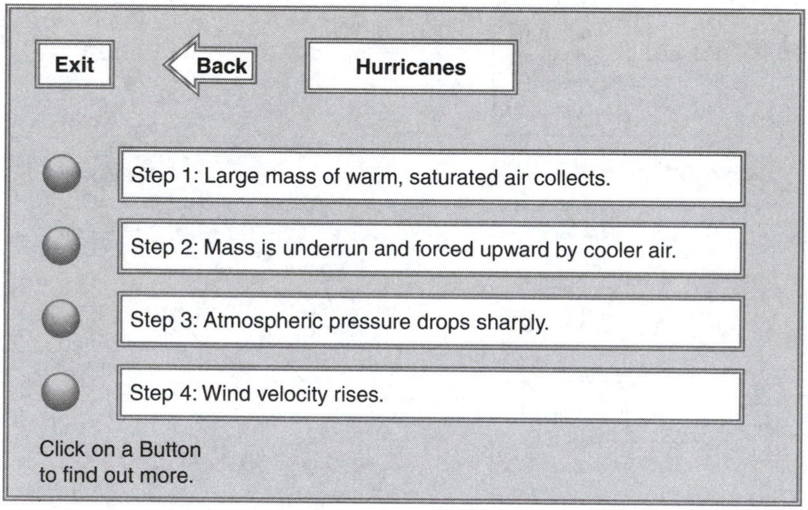

Embedded events in a cycle

Exit   ⬅ Back   Hurricanes

⬤   Step 1: Large mass of warm, saturated air collects.

⬤   Step 2: Mass is underrun and forced upward by cooler air.

⬤   Step 3: Atmospheric pressure drops sharply.

⬤   Step 4: Wind velocity rises.

Click on a Button
to find out more.

FIGURE D.10 ■ Destination Screen of First Choice from Main Menu

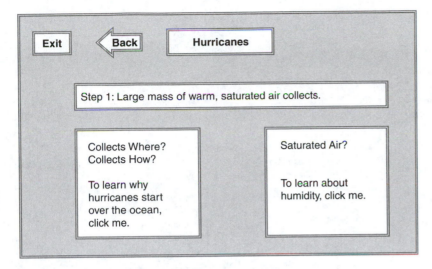

FIGURE D.11 ■ Destination Screen for Step 1

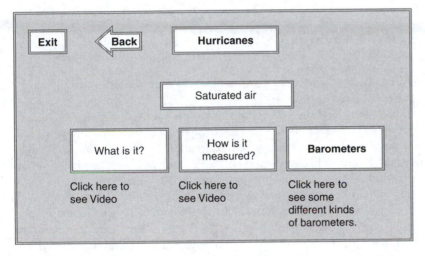

FIGURE D.12 ■ Final Screen Following Step 1 Branch to Humidity

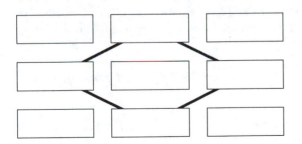

FIGURE D.13 ■ Cycle

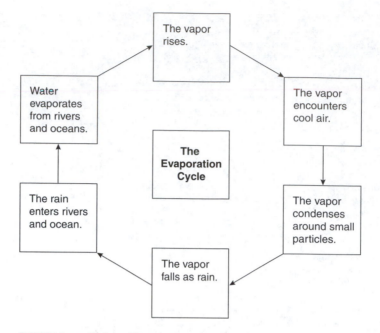

FIGURE D.14 ■ Event That Is a Process and Cycle

Both are chains which students need to comprehend in order to understand the evaporation cycle.

Now think about how students often study these events. They read about the Evaporation Cycle in their textbooks and learn vapor, precipitation, condense, and evaporate as vocabulary words. Ideally, the class might do an evaporation/condensation experiment, but most likely, students will learn evaporation or condensation by answering end-of-chapter questions and/or by memorizing definitions.

Students who are practiced at idea mapping and using presentation software, on the other hand, will be compelled to notice embedded concepts in their idea map, make boxes for them, and find out what belongs there. These students may then illustrate them, explain them with text, audio, or even make a narrated video of an evaporation/condensation experiment. Working in this way, students will do the organization and elaboration that they need to attach their new knowledge to old knowledge. This, in turn, will move The Evaporation Cycle and its embedded concepts and processes to their long-term memory, where these ideas will become part of their permanent store of knowledge.

Summarizing Events   Events are not difficult to recognize but here are two tips that will help you recognize them.

1. They are composed of segments in which one segment of action must always follow or precede another segment.
2. Certain words are a clue to processes and procedures: "precedes," "follows," "a step in," "is a stage in," "results from," "causes/is caused by," "influences/is influenced

by," "enables/originates from," "uses," "exploits/is exploited by," "consumes/is consumed by," "evolves," "provides/is provided by," or "regulates/is regulated by" (Jonassen, 2000).

Remember that events, though seemingly simple and linear on the surface, are often quite complex. Not only do they contain embedded concepts that are prerequisite knowledge for understanding the event, but may also contain embedded events. As students do their idea maps, they must be trained to find these ideas and explain them.

■ BRANCHING

Branching is a term used in computer programming to indicate the action of moving from one part of a program to another. As indicated previously, branches are the embedded concepts or events that students must understand in order to really know whatever it is they are studying. Branching in a presentation may take several forms. Students can use hot words, hot graphics, menus, or icons to allow their users to initiate the branching process.

Hot Words

Hot words are perhaps the simplest method of initiating a branch. Branches that result from these hot words should be very simple. A hot word, which is a word in the text of a presentation that indicates that the user may click on it for more information, should go to a short pop-up definition or graphic. Ideally, the user should never leave the original screen. If the user does leave the original screen, a Back button should be clearly visible and easily accessible with no other branches available. Use other methods for initiating branches for more complex ideas. Hot words are indicated several different ways. The way that your students will indicate hot words will, no doubt, depend on the software that you are using. Authors indicate hotwords to users by applying a different color to them, underlining them, or by having the cursor icon change shapes when the mouse is dragged over them. The cursor icon is the symbol that tells you the location of the cursor and what it can do at the moment. For example, an hourglass cursor icon tells you the computer is working and that you should wait until the cursor changes back to the shape of an arrow. When the cursor turns into the shape of a hand, you can move the object or click on it. In the presentation software that you use, you will see a menu item called either "Create Hot word," or "Create Link." Either of these will serve your purpose.

Uses for hot words

Hot Graphics

When your students are working with an idea that may be visualized and placed on the computer screen as a graphic, they may make portions of this graphic "hot," allowing their readers to click on this hot area for more information. There is no reason why a whole presentation may not be organized around a hot graphic. Such a graphic might be a main menu screen and the basis for all branches in the program. For example, your students could use their idea maps or modifications of them as the basis for their

Ideas for using hot graphics

main menu screens and even some of the branches. Such an approach will give your students added incentive for taking their idea maps seriously.

Another approach to using hot graphics as the basis for menu screens is for your students to find a metaphor into which their approach to their topic will fit. Web site designers and software developers successfully use these metaphors to organize software on a regular basis. One example of this technique is organizing a menu page like a floor map of a school with several classrooms, each indicating different topics or pieces of the presentation, a library where users can go to find definitions or other information, and a student recreation area where students can go to see graphics, videos, or animations about the topic they are working on.

Icons

The Back arrows in the figures to which you just referred are called icons. They are a special kind of graphics file often followed by an extension ".ico." You may buy libraries of these icons with many different kinds of pictures on them, or your students may make their own icons using a draw program. Icons are very simple diagrams that capture the meaning of a more complex idea. For example, a trashcan on your computer's desktop screen symbolizes the process that you use to delete a file. If, for example, your students were working on The Evaporation Cycle, they might do a simple text menu like the one in Figure D.9 and D.10. However, they could turn the buttons to the left of the text into icons that symbolically describe each step of the process. Figure D.15 is an example of an icon a student might make to describe evaporation. This icon is very simple, but it requires a conceptual understanding of the elements of evaporation. Making or choosing an icon makes the students translate content into a simple, summarized format that requires a significant cognitive effort.

Menus

Menus are the most typical navigational devices used to organize presentations. These may be as simple as a button followed by a line of descriptive text. The menus in Figures D.9 and D.10 are examples of this approach. They are helpful for users of the software because they always keep the organization of the topic clear.

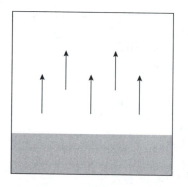

FIGURE D.15 ■ Icon for Evaporation

Branches That Help Users Get Around in the Software

There is another kind of branch that has nothing to do with content and everything to do with the usability of a presentation. These are the branches that get users back to where they came from, as well as entirely out of the program. Your students should be very careful to provide these options for their users. Figures D.9–D.10 illustrate this technique very simply. Notice two characteristics of the Back and Forward branches: they are illustrated with an arrow that is always the same, and these two icons are always in the same place on the screen. This is a fundamental presentation skill that students should become familiar with early in their use of presentation software.

> Consistency is the key to navigational branches

■ LOOKING AT THE BIG PICTURE

You have read a lot about idea maps and seen quite a few examples. You have learned about concepts and events. What you have learned about them is summarized in a short outline below.

1. Concepts are ideas (social class, war, love, kinds of themes in literature) or groups, things, or living creatures (the animal kingdom, kinds of clouds, kinds of rocks) and have:
   a. Properties that describe them
   b. Examples
2. Events are either:
   a. Chains (beginning and an end)
   b. Cycles (no beginning or end)

Your students should try to diagram these two basic kinds of knowledge in a way that makes sense to them and to you. If people understand the organization of what they are learning, they remember it better (Gagne et al., 1993). You have seen some basic patterns for mapping concepts and events, and there are more. Pause for a moment to study the diagrams in Figures D.16–D.21. Look at how they are alike and different. Think of the topics you teach and how they fit the diagrams.

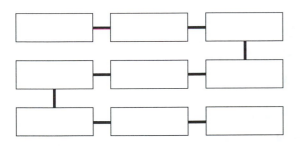

FIGURE D.16 ■ Chain

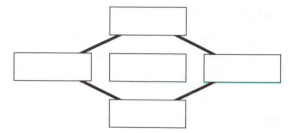

FIGURE D.17 ■ Another Cycle

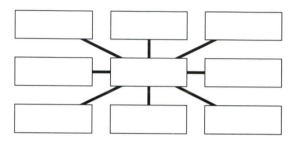

FIGURE D.18 ■ Star (For Concepts—Comparison/Contrast)

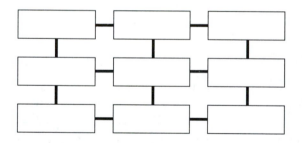

FIGURE D.19 ■ Grid (For Concepts—Like a Table—Column Headings Are Properties and Rows Are Examples)

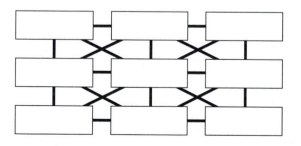

FIGURE D.20 ■ Web (For Concepts—Shows Relationships)

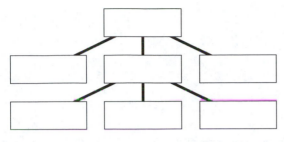

FIGURE D.21 ■ ■ Tree (For Concepts—Helps With Classification)

✔ CHECKING YOUR UNDERSTANDING

D.2

Now we are going to try another exercise. This time, the exercise will provide the topic and you must provide the map. Each topic will fit into one of the six figures (D.16–D.21). Study the shapes carefully. Then take a sheet of paper, and after covering the answers in italics, look at the cue (in bold) and write the answer to each of these two questions:

1. Is the cue a concept or an event? If it is an event, is it a cycle or a chain?

2. Which map would be most appropriate for describing the cue?

Cover the italicized words below and begin the exercise.

Cue: Mitosis

(*Event*)

(*Cycle*)

Cue: Forms of Government

(*Concept*)

(*Tree*)

Cue: Plot

(*Event*)

(*Chain*)

Cue: Volcanic Eruption

(*Event*)

(*Chain*)

Cue: The Four Seasons

(*Event*)

(*Cycle*)

Cue: Dinosaurs

(*Event*)

(*Tree or Brace*)

Cue: Passing a Bill in Congress

(*Event*)

(*Chain*)

Cue: Theme (in a short story or novel)

(*Concept*)

(*Properties diagram*)

Cue: Testing for pH

(*Event*)

(*Chain*)

Cue: Earthquake

(*Concept [think about what the characteristics of an earthquake are]*)

(*And/or [could be either]*)

(*Process [There is a beginning and an end, and the moments in between are somewhat predictable; i.e., the quake itself and then the aftershocks]*)

(*Properties map attached to a chain map*)

Sample Database for an English Class

■ AMERICAN SOCIETY REFLECTED IN FICTION

The stories and poems that you have read over the last semester represent different themes, settings, characters, plots, and historical periods. Fiction can tell you a lot about the people and time in which it was written. Your assignment is to write a paper analyzing changes in American society reflected in the American stories and poems that you have read this semester.

The way that authors handle theme, plot, character, and setting reflects the conflicts of the society in which they live. If you look for patterns in the key information about each story or novel and then think back to your reading, you will see that American attitudes toward many aspects of life have changed over the last 200 years. Your database will look something like Table E.1, but it will have many more fields.

Step 1

The first thing you should do is to get to know your database and think about how you might use it. Take a few moments to study the names of the fields below and think about the kind of information they provide for you.

1. Conflict (man against himself/other men/God/nature)
2. Setting in time
3. Gender of main character
4. SES (socio-economic status) of main character
5. Gender of antagonist
6. SES of antagonist
7. Setting (urban/rural)
8. Setting (name of continent)
9. Mood (tragic/comic/satire)
10. Plot (episodic/linear/*in medias res*)
11. Narrator (1st person/3rd person)
12. Nature (good/bad/no effect)

TABLE E.1 ■ Database of American Stories and Poems

Story	Theme	Setting in Time	Gender of Main Character	SES of Main Character
Rip Van Winkle	Man against himself	18th century	m	Lower class
Billy Budd	Man against society	19th century	m	Lower class
The Fall of the House of Usher	Man against himself	19th century	m	Upper class
The Outcasts of Poker Flat	Man against society	19th century	m	Lower class
The Pearl	Man against God	20th century	m	Lower class

13. City (good/bad/no effect)
14. Does anyone die violently? (yes/no)
15. If someone dies does the death have meaning? (yes/no)
16. Is there a romantic relationship? (yes/no)
17. If there is a romantic relationship, is it (happy/unhappy)?
18. Does the main character control his/her own destiny? (yes/no)
19. Is there heavy use of symbolism? (yes/no)
20. Date that the story was written
21. Does religion play a role in the story? (yes/no)

Again, your goal is to trace change in American attitudes about life and society over the past 200 years. To use the database, you will need to think of questions that are related to your goal.

Step 2

Before you actually start asking questions of the database, you must decide what you want to know. In the spaces below, list some of the items you think have changed over the past 200 years.

1. Role of women
2. An individual sense of who is in control
3. Attitudes toward nature
4. The role of violence in storytelling
5. The kind of people the public is interested in reading about
6. Attitudes toward religion
7. Respect for society and its rules

Step 3

Now that you have thought about some of the ideas that might help you analyze how American attitudes have changed over time, it is time to begin asking questions of the database. Use the hints below to help you work through all of the questions you listed in Step 2. When you key in your questions, remember that sometimes it might take you several tries to translate your question to a format that the computer understands. If the computer gives you an error message or won't give you an answer, try to think of another way to ask the question.

1. Ask a question about one of the ideas you listed in Step 2:

   _____

2. First, you must decide which available fields will give you information about this problem. What are they? _____
3. Next, you must decide how the information in these fields can help you make a comparison. You may only need to ask two questions or you may need to ask four or five to get the information you need to build a query. To help you ask questions, try to divide your thinking into two parts: the facts you need, and the conclusion that the facts point to.

   ■ Fact (evidence for what I want to know): _____
   ■ Fact (evidence for what I want to know): _____
   ■ Fact (evidence for what I want to know): _____
   ■ Conclusion (What I want to know): _____

Step 4

Now that you have asked questions of the database about all of the items that you listed in Step 2, you should have enough information to begin writing. Use quotes and examples from the stories to support your arguments about how American life and attitudes have changed over the last 150 years. You will present your ideas to the class. After you have listened to your classmates present their findings, answer the questions below.

What changes did you observe that others in the class did not find?

1. _____
2. _____
3. _____
4. _____
5. _____

What changes did others find that you did not find?

1. _____
2. _____
3. _____
4. _____
5. _____

Revise your paper to include the new information you have from your classmates. If you do not agree with one of their findings, argue against it. If you agree, add it to your own paper and support it.

As you have worked with this exercise, you have thought about stories in many different ways. The database helped you process and analyze information very quickly and accurately. You could have done all of the research "by hand," but it would have taken you much longer because you would have had to look up answers for every story each time you asked a question. The database did that work for you. Databases are useful tools that help you organize and think about large quantities of information. Databases are good for studying other topics besides stories. What other topics could a database help you study?

1. _____
2. _____
3. _____
4. _____
5. _____
6. _____
7. _____
8. _____

Index